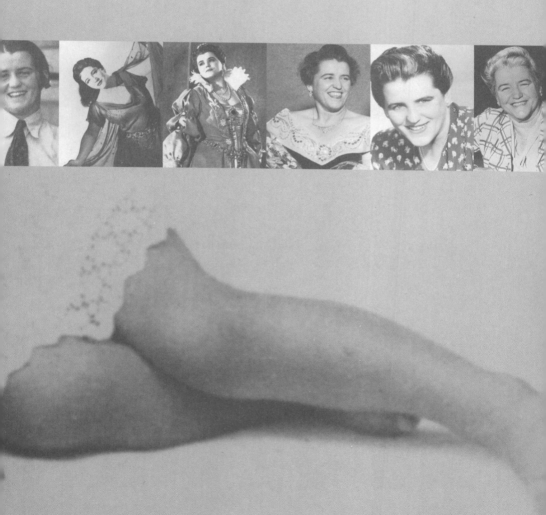

Dame JOAN HAMMOND

LOVE & MUSIC

Dame JOAN HAMMOND

LOVE & MUSIC

SARA HARDY

ALLEN&UNWIN

First published in 2008

Allen & Unwin
83 Alexander Street
Crows Nest NSW 2065
Australia
Phone: (61 2) 8425 0100
Fax: (61 2) 9906 2218
Email: info@allenandunwin.com
Web: www.allenandunwin.com

National Library of Australia
Cataloguing-in-Publication entry:
Hardy, Sara.
Dame Joan Hammond : love & music
ISBN: 978 1 74175 083 6 (hbk.)
Includes index. Bibliography.
1. Hammond, Joan, Dame, 1912–1996. 2. Sopranos
(Singers)–Australia–Biography. 3. Singing–Instruction and study.
782.1092

Jacket and text design by Ruth Grüner
Typeset by Ruth Grüner
Index by Fay Donlevy
Printed in Australia by McPherson's Printing Group

'Her voice, of course, exhibited its now
legendary character—its swooning depth
as if it had passed through half a dozen
Gothically vaulted cathedrals before
emerging from her lips . . .'

CONTENTS

PRELUDE

Joan Hammond was on tour in Australia with *Tosca*. The final performance was in Adelaide and there was a party afterwards in the theatre. Joan donated a crate or three of champagne and everyone had a great time. She was amongst the last to leave and when the small group reached the big iron gates at the back of the theatre they found them locked. The only way out was to go up and over. Joan climbed to the top of the gates with remarkable speed and hauled her companion of many years, Lolita Marriott, up after her. The descent on the other side was just as impressive— all done with much hilarity.

Second-hand anecdotes can be unreliable but this one turned out to be true.

I heard the anecdote in the 1980s when Joan was very much alive and living in Melbourne, my home town. It impressed me and stayed in my mind. I read Joan's autobiography and paid attention when she appeared in the paper or was interviewed for radio or television.

She died in 1996 at the age of 84 and the *Age* published an account of her life and career. I felt a connection with this life and was pleased to see such a glowing obituary, yet was annoyed by a phrase that appeared in the final paragraph: 'Dame Joan never married'. It was common knowledge in the arts community that Joan's companion was Lolita Marriott, and that the pair made no secret of the fact. I'd admired this openness tremendously and was appalled that their relationship had been brushed aside with such a hackneyed phrase. My letter of complaint to the *Age* was published:

> What a wonderful photograph of Dame Joan Hammond (the *Age*, 27/11) and what an extraordinary artistic life.
>
> Her obituary could only but glance at her great and significant achievements. However, it is a shame that the sentence 'Dame Joan never married' should so completely sweep aside a 40-year relationship that Dame Joan carefully acknowledged, with her usual charm and dignity, as the blessing of her life.
>
> Love comes in many guises and is not always legally bound. What's in a label? Whatever we might call her/him: friend, companion, partner, lover—isn't it time we allowed the 'significant other' a place? Silence only breeds silence, and ignorance.
>
> Bravo, Dame Joan Hammond. Rest in peace. And bravo her life-time friend Lolita Marriott who died in 1993 having 'never married'.

I was astonished to find that the letter had an immediate effect. Strangers rang up or sent letters to say how pleased they'd been to read it. I seemed to have hit a nerve. This too stayed in my mind.

When I eventually came to do my research for this biography I found that Joan's relationship with Lolita was not necessarily as it seemed. There were contrasting opinions; some saw them as a lesbian couple while others saw them as just good friends.

Defining someone's life in a biography is an enormous responsibility and I knew I had to check my facts very carefully before making any pronouncements. Yet the checking of facts proved especially difficult. Joan and Lolita lost their home and belongings in the devastating Ash Wednesday bushfire of 1983. Letters, diaries—everything perished on that terrible day. Strangely, this was a problem I'd had to deal with in my previous biography of Edna Walling, the landscape designer. Edna Walling's house burnt to the ground when she was 39, Joan, however, lost everything when she was 70.

I didn't want to pin the story of Joan's life to the question of her sexuality but I did want to clarify assumptions as far as I could. I discovered, after talking to a number of people, that there were no definitive answers—which is perhaps as it should be, 'truth' being so tricky.

Of all the interviews I conducted I found that Julie Wyer, Joan's niece, summed the issue up with succinct ease: 'They probably didn't explore the physical side of it—but who knows?—and who cares! It doesn't matter: they loved each other.' Julie Wyer knew Joan and Lolita from childhood and had once bartered her aunt's autograph for a quantity of tadpoles.

Joan's autobiography, *A Voice, A Life*, was published in 1970. It contains some remarkable details but there is much that she skimmed over or left out—and there were things about her family background that she never wanted discovered.

Joan was a very private person. There was a reserve about her that only close friends could penetrate. The private Joan was mischievous and teasing; the public Joan was gracious, and sometimes intimidating.

She wrote her autobiography when she was convalescing from the coronary that had forced her into early retirement. It was a cruel and untimely ending to a magnificent career: she was 52 and still in excellent voice. She and Lolita moved back to Australia after many years of living in England and settled down to what they thought would be a tranquil existence—golfing, sailing and gardening being the major passions. Then Joan's new career began. She became head of vocal studies at the Victorian College of the Arts and guided the talents of many young opera singers.

I never met Joan Hammond, though I fancy I saw her once driving down St Kilda Road in her famous Rolls-Royce (the 1950s model with the big front lamps). Newspapers, periodicals and post-1983 Ash Wednesday archived papers have helped to fill in the research gaps, but it's been the interviews with the people who knew her that have been invaluable.

Joan's athleticism was exceptional—as the gate-climbing anecdote shows. If she hadn't made her name as a singer then we'd doubtless remember her as one of Australia's top golfers. She was a golf champion when a teenager and won junior and senior championships back to back.

It was said that Joan's undoubted natural ability as a golfer was enhanced by her particular brand of 'perseverance, doggedness and intelligence'—the very talents she utilised when she focused on her singing career. When Joan set her sights on a goal she usually achieved it. Obstacles were there to be overcome: a locked gate, a championship-winning putt, a prima donna role—these were the challenges that brought a sparkle to her eye.

JOAN HAMMOND

Pianoforte - - IVOR NEWTON

Programme

I

Bist du bei mir	*Bach*
Widmung	*Schumann*
Aria: Dido's Lament from " Dido and Aeneas "	*Purcell*
Non piu d'amore	*Andre Falconieri*
Aria: Dove Sono? from " The Marriage of Figaro "	*Mozart*

II

Aria: 'Twill soon be midnight now from " Queen of Spades "	*Tchaikovsky*
The Tryst	*Sibelius*
Spring Waters	*Rachmaninov*
Aria: O Silver Moon from " Rusalka "	*Dvorak*

INTERVAL

III

Claire de lune	*Joseph Szulc*
Chanson triste	*Henri Duparc*
Ouvre tes yeux bleus	*Jules Massenet*
Aria: Pleurez mes yeux from " Le Cid "	*Jules Massenet*

IV

Charity	*Richard Hagemen*
At the Well	*Richard Hagemen*
She wandered down the mountain-side	*Frederic Clay*

V

Aria: Mimi's Farewell from " La Boheme "	*Giacomo Puccini*
O Primavera	*Tirindelli*
Aria: One Fine Day from " Madame Butterfly "	*Puccini*

NEXT CONCERT

November 10th—ISO ELINSON (Piano)

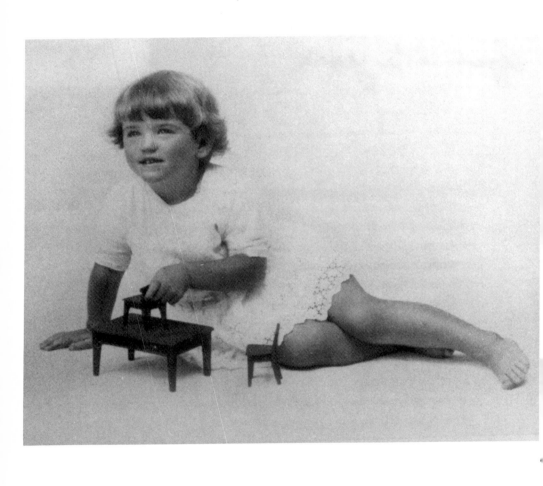

CHAPTER I

SPORT AND PLAY

JOAN WAS THREE YEARS OLD when she experienced her first adventure. It was a hot summer night, just before dawn. Her room was airless so she decided to kick off her bedclothes and go for a walk. She was wearing a nightdress and had nothing on her feet. She meandered through the house, into the garden, then to the bushland beyond—discarding her nightie as she went. She wandered naked, on and on, as the starlight faded and the sun rose. She must have come close to some fascinating yet potentially lethal encounters: cobwebs, reptiles, kangaroos . . . It's fortunate that the family dog accompanied her on this journey, for it was through this dog that she was eventually found. A neighbour spotted the dog and the dog led her to the naked child. Joan was too young to remember the experience but her parents never forgot it.

At heart Joan was a childlike free spirit, blissfully following her own course, unaware of dangers ahead. Strangely enough, there would almost always be a devoted friend keeping watch nearby— usually human but sometimes a dog.

THE NIGHT SKY lit up each year when it came to Joan's birthday. May 24 was Empire Day—Queen Victoria's birthday, later called Commonwealth Day—and Australians celebrated with fireworks. Bonfires burned, catherine wheels twirled and rockets burst into particles of brilliance. Samuel, Joan's father, told her that cracker night was held in her honour, and of course she believed him.

It was a harmless fantasy, like Father Christmas or the Tooth Fairy, but in later years Joan found that Samuel tended to give misinformation about a number of things. In fact he fabricated to such a degree that she began to question everything he said.

Joan had a neat way of summing up her origins: 'I was conceived in England, born in New Zealand and raised in Australia.' This was entirely true. She was conceived in a well-appointed house that overlooked Wimbledon Common, was born in a small rented house in Christchurch, and grew up in comfort on the North Shore of Sydney. Yet behind these simple facts was a hidden story.

Two of Joan's nieces alerted me to the 'skeleton' in the family closet. Both said there was something odd about Samuel and Hilda Hammond's marriage. They remembered the flurry there'd been when someone offered to do Joan's family tree—there was a very definite 'No! No thanks.' They suggested, with a certain sense of humour, that the problem was probably that Samuel and Hilda had never married, or that Samuel was a bigamist. The core of the issue was Samuel's name. His birth name was Samuel *Hood*, and for reasons no one knew (Samuel's explanations being weak and unbelievable), the family accepted that at some point he'd sidelined the 'Hood' and added the 'Hammond'. It was a long time ago and there was no documentation.

One clue did come to light. Embedded in Joan's papers (held by the National Library of Australia) was a scrap of handwritten paper that traced the ancestry of Joyce Calcutt, Joan's paternal grandmother. From this clue I was able to piece together some of Samuel's story. It goes like this:

Samuel Hood was a working-class lad who'd grown up in the East End of London in the 1880s. His father had been an engineer's fitter and his mother died young. Samuel developed into a handsome, lean young man who was fond of a laugh, a drink and a gamble — and he was always on the lookout for a likely opportunity. He saw that opportunity in electricity. He became an electrical engineer and started his own business. At about the same time, meanwhile, he met and married Edith, a girl from St Pancras. By 1901 they'd settled in a house in East Ham. Samuel aged twenty-five, Edith almost thirty.

Two or three years passed and then Samuel met Hilda Blandford, a smiling seventeen year old from the Isle of Wight. Samuel found Hilda Blandford very attractive . . .

So now there was Edith in East Ham and Hilda wearing a wedding ring and nursing a baby on Wimbledon Common. Thankfully, Samuel managed to turn his electrical business into a highly profitable venture, but some of his shadier business dealings were causing him problems. Things became increasingly tricky, so much so that he decided to make a few protective 'adjustments', one of which was to alter his name. He became Samuel H. Hammond, the 'H' for 'Hood' sitting silently in the middle. It was a made-up name, and never changed legally.

Samuel opened a business in the city and boldly registered it in the 1909 London Directory as 'Samuel Hammond & Co, Electrical Engineers, 107 Cannon St, EC'. It was an excellent location and he prospered.

Hilda, meanwhile, had accepted Samuel's explanations concerning the lack of a marriage certificate and was remarkably happy. By 1908 she had two little boys, Noel and Len. Life was good for the Hammonds (but it's unclear how life was for Edith Hood). Samuel took to wearing a bowler hat and well-tailored suits and contemplated taking up golf. Even so, the bad odour of his past hung about him. He thought that a new start in the colonies could be just the thing, New Zealand for instance, or Australia. Hilda was dismayed, but Samuel was so enthusiastic she was soon persuaded that a new land was just what they needed.

In early 1912 Samuel, Hilda and their two boys boarded the Shaw Savill liner that was to take them to the Antipodes—Hilda heavily pregnant with her third child. There were storms off the Cape of Good Hope and all manner of delays during the voyage. Samuel wanted to attend to business prospects in Sydney but Hilda wanted to be comfortably settled and definitely off the ship before her baby was born. By the time their ship reached Christchurch, New Zealand, they decided it was wise to disembark.

The promotional publicity for New Zealand had promised wealth, health and sunshine, but Samuel was disturbed to discover that business opportunities were limited and there was a shortage of suitable housing. Had prospects been more positive, the Hammonds may well have bought land and settled in Christchurch. As it turned out, Samuel rented a small house as a temporary measure. This was done just in time, for Hilda went into labour on 24 May 1912. All went well and a baby girl was born. A few weeks later she was baptised 'Joan Hilda Hood Hammond', Hammond being the surname.

Samuel left for Sydney a few weeks later, leaving Hilda and the little ones behind. It was six months before he sent word that they were to follow. It's unclear what business dealings he put together during those months but the outcome was that he was able to settle his family in a large house with ample grounds that adjoined bushland. The location was Beecroft, a semi-rural area in the Hills District of Sydney.

So Samuel and Hilda made their way in the new country as Mr and Mrs Hammond, and of course neither their children nor anyone else thought to question their legitimacy—not at that time anyway.

JOAN'S FIRST SEVEN YEARS were free-flowing. Both Hilda and Samuel had come from humble beginnings. Both had lost a parent early on, and two of Hilda's sisters had died from tuberculosis. Samuel and Hilda obviously wanted their children to have a good start. Their way of achieving this was to send them to boarding school at a young age. Noel and Len were sent aged five, while Joan was sent aged seven.

The school chosen for Joan was rather unusual. Glen Carron, The Garden School, was situated in an old mansion in the suburb of Mosman on Sydney's North Shore. It was co-educational and run by Miss Arnold and Miss Macdonald. These two women were disciples of The Order of the Star of the East, an order founded by the Theosophical community based near Madras, India. Theosophy was a brand of spiritualism popular at that time. Committed Theosophists tended to be unconventional in their dress and habits—they favoured loose casual clothes and a vegetarian diet. The tone of the school was progressive, and free-flowing play, especially in terms of music and movement, was encouraged.

Hilda and Samuel probably chose this school because of its reputation, for it's unlikely they were Theosophists. The freedom suited Joan well. It was here that she started to play the violin, here that she discovered her athleticism, and here that she danced through the garden waving silken scarves in time to rather unusual music.

She was a robust little girl who could channel her energies with astonishing concentration—if she liked what she was doing. She especially liked to play the violin and felt connected to the instrument. She knew that the strings could be made to speak, to sing, with a supreme eloquence—and she worked hard to release that voice. Yet there was another element, something she didn't pay much attention to: her teachers began to notice that she had a very attractive singing voice. But it was the violin she wanted to master, and her progress was very good.

SAMUEL'S PROGRESS WAS ALSO VERY GOOD. He'd become a merchant/agent—an importer of goods ranging from Packard cars to dry ice. His entrepreneurial activities had earned him a prestigious business address in George Street in the city, and his success was such that he could afford to build his dream home. He bought a large plot in Lindfield, an underdeveloped suburb on the upper North Shore, conveniently close to the railway station. The house was two storey, had a small ballroom, leadlight windows bearing the Hammond 'coat of arms', and had Samuel's initials carved into the wooden fixtures (the S superimposed over the H was later mistaken for the dollar sign!). There was a terraced garden, a tennis court, and a cricket lawn that gave on to bushland and then drifted down to a creek with dainty ferns and sandstone rock pools. He named the house 'Walbrook' after the ward of Walbrook in the City of London where he'd run his electrical business. It was completed in time to accommodate Tony, born in 1920, the final addition to the family.

Samuel was doing so well that he built a holiday house at Palm Beach. It was a wonderful location: the house was next to the sea and it overlooked the narrow neck of land connecting Palm Beach to the Barrenjoey headland (which separates the Pacific Ocean from Pittwater). There was the beginnings of a simple golf course on this land, and this was developed into a nine-hole links. Samuel and Hilda were keen golfers by this time and Samuel became a founding member of the Palm Beach Golf Club. The front veranda of the holiday house overlooked the ninth green and young Joan was given a miniature set of golf clubs and encouraged to try her hand. Golf would become a major passion one day, but for the moment it was the sea and nothing but the sea that took her fancy.

Joan and her elder brothers would go swimming, sailing and surfing. Whatever Noel and Len could do, Joan would do too. She was tall for her age, strong and fearless. Eldest brother Noel would go looking for his surfboard to find that his little sister had gone off with it. She adored surfing, and was one of the first of the girls to be seen catching a wave at Palm Beach—it was impressive, given that the boards were so big and heavy in those days.

IT ALL SOUNDS IDYLLIC. The large family home, the holiday house, the upper-middle-class comforts. Yet Joan's niece, Aurora, told me that Len couldn't think of one kind word to say about his mother, and he described his father as a drinker and a gambler. Len was adamant that he never received parental love. The Hammond children were showered with material things but starved of affection. Len remembered going to visit his little brother Tony at boarding school because his parents neglected to do so.

When Joan was quizzed about her parents she declined to answer. The most she would say was that Hilda wasn't maternal.

A close friend of Joan told me that the family was known as 'the fighting Hammonds'. They were a lively bunch, 'full of personality' and forever arguing—and there was much estrangement between siblings and parents in later life.

IT WAS 1925 and Joan was twelve years old when Samuel gave the children a new bicycle. It was a lovely sporty type of 'grown-up' bicycle with attractively curved handlebars—a boy's bicycle. Joan and her brothers loved to put it through its paces. One of Joan's tricks was to ride with her feet on the handlebars. The bike was kept at 'Walbrook' and she especially enjoyed riding around the quiet roads of Lindfield. They were steep, gritty, unmade roads, with lots of bends and blind corners. She liked to career around these roads as if she was on a speed track doing a time trial. On one particular day she'd done about four laps of this 'track' and was feeling full of bravado. She took a bend too wide and was on the wrong side of the road just

as a car was coming up the hill the other way. It was the sort of car that had large lamps, wide running boards and spoke-wheels. She slammed into the passenger side of the car, threw out her left arm to protect herself and caught her forearm in between the spokes of the front wheel. It was only a matter of seconds till the car could stop, but during that time her left arm was twisted round and round as her body was dragged along the ground.

She remembers being completely numb as the driver laid her in the back of the car. He drove her to a doctor who immediately sent her to the nearest hospital. It was decided that the arm would have to be amputated from the elbow. Fortunately, a young surgeon was rushed to the hospital and his opinion held sway. He detected a faint pulse and thought that he could save the arm. The operation was a success, but then Joan had to endure four more operations over the next twelve months. It was a ghastly cycle of pain: surgery would be done, the arm would be strung up for some time, the fingers waxed to keep them straight, the arm would heal, some movement would be gained, and then the whole horrible cycle would have to be gone through again. The fifth operation involved a skin graft. Skin was removed from her inner thigh and placed around the wrist area. She remembered this as one of the worst experiences.

She was out of action for a year. Her left arm was now two inches shorter than her right and movement was painful and limited. The wound was raw-looking, blotchy, bumpy and reddish blue. There was also a nasty scar on her thigh where the skin graft had been taken. She fought these difficulties with a steely determination, fired by her desire to resume her two great loves, sport and music, and by music she meant playing the violin. She had dreamed of becoming a professional violinist.

She worked to recover strength and agility in her arm and fingers, but the first time she attempted to play her violin she couldn't even raise the instrument higher than her waist. It was months before she could place it under her chin, but gradually, gradually, she was able to play again. She must have discovered extraordinary depths of will-power and patience. Strengths she would call upon in later life.

She spent several months at home while her arm healed. She read, painted and listened to records on her wind-up gramophone. Her brothers had piles of jazz records and she enjoyed these as well as pop songs, but it was classical music that she loved. Hilda encouraged her to listen to a range of classical music and bought her some music scores.

Hilda's background was even more humble than Samuel's. Her father had been a mariner but had died when she was young. Matilda, her widowed mother, was left with five young children to bring up and she probably achieved this by working as a laundress. Hilda is variously described as shy, smiling, pleasant and not so pleasant (depending on whom I interviewed). Slim and good looking in her youth, she became a stocky woman with a square face and wide smile. She can't have had much of an education—brought up on little money on the Isle of Wight—so it's significant that she was so enthusiastic about Joan's interest in classical music. Joan always said that it was Hilda rather than Samuel who had the 'singing gene' in the family. Samuel tried to take some credit by saying he used to sing at Westminster Abbey, but Joan never believed him—he didn't have much of a voice.

WHEN JOAN WAS well enough to go back to school she was sent to the Presbyterian Ladies' College at Pymble (the Hammonds were Church of England but PLC took all-comers). Pymble was just a short train ride from Lindfield, yet Joan was a boarder. She didn't seem to mind, in fact she enjoyed her sense of superiority over the 'day-bugs' (day girls). She also enjoyed the camaraderie and general high jinks. She had a good sense of fun and became popular very quickly—not so easy when you're a new girl arriving mid-year.

She involved herself in every sports activity available and wore an arm shield for rougher games like hockey. Photos of her at this time show a girl in school uniform or gym slip with one sleeve rolled up and the other buttoned down. If she was sleeveless, or in a swimming costume, the left arm was placed so it was out of sight of the camera.

Her bike accident had occurred when she was on the cusp of puberty, a delicate time. The scarring on her arm and thigh was a constant embarrassment, something that probably made her more self-conscious than she might have been if the accident had never happened.

Her swift promotion to the 'A' teams for tennis, hockey and netball, her perpetual first or second placement in swimming, springboard diving and running endeared her to the whole school. Opposing teams would hear the mystifying chant of 'Ham'nd eggs, Ham'nd eggs!' or simply 'Ham, Ham, Ham!' as they cheered on their champion.

Joan loved to rise to a sporting challenge, and she loved to win. She was a 'good sport' at all times—but the point of playing any game was to win.

She took singing, violin and piano as extra subjects and contrived to avoid mathematics whenever it appeared on her timetable. Her excuse was that most unfortunately she was already booked for one of her extra classes. This strategy worked for a surprisingly long time.

Her school house (with the promising title of 'Goodlet') was conveniently close to two of her favourite places: the outdoor swimming pool and the newly established Avondale golf course. She'd absent herself and disappear into one of the music rooms, or perhaps wander down to the pool and swim a few laps, and then, should there still be time before tea, she'd practise some putting on the nearest green.

Sport and music were her consummate passions and everyone knew it. Everyone knew it—including Miss Jobson, the headmistress. Miss Jobson was loved by most and revered by all. She knew what her girls were up to, often before they did, and she tended to know what was good for them.

There came a day when Joan received her comeuppance. She was enjoying an illicit swim when a breathless day-bug arrived to say that Miss Jobson wanted to see her immediately. The interview that followed was an uncomfortable yet salutary experience.

Miss Jobson expressed her disappointment in Joan's behaviour, below-average class marks—and no marks at all for maths. The allotted punishment cut to the quick: she was demoted from her position as Class Captain and given a long list of psalms to learn instead of playing sports. Having achieved the desired effect, Miss Jobson then offered her a challenge. She appointed her House Prefect and asked her to live up to the honour.

It was a clever move. Joan was never a model student but she took her new responsibilities seriously. She also learnt something interesting from having to memorise so many psalms: she had a talent for learning large quantities of material at great speed, an ability that would come in useful later on.

Joan was at PLC Pymble for just a little over two years but she left her mark. She won the Feldwick Prize for singing and twice won the Jobson Shield for swimming. Her good singing voice must have been obvious, for she sang a solo in the Christmas concert at the end of her first term. The song she sang was prophetic because it became one of her best-selling records—'The Green Hills o' Somerset'—an unlikely choice for a 13-year-old Australian girl. The following year she played a violin solo, which suggests she'd returned to a good standard of playing. She also acted in Shakespearian scenes and humorous playlets, her height and boyish demeanour casting her in the male roles. She had fairly short black hair with an off-centre parting. It had a natural wave but she kept it straight with hair cream—otherwise she didn't pay much attention to her appearance.

Joan's violin teacher was Henri Staëll, a leading Sydney violinist.

Her singing teacher was Madame Tasma, who described herself as a former 'pupil of Mme. Marchesi and Mme. Melba'—good credentials considering it was Marchesi who taught Melba in Paris. Joan was fortunate that her early singing teachers didn't introduce bad habits, for there were many charlatans with pet vocal techniques that could have crippled her natural talent. The school magazine congratulated her for 'ably filling the breach' when Madame Tasma was unable to sing at a fundraising concert in 1928. What a nerve-racking yet exhilarating moment it must have been, to fill the shoes of her teacher.

Joan was a 'golden girl'. Popular and successful and blissfully un-aware of the social advantages that came with having a wealthy father. She simply knew that it was better to be a boarder than a day-bug.

When the school holidays came around she would take off with one of her best friends: Heather Field, nicknamed 'Prairie'. 'Prairie' and 'Ham' would spend the summer holidays at Palm Beach. Winter breaks were spent at Heather's family property at Narrabri in the northern part of New South Wales. They'd go horse riding, polo playing (which Joan didn't take to), and droving. The droving meant long days in the saddle and a sore backside, but the evenings were deliciously romantic. The tents would be pitched and a camp fire lit while the sun set behind the hills. The billy would be simmering while potatoes were cooking in the glowing ashes. After a simple meal and gentle talk, Joan would be asked to sing. She'd give them a song or two and her voice would sound especially beautiful, hanging in the air between starlight and ember glow.

She was serious about her singing, but she also liked to have fun. She'd turn 'the *green* hills of Somerset' into 'the *blue* hills of some-where else', or she'd sing one of the popular numbers:

Izzie an Ozzie, izzie, Lizzie?
Izzie an Ozzie, izzie, eh?

Is it because he is an Ozzie,
That he makes you dizzy Lizzie?

By Flotsam and Jetsam

LIFE WAS GOOD. Joan especially adored her days at Palm Beach because she loved surfing and sailing so much. Samuel had given her a cabin cruiser called *Alawa* which she spent much time on. She also went sailing on other people's yachts, and raced on Sydney Harbour in a twelve-footer called *Stormalong* with her brother Tony, gathering a few trophies along the way.

Yet the sea also brought unpleasant experiences. She was surfing at Palm Beach and was way out beyond the breakers when she saw the fin of a shark cutting slowly through the water just as the warning bell rang. Her mind said swim but her body just froze. Then a massive wave rose up and pushed her into action. She caught it and rode to shore. Hilda tried to make her promise never to swim beyond the breakers again, but Joan knew herself too well to promise.

And then there was golf. Joan was one of the few girls to take advantage of the open invitation to use the Avondale golf links alongside PLC (she became an associate member of this club after she left the school). At Palm Beach she could step off the front veranda and saunter on to the ninth green and do some chipping or putting whenever she pleased. Her parents were average players but three of Samuel's business friends were good golfers, and they had a marked influence on her game. Percy Hunter, Alan Box and Mr Moses were well-known businessmen from Sydney. They holidayed at Palm Beach and played every day. They called over the fence one morning to ask if she'd like to make up a four.

She had a natural game which these three men encouraged. She *had* to improve her drive and her putting just to keep up with them.

Joan with her father and brothers

She learnt from observing and from the helpful hints they offered, and never had a lesson—which is why she learnt how to play a man's game rather than a woman's game.

SHE CELEBRATED HER fifteenth birthday at school on 24 May 1927. On the very next day, quietly and privately, Samuel and Hilda went to the District Registrar's Office in Chatswood and officially became husband and wife. Why they chose to get married at this particular time is anybody's guess. Samuel declared on the marriage certificate that he was a widower, so perhaps Edith Hood had died, but Samuel also stated that his father's surname was Hammond, which was untrue. Whatever the reasons, the marriage was at last legal. Their past was their past, and no one need ever know about it—especially their children.

The couple continued to be known as Mr and Mrs Samuel H. Hammond, the 'H' standing silently for 'Hood' as always.

JOAN MADE SOME choices towards the end of 1928. She decided to study violin at the State Conservatorium of Music. Her left arm gave her pain when she played but her standard was good. Good enough to become a teacher of violin at PLC Pymble. Her name was listed in the PLC prospectus beneath the name of her own teacher. Henri Staëll charged £4 4s per term and Joan charged the same. It's unclear whether anyone actually engaged her services, but it was a significant development. Finances, as much as talent, may have been at the back of this move because Joan's world of luxury and social advantage was coming to an end. Samuel H. Hammond was beginning to lose all his money.

Presbyterian Ladies' College
Pymble

... Prize ...

Singing
Feldwick Memorial Prize

Awarded to
Joan Hammond

Class 6R.

~~signature~~ Chairman

Anna Drennan, (M.A.) (Edin) *Principal*

Year, 192 5

CHAPTER 2

A POWERFUL DRIVE

THE HAMMONDS WERE WEALTHY on the Monday and poor by
the Saturday. Palm Beach was the first of the family properties to be
sold and 'Walbrook' was the last (bought by Billy Hughes, a former
prime minister). It was the Wall Street crash, the beginning of the
Great Depression. For the first time in her life, Joan had to think
about how she was going to earn a living—to assist her family as well
as herself.

The Hammonds eventually moved to a small flat in Kirribilli on the
North Shore. Noel and Len were making their own way by this time
so it was just the four of them—plus a paying guest, 'Tweet' Mcindoe,
a young woman from New Zealand whose father was wealthy. The
block of flats was called 'Renown' after a ship, and was close to
Admiralty House. Conditions were cramped compared to what they'd
been used to, but at least the location was good. Their top-floor flat
had a fabulous view of the harbour, and the garden went down to the
sea. It was also conveniently close to the city. Joan could catch the
ferry and be at Circular Quay within a matter of minutes. Then all she
had to do was walk up the hill to the Royal Botanic Gardens. There,
in all its glory, stood the State Conservatorium of Music.

The New South Wales State Conservatorium of Music, or 'the Con' as it was affectionately known, was a strange building in a magnificent setting overlooking the bay. It had sixteen turrets and eight large gateways and looked like a castle in a fairytale. The original purpose of the building was to house the Governor's horses, but with the advent of the motor car the place fell into decay. It was reborn as the State Conservatorium in 1915, and thereafter attracted excellent teachers, talented students, and high-profile visiting artists.

Joan studied diligently and was soon rewarded with a place in the second violins of the Sydney Philharmonic Orchestra. Dr Orchard was the conductor as well as director of the Con, so it was a positive step to be playing under his baton.

Rehearsals for her first major concert progressed well—except that sustained playing caused pain in her arm. The discomfort could become so acute that she'd be forced to rest while all around were playing. The conductor understood the problem but it didn't help her embarrassment—especially when it happened on the night of the performance. Her fantasy had been that the exhilaration of the evening would carry her through—so to fail so publicly was a crushing blow. She had to accept that a career as a violinist was out of the question.

A lesser being might have fallen into a depressed heap after all these difficulties, but not Joan. She kept pushing forward at full steam and put all her energies into singing.

Her first professional engagement came with relative ease. Dr Orchard was looking for a soprano to sing a short but difficult solo in a forthcoming concert. Perhaps he'd heard that Joan had potential, for he went to the studio where she was having a singing lesson and listened outside the door. The composition he required a soloist for was Vaughan Williams's *Pastoral* symphony, a haunting work inspired by the composer's experiences while serving in France during the First World War. The solo comes in the final movement. The soprano's voice creates a poignant lyricism which is undercut by the soft but menacing sound of solo timpani. The special difficulty for the soprano is that she must begin unaccompanied and still be in tune when the orchestra picks up the theme where she's finished off. Dr Orchard thought Joan could do it. After the first rehearsal the job was hers.

The score stipulates that the soprano must be 'distant' and Dr Orchard interpreted this as 'out of sight', so Joan was heard and not seen at her debut professional performance.

JOAN STILL FOUND TIME to play golf, despite the financial pressures. Golf was a very necessary part of her life—though even this gave her some pain in her left arm.

She started playing more regularly and competing more seriously. She'd won the easy-going Palm Beach Championship three times (1926 to 1928), but her first real test came when she competed in the inaugural Junior State Championship in 1929, just a few days after her seventeenth birthday. The somewhat formidable New South Wales Ladies' Golf Union had decided to mount a junior event to encourage younger players into the game. The event was held at Rose Bay, home of the Royal Sydney Golf Club—of which Joan later became a member.

She was a clear winner. She also amazed officials by establishing a handicap of nine, a figure that most players of any age would envy in the extreme. She won the junior title again in 1930, and was also runner-up in the senior championship. This was an extraordinary achievement, not least because she'd suffered two miserable events during the week of competition. A cyclone had passed through Sydney and wrecked her boat (one of her last assets), and her dog had died from tick poisoning on the morning of the final.

Joan's opponent in the senior final was her new friend Odette Lefebvre, who was young, tall and attractive. She was engaged to a well-known golfer, Tom McKay, and received professional coaching.

Odette possessed an air of French elegance, and her playing style was graceful. Joan's style was less attractive but her play had more punch. Both players had a following and by the time the two young women reached the final the crowd was extremely large—and enthralled. It was a ground-breaking contest. No one could recall a more exciting final in the history of the championship (a history that went back to 1903). A new era in women's golf had begun.

For the next few years Joan would be known as 'the famous golfer'. Newspaper articles and photographs celebrated her powerful drive, sporty image, and intelligent approach to the game. It was noted that her putting sometimes let her down, but her swing was often photographed, and even appeared on the front cover of a golfing magazine as an example of how it should be done. Odette Lefebvre was also featured in articles, though observations regarding her looks sometimes outweighed comments on her game. The basic outfit for associate players (i.e. women) was: shirt and tie, lengthy skirt, and stockings—to be worn with or without socks, but bare legs were forbidden. The dress code was strict. An official once ordered Joan off the first tee at Rose Bay 'to return only if bestockinged'.

Journalists characterised Joan as a robust all-rounder. She was 'charmingly natural' with an interest in music and an ability to tackle practical things like repairing a car engine or outboard motor. She was also reported as knowing all the golf rules by heart. When more experienced players challenged her on a technicality they invariably found she was correct when they got back to the clubhouse and checked the rule book.

One of the significant things about Joan's growing fame was that she started to highlight the 'Hood' in her name. Newspaper articles and championship honour rolls of the early 1930s would list her as Joan Hood-Hammond, with or without the hyphen. It was inconsistent, but the Ladies' Golf Union certainly used this form. The reason isn't clear. Joan was too straightforward for affectation so perhaps Samuel

D 1933
XV., No. 6

PUBLISHED MONTHLY IN ALL STATES.

Registered at the G.P.O., Melbourne,
for transmission by post as a newspaper.

The Australian
GOLF & TENNIS
MAGAZINE

MISS JOAN HAMMOND'S POWERFUL DRIVE

LEFT ELBOW CLOSE TO SIDE

RIGHT SHOULDER HAS GONE UNDER & THROUGH BUT THE HEAD HAS BEEN HELD BACK

The New South Wales Champion will be defending her title next month at the Australia Club, Kensington

WEIGHT TRANSFERRED TO LEFT FOOT

6D

SEE YOURSELF AS OTHERS SEE YOU — Page 189
VINES OPPOSES OPEN CHAMPIONSHIPS — Page 211

had revealed something about the true value of her middle name. She signed herself as Joan Hood Hammond, on and off, for a couple of years, then the 'Hood' disappeared from view again.

SHE CONTINUED TO STUDY singing at the Con, but the most significant new influence on her development was Lute Drummond, a talented opera coach. Lute Drummond (1879–1949), and her sister Jean, had spent their early years travelling and studying music in Europe. Lute was an accomplished pianist and her sister was a dramatic soprano who'd sung professionally in Italy. They settled back in Sydney for good in 1930 and Lute established a tiny roof-top studio in Bond Street where she coached singers and taught languages. She was an excellent linguist, and had an encyclopaedic musical knowledge, especially of opera. Lute passionately believed that there should be a 'National Opera House' and did a great deal to foster this idea.

The sisters had enjoyed some wonderful musical experiences. They'd heard Richard Strauss conduct *Der Rosenkavalier* in 1911 and later attended a performance of *Eugene Onegin* at Petrograd, in the Soviet Union. They'd seen the best the world had to offer. When Joan first sang in the tiny roof-top studio, the sisters realised they were listening to a voice with a future. They did everything they could to assist her.

Joan attended Lute's German, French and Italian classes, as well as studying opera and song. Lute suggested a richly diverse repertoire, unusual arias such as Puccini's '*In quelle trine morbide*' ('In that soft lace') from *Manon Lescaut* and Marietta's Song from *Die Tote Stadt* (The dead city) by Korngold. She added the works of Duparc, Debussy, Strauss, Schubert, Wolf and Marx to her repertoire, plus contemporary English composers such as Delius, Quilter, Bax, Vaughan Williams and Armstrong Gibbs. Her schoolgirl repertoire was cast aside, though she kept some sentimental favourites, including 'The Green Hills o' Somerset'.

She began to understand the subtleties and importance of interpretation: that singing was about mood, emotion and placement, as well as technique; that each song must be invested with total commitment if it was to come alive and truly communicate. She discovered that she wanted to achieve this miracle of communication more than anything: she wanted to be an opera singer. But it was a notoriously difficult ambition to fulfil, especially for someone living in Australia. Melba was the magnificent example, but the road she'd travelled was littered with singers who'd faltered at one point or another.

Opera productions were infrequent in Australia at that time. They were presented using imported artists, and only included Australians if they'd made a name for themselves overseas. Joan had seen her first production in 1928 when the Melba-Williamson Company toured with a predominantly Italian cast. It was Hilda's idea that her daughter should see an opera. They were unable to get tickets to hear Melba, but they did see a good production of Massenet's *Thais*. Joan was enthralled. The performances of the soprano, Lina Scavizzi, and Melba's protégé, the Australian baritone John Brownlee, impressed her enormously.

There was excitement, therefore, in 1932, when it was announced that the Williamson Imperial Grand Opera Company was organising a major tour. Italian singers were to be imported for the principal roles but auditions were to be held for minor roles, chorus, ballet dancers and orchestra. It was a great opportunity for Australian talent. About six hundred singers applied to audition, and Joan was one of them. The selection process was brutal. Everyone was seen briefly in the first round, then the culling began. Joan had an agonising wait before she heard she'd made it to round two, and then round three . . . her name was on the list when the final selection was pinned to the notice board. She joined the chorus as a permanent member of the company with fifteen women and six men, and was the youngest in the group.

The first day of rehearsal got off to a bad start. Some of the rejected singers gathered at the stage door and made nasty personal comments as the 'lucky ones' passed through. It was an early indication of how resilient she'd have to be to survive.

The company presented seventeen operas over a five-month period beginning in Sydney at Her Majesty's Theatre in April and ending in Melbourne at The Theatre Royal in September. The premiere was *Aida*. She found that her abilities were stretched to the limit: she had some knowledge of singing in Italian but had no idea about stagecraft—and wasn't given much help. The chorus was 'herded' with instructions from all sides. The Maestro and Stage Director only spoke Italian, so translations were 'barked' by assistants. She found that singing while acting was really difficult, for her dominant urge was to stare at the conductor at all times. She even had to dance in some of the operas because chorus members with dancing ability were used to bolster the corps de ballet. She was reminded of her childhood when she danced through the school garden waving silken scarves—a memory that would be echoed years later when she played Salome.

The first costume call for *Aida* was a lesson in itself. Joan assumed she'd be fitted by the Wardrobe Mistress, but the reality was like a scrummage at a jumble sale. There were piles of 'Egyptian' costumes, mismatched and with the whiff of body odour, and everyone had to dive in and grab what they could. Joan soon found that her new friends had sharp elbows.

She managed her duties well, though there was one incident in *Madam Butterfly* that caused her to blush. She was 'fluttering' on stage as one of Butterfly's relatives when she felt a cool breeze around her head. A fellow flutterer pointed upwards and she saw her wig dangling from a cherry blossom branch. Mortified, she made a hasty exit but ran straight into the Stage Manager. She thought he'd give her the sack but he just said: 'Gor blimey 'ammond, can't you keep your ruddy roof on?'

Dismissal wasn't out of the question. One night in *Aida* four spear carriers snagged a rope and almost brought the scenery down. They were fired on the spot.

Joan learnt on the job and began to fall in love with theatre life. She enjoyed the backstage rough-and-tumble just as much as the illusion that was being played out onstage. She liked the rituals: the half-hour call shouted by the call-boy, the sound of the orchestra tuning up, the application of make-up, becoming a pale Japanese or a dark Egyptian depending on the night, the costume hanging on the rack with 'Hammond' written on the name tag, the shoes that didn't quite fit; the transformation. The backstage ebb and flow of chaos and order, the waiting in the wings, the nervous excitement, the cue to go on stage. Then of course there was the pleasure of observing the Italians going about their work, the colourful personalities, the arguments, the kindnesses, the performances, the audience applause, the after-show banter back in the dressing room as the greasepaint came off. The 'good night Miss Hammond' from the stage doorman as she re-entered the real world beneath real starlight. It was a strange but exhilarating life.

She was earning £3 a week from the Williamson opera company, and half of that, 30 shillings, went to Samuel for general upkeep. There wasn't much money to spare for essentials, let alone luxuries. To give an idea of prices at this time: a good pair of golf shoes cost 45s, a fitted golf shirt 16s 6d, and a set of golf clubs ranged from £10 to £18. The most expensive seat at the opera cost about 12s 6d.

It was terrific news, therefore, when she was selected to stay with the company for the Melbourne tour. She was given a minor role and the chance to understudy.

The minor role was Giovanna in *Rigoletto* — maid-cum-guardian to the heroine and somewhat older than Joan's fresh-faced 20. It was

a marvellous experience to perform opposite principals who'd sung at
La Scala, though the role was especially small, seven bars in all:

Rigoletto:
Is the gate to the street always kept locked?
Giovanna:
Yes, always.

Rigoletto, Act 1

It was her first visit to Melbourne so it was all very thrilling—except for
the accommodation. She was given a living allowance of 10 shillings
but Samuel insisted that this 'extra money' be sent back home, and
Joan complied. Cheap digs with ghastly meals and uncomfortable
beds made her realise how much she'd taken for granted. Hilda may
have had her shortcomings but she always had a nice meal waiting
when she got home. The Melbourne tour was Joan's first experience
of looking after herself.

One of her discoveries on the tour was that Italian men can have
unwelcome 'habits'. Roving hands was one, and hawking another.
'Hawking' was a new word for Joan. All singers have to clear their
throats, but the Italian males never seemed to care where their
projectile ended up! It was common practice but she never got used
to it, not ever.

SHE WAS DISAPPOINTED she couldn't compete in the New South
Wales Golf Championship that year; she'd registered to play but
then discovered the dates clashed with the Melbourne tour. Certain
members of the golfing community were similarly disappointed and
they tried to do something about it. Unknown to her, a particularly
forceful member of the Ladies' Golf Union approached E. J. Tait,

one of the owners of the Williamson Company, and explained the situation. Tait happened to be a keen golfer, but hadn't realised that the Hammond on his payroll was the Hammond who was the golfer. The upshot was that he gave Joan leave of absence to compete. So halfway through the Melbourne tour she caught the train back to Sydney.

There was a huge crowd at Rose Bay to watch the event. Supporters, dignitaries, caddies, punters, they'd all turned up to see what the young champion could do. Pre-game nerves were ghastly but she overcame them and played her best golf ever. She beat Odette Lefebvre in the semi-finals, and triumphed over a top rank competitor to win the final. 'Miss J. Hood-Hammond' became the New South Wales Golf Champion of 1932. She was awarded a trophy and a cash prize.

When the train brought her back to Melbourne she found the entire opera company waiting to greet her at Spencer Street station—even the Maestro—and when she stepped from the train they sang 'For she's a jolly good fellow' at full volume.

Joan's stay in Melbourne improved considerably after that. She was embraced by the golfing community and quickly made new friends. These friends included the Marriott family. Nance Marriott was President of the Yarra Yarra Golf Club, and was a generous host when it came to entertaining visiting golfers. Her husband, Clarence Marriott, was Managing Director and owner of Hecla Electrics, the largest manufacturer of electrical heating appliances in Australia. (If you wanted a kettle or a toaster you were bound to end up with a 'Hecla'.)

The Marriotts lived in a mansion called 'Hawthroy' in Albany Road, Toorak, and they had two children, Ron and Lolita. Ron was studying science at university and was destined to join his father in the business. Lolita was seventeen and spent most of her days playing golf and having a pleasant time. Joan became very fond of the whole family, and Lolita eventually became one of the most important people in her life. But for the moment, in 1932, Lolita was a teenager with thick plaits, a dominant mother, and no particular focus. She was a good golfer, played violin, enjoyed the sea and loved dogs—so Joan found her very easy to get on with. Joan became a welcome guest at the Marriotts whenever she was visiting Melbourne, and in following years she would spend holidays with them.

Joan's shyness was less pronounced after all these experiences, but she still felt intensely self-conscious in formal situations. Talking with dignitaries after a golf tournament made her so uncomfortable that she broke out in a cold sweat.

The shyness fell away when she relaxed with friends. She was a terrific mimic and could imitate almost anyone to great effect, with actions. She liked to lark about and do silly things—simple pleasures like a trip to Luna Park with friends. She also liked to tease. This was usually harmless but not always. She had her blind spots and one of them was intolerance toward Catholics (not uncommon at the time). Interestingly, the Marriotts were Catholic, as were most of the Italians in the opera company, so she probably 'adjusted' her comments accordingly.

Joan was solidly Church of England. She didn't attend church very often but she uttered the occasional prayer—especially if she had a competition-winning putt to sink.

SHE HAD TO DECIDE whether to go with the opera company to New Zealand, or stay in Australia and compete in the National Golf Championship. The golfing community was pressing her to play, but there was no way of doing both. It's interesting that she hesitated, just for a moment, before making her choice.

The New Zealand tour was enjoyable except that it brought the grand opera season to a close. When the curtain fell on the last night it meant the company would disband forever. There were tears mixed with cheers and everyone was emotional. Joan didn't feel too sentimental, for she stayed in New Zealand rather than travel back with the rest of the company. She'd somehow managed to procure a singing engagement at a new cinema in Auckland. The deal was that she would sing the aria 'One fine day', plus two songs of her choosing, twice daily for three weeks. Maybe it was a working holiday, or maybe she felt she had to take whatever singing work she could get. The financial situation at home wasn't getting any better.

When she got back to Sydney she made it known that she was available for weddings, parties, fashion parades, anything—and engagements began to trickle in. Grace Brothers, the department store, held a fashion week and she was employed to sing something 'suitable' while the ladies consumed tea and the models went up and down the catwalk. She sang 'Because' when bridal gowns were on parade. Music clubs were popular, despite the Depression, and offered good fees for recitals. She could earn 2 guineas (£2 2s) for singing two groups of songs at a music club, whereas Grace Brothers only paid 4 guineas (£4 4s) for the full week.

Hilda often accompanied Joan on these engagements, as support, but also as a way of enjoying some reflected success. Hilda was happy to be 'Joan Hammond's mother', especially in later years. Her world had crumbled and there was little hope of restoration: gone was the big house, the Packard car, the domestic servants. She blamed Samuel rather than Wall Street for their losses, and never forgave him. It's difficult to know what Joan's attitude was toward her mother, given that she'd never talk about her. It may be significant that Joan stopped calling her 'Mother' and started using the nickname 'Darls'. 'Darls' or 'darling' is a term of endearment, but in theatrical circles it's too overused to have value. Joan didn't give her father a nickname, and perhaps she didn't speak to him much at all. Samuel's reputation was shaky. It was rumoured he'd been involved in dishonest dealings concerning the management of a golf club. Whatever happened, he'd

Hilda and Joan, Tony and Samuel

been dismissed from the job and was drinking heavily. Samuel and Hilda were only surviving financially because Joan, and her eldest brother Noel, were sharing much of the load. (Noel had married the daughter of the publican who owned The Ship Inn on Circular Quay, Len was in Queensland, and Tony was still at school.)

Despite all this, Joan continued her lessons with Lute Drummond, and attended harmony and theory classes at the Con. It was through two teachers at the Con that she got her next big singing job. Lindley Evans and Frank Hutchens had made a name for themselves as duo pianists. They gave recitals all over Australia and played regularly for the Australian Broadcasting Commission (ABC radio). When they were looking for a vocalist to join them on a tour they thought of Joan. She jumped at the opportunity but the ABC wasn't so sure; they'd never heard of her. The producers were still uncertain after she'd auditioned, but Evans and Hutchens insisted. They said that none of the better known artists would do such a tour for the low fee that the ABC was offering, especially over Christmas, so Joan got the job.

The six-week tour included Melbourne, Adelaide and Tasmania. Evans and Hutchens were superb musicians and their advice during this period was invaluable. They were also great fun. The fourth member of the party was Marie, Lindley Evans's wife, who went along for the ride. The trio performed a number of recitals in the ABC studio of each city. Joan's job was to sing two short groups of songs between the longer piano duets. They found Adelaide the most problematic because of the heat. Some nights were so sweltering that they slept on the lawn of their digs. Hot or not, they still had to wear full evening dress for their radio performances—despite the fact that no one could see them. The last part of their tour was spent in Tasmania. Marie brought her car, so they were able to do some sightseeing on their days off. This led to drama on their final day because a serious bushfire caused them to lose their way. Thick smoke and fierce wind, plus the added tension of needing to be in Hobart to catch their home-going ferry, made it a memorable journey. Otherwise it was a great experience.

But it was golf rather than singing that began to bring the better income. Anyone who read the sports pages knew that Joan Hammond was the famous young golfer. Newspapers began to capitalise on this by offering her work as a sports reporter. She started in a small way, reporting golf results for the *Observer*, and within the year she went to the *Mail* and then the *Telegraph*. She stayed with the *Telegraph* from 1933 to 1936 and really enjoyed it. Golf was her primary area but she was sometimes asked to cover other events. A dog show was fine, but if she was asked to cover a fashion parade or a classical concert she panicked. Fashion was too nonsensical for words, while concerts were too big a responsibility. She felt she lacked the depth of musical knowledge required. Joan was ambitious but she wasn't arrogant.

Her good friend and fellow golfer, Odette Lefebvre (now Mrs McKay), was also writing occasional articles. The pair could write about each other, but they couldn't report more than score details about themselves. Journalists usually wrote glowing articles about Joan's golfing prowess, but there were times when she was criticised for 'biffing' the ball (whacking it in a graceless style). Joan was annoyed by the criticism and retaliated by writing an article about a hypothetical 'younger player' who got results despite her style: '. . . unfortunately there are many players who have ruined their natural swing through trying to look nice, instead of trying to hit the ball'.

Her job was to collate all the match scores for the day, and if there were other things to write about she'd stay at her desk till late in the evening. The newspaper office had an atmosphere she enjoyed. Young journalists and copy boys would drop by for a chat. Cadets sometimes wrote articles about her for the in-house *Sun Junior*, and she wrote occasional pieces herself. She even managed a minor but rather clever scoop. Two top New Zealand players were arriving by liner to play in the Ladies' Amateur Golf Championship. Joan wangled a lift in the pilot boat, climbed aboard the ship via the rope ladder, found the players, interviewed them, and was back ashore before the liner docked. Her article came out in the first editions of the *Telegraph* while her colleagues were still waiting to greet the players.

Sports reporting meant that Joan became extremely busy, but it was a lifesaver as far as income was concerned. Her basic weekly wage was £5 5s, and she often earned more with extra articles. It was a good wage and certainly helped to keep the Hammond ship afloat. It also pushed her to improve her golf. She won a number of competitions in spectacular fashion, breaking all sorts of course records along the way. She reduced her handicap from four to two, and only just missed out on reducing it to one. She held the lowest women's handicap in Australia for two years.

Joan and Odette often played together when they were representing New South Wales. On one occasion they travelled to Melbourne to play in a big interstate tournament at Sandringham. The other Sydney players were staying at the guesthouse nearest the golf course but Odette and Joan decided to stay in a hotel in the city. They wanted freedom from the LGU officials. They also knew from past experience that the older ladies hogged the armchairs by the fireplace, leaving the rest of the girls to freeze. They caught the train out to Sandringham in good time on the morning of the tournament but when they arrived they found there were no taxis to take them to the golf course. Catastrophe. If they didn't arrive within half an hour they'd be scratched from the tournament and be a disgrace to their team. There was nothing for it but to start walking. They had their golf clubs and their day bags and it was a very long distance but there was nothing else to do. Then a vehicle came into view, going their way. It was a horse-drawn milk cart. Joan looked at Odette and Odette looked at Joan and they both made a beeline for the milkman. Joan

Odette and Joan

did the talking and Odette did the smiling, a very sweet coquettish French smile, and although the milkman said he really shouldn't he found himself saying that he would. So they hauled themselves and their bags on to the cart and the horse went clip-clop through the streets of Sandringham all the way to the club house door. It was only then, when they saw the horrified faces of the other golfers, that they realised what a sight they must be. Undeterred, Odette lowered

herself from the cart with immaculate dignity and Joan hopped down
as if she were the milkman's daughter. They gathered up their bags,
registered for the tournament, played their games like demons, and
won the cup for their team!

> Hoyotoho! Hoyotoho!
> Brünnhilde! hi!
>
> *Die Walküre*, Wagner

SIR BENJAMIN FULLER'S GRAND OPERA COMPANY came to
Sydney in 1935, bringing a distinguished cast of British singers, many
of them from the British National Opera. Soloists included Australian
expatriates, and top of the bill was Florence Austral, famous for her
Wagnerian roles. Operas by Verdi, Puccini, Wagner and others were
presented in English in the hope of attracting a wide audience. Prices
were low, production values high, and the staging more refined than
the Italian approach.

The Fuller company had opened its season in Melbourne, which
is perhaps why Joan wasn't involved when the company toured to
Sydney. Yet everything changed when the Conservatorium received
an emergency phone call from Benjamin Fuller. The soprano playing
Venus in *Tannhäuser* had suddenly withdrawn and they needed a
replacement by the end of the week: did they know of anyone? It was a
substantial role and Joan had twenty-four hours in which to learn it.

It was a huge undertaking. Everything else was put aside, including
sleep. She played the music on her violin all through the night (thus
saving her voice), and she put the words to the notes in the morning.
When she arrived at the theatre and sang for the coach she was music
and word perfect.

Wagner had never been on Joan's study list, and Venus is not an
easy role, especially for a naïve young woman of 23. Venus is supposed

to be a sexy pagan goddess who seduces Tannhäuser and causes his downfall. Joan had no illusions, she knew it wasn't a part for her— but she gave it her best shot. How terrifying it must have been to go onstage with so little preparation. The unfamiliar set, costume, props, stage directions, singers, conductor. The coach supported from the wings but she did her first performance without ever having had an orchestral rehearsal. She wasn't an overnight sensation but she survived. She was then given Helmwige, one of the Valkyries in *Die Walkure*, and also Siebel in *Faust*—a sizeable role and her first 'breeches' part. Siebel is a young man in love with Marguerite:

Siebel:
May she be acquainted with
The passion she has roused
And of which my troubled heart
Has not breathed a word.

Faust, Act 3

It rounded off her Fuller Grand Opera excursion very nicely.

JOAN MADE FULL USE of all these opportunities but she'd always known that progress could only be made by studying overseas. One had to have talent *and* money to succeed—plus a sponsor who could help to open doors. Joan believed in destiny. She kept faith with her talent, worked hard, and hoped that Fate would look after the rest. Oddly enough, Fate obliged.

Lute Drummond, ever vigilant in her effort to assist her student, put her name forward to sing at a prestigious reception to be held in honour of the Governor's wife. The name of this dignitary was Lady Hore-Ruthven, but as her husband was about to be made the

Governor-General of Australia with the new title of Lord Gowrie she will be referred to as Lady Gowrie from now on. The committee that was organising the prestigious function, as well as some of the 'name' artists booked to perform, felt that Joan was too young and inexperienced to have the honour of singing in front of the King's Representative. Besides, she was semi-amateur while all the other artists were professional. Fortunately Lute Drummond had a strong ally on the committee and her will prevailed. Even so, there was a strong undercurrent of resistance.

It was a hot afternoon, and the Australia Hotel, where the function was to take place, was stuffy—in more senses than one. Joan was again surprised at how resentful some artists could be. The 'big names' treated her with disdain in the dressing room, and the co-ordinator told her to 'keep it short and get off quick'. Joan knew that her dress wasn't quite right—especially with its unfashionably long sleeves which were necessary to cover the scar on her arm—and she knew that she was gauche. She sat in a corner and tried to keep calm while she waited for her turn, which came after interval. She sang a couple of songs and got off quickly as instructed. She had gathered her things and was heading for the door when a committee member came to say that Lady Gowrie had expressed the wish that Miss Hammond sing again. An icy chill rushed round the room. Yes, Lady Gowrie was quite specific, she wished to hear Miss Hammond sing 'The Green Hills o' Somerset' again, and any other song of her choosing. Royalty had spoken, so of course Joan, and everyone else, obeyed.

Lady Gowrie did not come from Somerset but she was rather fond of 'green hills'. She was born in County Galway, Ireland, and her original name was Zara Eileen Pollok. She was a splendid woman: warm, intelligent, witty, dedicated. Now in her mid-fifties, her many talents included a knowledge of music—in fact she had studied music in Vienna when young.

45

A few days after the reception Lady Gowrie sent Joan an invitation to visit her at Government House. Joan was nervous when she arrived but Lady Gowrie gently put her at ease by taking her to a comfortable alcove. She gave her tea and cucumber sandwiches and described her own experience of the reception: it had been hot and stuffy, and after interval she felt her eyelids grow heavy, very heavy. Then suddenly she was lifted from her drowsiness by a wonderful voice, 'a peerless young voice'. She looked down at the stage and saw a girl in a long-sleeved dress. The audience applauded long and loud but the girl dashed from the stage and would not return for an encore. That was a shame, thought Lady Gowrie, and she requested that her aide see what she could do about it . . . Lady Gowrie asked Joan about her circumstances and intentions and was surprised to be told that they'd met once before, when she presented Joan with her first senior golf trophy. They talked earnestly about her singing aspirations and general financial circumstances. Lady Gowrie assessed the situation quickly and astutely. Something had to be done to assist this young singer, and she was going to do all in her power to help.

Lady Gowrie was true to her word, in this and many instances that followed. It was as if Joan had found her Fairy Godmother: 'You *shall* go to Europe and study singing!'

The magic didn't end there. Fate, or a remarkable coincidence, brought the Vienna Boys' Choir to Sydney at exactly this time. The director of the choir was Rector Joseph Schnitt, the man who'd guided the choir to international success. Lady Gowrie asked Rector Schnitt to hear Joan sing. He listened and responded by suggesting that she complete her studies in Vienna under his supervision. It was the key to the door.

Lady Gowrie wasn't wealthy, but she had friends who were. She began her campaign by holding two large dinner parties at Government House. The wine flowed, Joan sang, and cheque books opened. This spread the word and attracted prestigious dignitaries to serve on the fundraising committee. A 'Joan Hammond Fund' was set up with the aim of raising £1000 within twelve months. This was a staggering sum when one remembers that Joan's weekly wage was less than £6. On Joan's suggestion they invited Miss Leo Wray, a highly regarded golfing celebrity, to act as manager and fundraising co-ordinator. This was an inspired choice because she had contacts that went deep into the inner networks of the Ladies' Golf Union. Funds came from a multitude of sources, but it was the New South Wales Ladies' Golf Union that pushed the hardest to reach that target.

Initial meetings showed promise. A public gathering in November 1935 attracted nearly a hundred people. Lady Gowrie, Sir Henry Braddon MP, Lute Drummond, and Madame Cherniasvksy made glowing speeches about the outstanding prospects that awaited Joan if she were to study overseas—and there was a generous response. Several donations were received on the night and representatives from fourteen golf clubs offered to raise funds through their club's efforts. By the end of the evening the Joan Hammond Fund stood at £120, by February 1936 it had reached £600.

Joan was overwhelmed, so much so that she could hardly string two words together. She felt an enormous pressure to prove herself worthy of all the effort, and told a friend, with great earnestness, that she would repay the money one day. The friend was Bertie Lloyd (nicknamed 'Boo' by Joan), and although Bertie loved Joan dearly and believed in her voice, she couldn't see how such a repayment could ever be made. But Joan was determined. It was like a force inside her that drove her on: she *would* repay somehow, some day.

Bertie Lloyd was a good friend to Joan. Bertie and her family made sure that Joan sometimes had a weekend off. They'd go for a picnic, see a film, or have fun at Luna Park. On one memorable occasion they'd been to a Saturday night film. Mrs Lloyd (as Joan called her) was preparing supper in the kitchen and Joan was leaning against the draining board singing something she'd just learnt. She often sang in the kitchen because Mrs Lloyd liked it. The aria rose high and Joan sang softly. Then she said 'Shall I let it go?' and Mrs Lloyd said 'Yes' — and her voice soared up, rich and powerful. And as she sang, the lights in the houses all around started to come on, one by one, and people stood at their windows and listened. And for the next few days people kept saying to Mrs Lloyd, 'You know, we did enjoy that concert.'

Socialising with the Lloyds was the kind of friendship that suited Joan. Work was her focus and it's unlikely she looked for something deeper in terms of 'a relationship'. She liked to have a mate come along for the ride and Bertie was often that person. Bertie was the same age and she'd attended PLC Pymble — as had another good friend, 'Mickey' McCay. The McCay family, like the Lloyds, took Joan on outings. They were very fond of her, as were so many people.

Bertie Lloyd, Mrs McCay and Joan

THINGS MOVED VERY QUICKLY under Lady Gowrie's command. Joan's passage to Vienna was booked for 4 April 1936 and a 'farewell and thankyou' concert was held at the Sydney Town Hall a couple of days before she left.

It was a superb evening. The hall was packed and there was a wonderful line-up of performers, including Gladys Moncrieff. As one journalist commented: 'If Joan Hammond's four years of study abroad are paved with as many flowers as were showered upon her at the Town Hall last night—her life, literally, will be a bed of roses'.

There were more flowers showered upon her when she boarded the MS *Dagfred*. Almost a hundred people came to see her off. Joan's parents and brothers, the Lloyds, the McCays, Lute Drummond, Leo Wray, golfing friends, musician friends, so many were there, and almost everyone brought a gift—something 'useful' for the journey.

Joan smiled for the cameras and joked and laughed, and held her bouquets and threw out the streamers, and waved and waved. But there was anxiety in her eyes. What lay ahead?

CHAPTER 3

INNOCENT ABROAD

JOAN FELT THE THROB of the turbines as the *Dagfred* eased away from the wharf. Familiar landmarks came and went. There was Circular Quay on the south shore, Kirribilli and Admiralty House on the north shore. Then there was the green sweep of the Botanic Gardens and the small white 'castle' that was the Conservatorium in its prime position overlooking the bay. Then the awesome contour of the Sydney Harbour Bridge, getting smaller and yet smaller, till gone from view.

The *Dagfred* was a modern Norwegian cargo ship equipped with two spacious cabins for passengers. Joan shared a cabin with a French Moroccan woman while three Italian men shared the other cabin. There was a small saloon that served as a dining and sitting area but otherwise there were no special amenities for passengers.

The ship ran into storms within hours of leaving Sydney and the freighter, light of load, was tossed around in violent fashion on the Tasman Sea. Joan found it exhilarating but her fellow passengers became seasick. They retired to their bunks and stayed there for several days. She was the only passenger to turn up for meals, so she was able to share some seafaring camaraderie with her fellow diners, the Captain and First Mate. The Norwegian Captain spoke German and English and had agreed to take responsibility for her until they reached Genoa—a voyage of six weeks.

When the freighter reached Melbourne there was a group of well-wishers waiting on the pier. Lolita Marriott was among them and was the last to say goodbye. The *Dagfred* went to Adelaide, then Fremantle, then at last turned toward the north-west and the Indian Ocean. The ship would cross the Tropic of Capricorn and the Equator before reaching the next port of call: Colombo, the capital of Ceylon (Sri Lanka).

The Italian passengers were the first to find their sea legs. Joan grew to like them later, but felt awkward with them initially. They spoke good English but their conversation included what she realised must be vulgar jokes and innuendo. She laughed in what she hoped were the right places. But it was the female passenger who caused her the most problems. The French Moroccan was in her early fifties and preoccupied with the idea of having a shipboard romance. The woman found Joan's presence—albeit innocent and inexperienced—a threat to this objective and started treating her very unpleasantly. She became so hostile and erratic that the Captain moved Joan to another cabin. It was a small single-berth cabin on the lower bridge, close to the hub of the ship's activities, and she felt much happier there.

She made the best of things thereafter. There were very few organised activities on board, but when the others played deck games or card games she joined in. One of the best things about the voyage was that the Captain allowed her to spend a lot of time on the bridge and in the chart room. She learnt how to use a Morse light and was given lessons in navigation by the stars. She understood coastal navigation but had never studied the celestial variety and found it fascinating. She saw the Great Bear and Polar Star for the first time, and kept an eye on the Southern Cross, her last sign of home.

As the days passed it became hotter and more humid. Mrs McCay had given her a fountain pen and Mrs Lloyd a five-year diary so she put the two together and started writing every day. She'd brought various things with which to amuse herself—from violin and wind-up gramophone to skipping-rope—but as the journey progressed she spent more and more time just gazing at the sea. The same question kept rolling around in her head: 'Will I succeed?' She felt lonely and homesick.

The night sky changed and changed again as the weeks went by, and the Southern Cross drifted out of view.

When the *Dagfred* docked at Colombo the Captain took her ashore. All her senses were thrown into a state of shock. The smell in particular was overpowering—a mix of cinnamon and rotting refuse—intensified by the heavy warm air. The colours of the fruits and spices, the noise and bustle of the people and traffic, the monkey hanging off the telephone wire, the women in their saris, the images of elephants, the Buddhist monks in their robes, the market stalls, the temples, the white men in their white suits, and the overwhelming sense of brown-skinned people going about their business—many of them in a state of extreme poverty. The Captain took her to various sites of interest and she was stunned and fascinated and disturbed by turns. Even the mode of transport gave her much to think about. It was a rickshaw pedalled by a man so emaciated she felt embarrassed by her own well-fed state. The whole experience was exotic in the extreme, an assault on every sense.

The days passed slowly as the *Dagfred* headed towards the Arabian Sea. Joan busied herself in the chart room and learnt what she could about the inner workings of the ship. She did her daily skipping exercises, wrote in her diary, stuck assorted photos into an album, wrote letters, sang scales, read, but more often than not she found herself looking at the sea. The rhythmic throb of the engine was a mesmerising sound, night and day, day and night. The Captain and crew were solicitous. They put up a hammock for her, sent a cold beer to her cabin by noon each day—the only drink that seemed to cool her down—and they asked what food she liked best. The heat was always intense and the tropical rain storms made the humidity worse. She wore a simple top and red pyjama trousers, and sat or lay wherever she could catch a hint of a breeze. The nights were no cooler but the night sky was intoxicating, so many constellations, and she made wish after wish for every shooting star.

There were occasional 'sing-song' nights helped along with quantities of alcohol. Apart from their voices, the Italians had some musical instruments, a guitar, a mandolin, and a ukulele, the last immediately co-opted by Joan. Everybody sang (except the French Moroccan who continued to be sour) and Joan added her violin to the general mix. They were raucous, ridiculous nights, thoroughly enjoyable. She practised her German with the Captain, her Italian with the Italians but rarely bothered with French.

The *Dagfred* entered the Gulf of Aden and then the Red Sea. There were hundreds of flying fish all around the boat by day, and the glitter of phosphorescence by night. She could see the shoreline on both sides when the ship reached the Gulf of Suez, and just visible to the east was the outline of Mount Sinai. There was Egypt on the left and Saudi Arabia on the right. Amazing!

The Captain took her ashore at Suez and Port Said, and she experienced the same barrage of mixed emotions and sensory extremes. The ancient history, the different cultures and religions were so extraordinary; but the extremes of poverty hit her the most. She realised how ignorant she was, how unaware, how powerless. The vastness of it all made her feel inconsequential, like a grain of sand in the desert. Her own little world seemed terribly insular by comparison. It was all deeply disturbing.

The ship pushed on into the Mediterranean Sea. The water was so blue, so clear, she wanted to throw herself in. She wondered when she'd go surfing again, when she'd see home again. The days passed and the weather cooled a little. It seemed an age before they reached

Malta, but it was very pleasant when they did. The Captain gave her a tour of the whole island and she enjoyed it very much. She was particularly taken by the sight of goats being milked in the streets of Valetta and people buying the milk direct—from bucket to jug.

The *Dagfred* skirted Sicily and entered the Tyrrhenian Sea. Italy, birthplace of Verdi and Puccini, was but a couple of days away. Naples was the next port of call and after that would be Genoa, her disembarkation point. Joan had felt calm in the middle of the Mediterranean, but now her stomach was aflutter.

They reached Genoa on 16 May 1936. The Captain showed her the sights, helped her through customs, gave her a special dinner, and waved her off on the 9.20 p.m. train to Vienna. It was a weird transition, from sea to train. Every sound, movement, smell was so very different. She travelled all night through the Italian countryside, unable to see more than the occasional light in the distance, but as the dawn broke she saw an undulating landscape, an extraordinary palette of reds, yellows, and many shades of green.

It was the European spring. The lushness, the hills and mountains, the trees, the villages, the patchwork fields, the rivers and valleys. The changes in the landscape were frequent and dramatic. The architecture of the towns, the roof-lines of the farmhouses—even the sheep looked different. The air cooled just a little as the train crossed the border into Austria; the colours, especially the greens, intensified. Then the sun started to set and it grew dark again.

Rector Schnitt was waiting on the platform in his distinctive black robes when the train rolled into Vienna. She was pleased to recognise his round smiling face. The chauffeur loaded her trunks into a large black car and they drove out of Vienna and up a winding hill for about half an hour. It was late at night and he took her straight to her room. She slept fitfully and when she awoke she found herself in fairyland. Even the air was rarefied.

She had woken in a palace.

The Schloss Wilhelminenberg was a palace on the edge of the Vienna Woods. The palace had seen better days but it showed all the hallmarks of past grandeur. Built in 1781 by Crown Prince Rudolf, and rebuilt in the 'Neo-Empire' style in 1904, it had a panoramic view of the woods and overlooked Vienna.

Rector Schnitt had placed Joan in her own quarters with a sizeable sitting room, bedroom and washroom. The ceiling was very high and all the fittings were ornate. The windows were tall and had a 'double door' arrangement, the first set opened in, the second set opened out—and the view was astonishing! A forest of trees on a steep hillside sweeping down to an old-world city far below.

Her first problem concerned the washroom. It had a toilet and basin but no shower, so in true Australian fashion she set forth in her dressing-gown to look for one. She wandered along magnificent corridors, up and down extravagant staircases, but couldn't find one. She at last came to a hallway leading to a ballroom and bumped into Rector Schnitt, who looked astonished. She had a towel over her shoulder and a wash bag under her arm but he still seemed bewildered by her request for a bathroom. He repeated the word bathroom several times 'You mean you wish to wash, *now*?' Yes, she did wish to wash now, in fact she wished to have a bath or shower every morning. It was something he found extremely difficult to understand, conceptually rather than linguistically. His face turned red with exasperation but she stood her ground. 'I shall have to ask the Countess,' he said, and scurried off through a side door.

When he returned he was all smiles. 'Yes, the Countess says you may use her bathroom every morning between 7 and 7.30' and he directed her through marbled corridors to the grandest bathroom she'd ever seen. It had been used by the royal family and their illustrious guests. 'It's the only bathroom in the palace,' said Rector Schnitt significantly, and left her to it. She was confused but it seemed that a special favour had been granted.

The Schloss Wilhelminenberg had been the home and boarding school of the Vienna Boys' Choir since 1934. The choir, which consisted of four or more separate choirs plus new boys in training, had only prospered during the post-war years due to the efforts and financial generosity of Rector Schnitt. His approach to business matters was her next shock. He expected her to pay for board and lodging a month in advance. Further to this, Herr Gomboz, chief conductor of the choir, expected the same prepayment for his coaching. Then she found that her singing teacher also wanted payment a month in advance. The arrangement regarding the Joan Hammond Fund was that Miss Wray would send a cheque from Sydney at the end of each month. There was a nerve-racking time gap between outgoings and incomings as a consequence.

The next surprise was the food. She'd enjoyed lovely meals on the *Dagfred* but culinary delights would now be a memory. Dark meat swimming in a boiled mush was the main meal. It was difficult to digest and she quickly turned to black bread and jam as a filler. Meals were taken in the dining hall and reminded her of boarding school, except she was now sitting with the teaching staff, all male. When she arrived at the palace she was noticeably overweight. She'd always been solid but during the last few months her athletic figure had been covered with a layer of fat. Perhaps there'd been less time to exercise, or perhaps she'd overeaten due to anxiety about her overseas trip. Whatever the cause, the weight came off rapidly and she became slim, or even thin, very quickly.

It was an especially pleasant surprise to meet the Countess, not least because she was the only other woman living at the palace. Countess Kinsky was elderly, gracious, and still remarkably attractive. She had once been a famous opera singer and the pair warmed to each other immediately. Countess Kinsky offered to help Joan with her German and they agreed to converse every day. To Joan she was like a ray of sunlight on a frosty morning.

Joan had her twenty-fourth birthday a week after arriving at the palace. Cards arrived from friends and family but she felt especially lonely on that day.

Excitement overcame loneliness when she was told she was to sing to an invited audience at the end of the month—in two weeks. Countess Kinsky and Rector Schnitt had organised the gathering and very important people, including the director of the Vienna State Opera and the famous soprano Elisabeth Schumann, had agreed to attend. The pressure must have been enormous—especially as she sang a number of German songs—but she sailed through with flying colours. Important people said nice things to her afterwards and they were complimentary about her German accent. It was a good start.

HER SINGING TEACHER was Frau Eibenschütz. She had an apartment in Vienna in the second district. The senior boys (ex-choir boys who'd stayed at the school to finish their education) told Joan that this was in the Jewish quarter.

Joan was unaware of the political climate in Europe at the time, though she'd picked up two new words: Fascist and Nazi. Her pocket English–German dictionary was constantly to hand, but it was inadequate when it came to political terms. The senior boys in the Schloss discussed politics all the time and grilled her about life and circumstances in Australia. Some of these boys were Nazis, and enthusiastic about a man called Hitler.

The days soon settled into a routine. She would rise at 6.30 and exercise with her skipping-rope, then spend her allotted time, 7.00 to 7.30, in Countess Kinsky's bathroom. She'd dress in her warmest clothes and breakfast in the dining hall. Then there'd be a 20-minute walk down the hill to catch the tram, followed by a half-hour ride into the city. If the weather was bad she'd catch a bus from the State Opera House (Staatsoper), otherwise she'd walk to Frau Eibenschütz's apartment for her singing lesson. Then she'd go back to the Schloss in time for lunch (dinner). All her meals were accompanied by the loud din of the choir boys, their chatter and clatter echoing around the dining hall to a mind-numbing degree. The next couple of hours were spent in her sitting-room memorising music, then at 4 p.m. she'd go to Herr Gomboz for coaching. The evening meal would be a kind of high tea (black bread and jam). Then she'd read, or converse with Countess Kinsky, or talk with the senior boys. She'd do a few golf exercises, write in her diary, and be in bed by 9.30.

On most Sundays she was taken to the Burgkapelle to hear the boys sing the Mass. The chapel was originally constructed in 1296 (but modified 150 years later) and had Gothic statuary in canopied niches. She could observe from a private box once used by the royal family. It was from this discreet position that she listened to Masses by Haydn, Mozart and Beethoven, and found the music deeply moving.

There were fabulous opportunities to see opera and theatre and Joan attended these as often as she could. Rector Schnitt wouldn't allow her to go on her own so Eber, one of the senior boys, was assigned as chaperone. This annoyed her because it meant she had to pay for two instead of one. Yet Eber turned out to be good company. She was going to her room one evening when she heard jazz floating through the corridors of the palace. Jazz was such an oddity in a place committed to classical music, so she pursued the sound to its source. She eventually discovered a jazz band, with Eber at the centre playing saxophone.

Eber explained that the jazz band had a purpose. They were preparing for the midsummer break when all the boys moved to a pension in a mountain village. It was a working holiday because the boys had to help run the pension and entertain the guests—which helped to keep the choir's finances afloat. She soon learnt that she too would be going to the mountain village because the Schloss closed during the summer period.

She'd been packing her trunk in preparation for her trip to Hinterbichl, the mountain village, when she felt the need to practise one of the songs she was learning—a difficult song by Strauss. She did all her practice in the ballroom, just down the corridor, and this is where she spent the next twenty minutes. Then she had the strangest feeling that someone was in her room. She kept singing as she walked back along the corridor and just as she neared her door a boy rushed out and ran down the staircase. She chased him. Down and around and down again till he reached the basement. The basement was out of bounds for Joan, it was where the boys slept and washed, yet she pursued him anyway. She saw where he went but also heard the sound of boys washing and knew she could go no further. When she got back to her room and investigated she found that 30 schillings was missing, plus the only jewellery she possessed: a diamond ring given by her parents for her twenty-first birthday, and a gold bracelet. She knew who the boy was, so assumed it wouldn't be too difficult to recover the items. But she was wrong. Had Rector Schnitt been at the Schloss things might have turned out differently, but he'd already left for Hinterbichl. Remaining staff proved unhelpful. She herself left for the mountain village next day, and by the time she returned it was all too late. She didn't see the boy again, though he did return to the Schloss once she'd left. The boy was blond and attractive, popular with the staff and Rector Schnitt in particular. Joan couldn't prove it, but felt Schnitt protected the boy from further investigation.

Earning a place in the Vienna Boys' Choir meant that a boy received an excellent education and the chance to tour the world as a 'singing ambassador for Austria'. Foreigners were assumed to be wealthy, especially if they spoke English. Little wonder then that the staff, and even the police, closed ranks against her. She had to let it go, but the experience left her feeling low. Apart from the sentimental value, they were the only two items she possessed of real monetary value.

Herr Gomboz went to Hinterbichl as well, so coaching continued even in the mountains. The only piano was in the dining room of the pension, which made practice difficult but never impossible. She had problems finding a bath—and hot water to put in it—but at last began to appreciate just why this was a practical as well as costly difficulty. She resolved to do as the Austrians did and have a basin wash instead, and make use of that thing called a bidet. On Sundays the jazz band transformed into a little orchestra and accompanied the boys singing Mass. There was only one violinist so Joan was asked to join them with her fiddle, which is how she came to learn the Mass by Schubert, another wonderful piece. There was a Tyrolean Festival with much singing and dance, complete with lederhosen and dirndl skirts; and a memorable but never to be repeated mountaineering expedition.

Eber challenged her to tackle a mountain hike and she rose to the bait. Someone lent her a warm jacket, an alpenstock, and a pair of heavy-duty walking boots, and off she went with Eber, an experienced guide, and two Yugoslav lads. They were heading for the Grosse Venediger, one of the highest peaks in the area, and would be at the peak in time for sunrise next day. A spectacular sight by all accounts.

Joan realised her terrible mistake after an hour or so of walking. Her boots were too big. Blisters began to form and the problem got worse and worse. Five hours later they reached the hut where they were to spend the night. What a relief to remove those boots, and what a surprise to find that males and females slept in the same room!—albeit with their clothes on. She had never come across such an informal arrangement before. Nor had she slept on such a hard board for a 'bed'. It was rough, really rough, but she gritted her teeth and stuck with it, not that she had an alternative.

They rose well before dawn, ate a Spartan breakfast, and proceeded towards the peak. Snow was falling heavily, there was a strong wind, and it was four degrees below zero. Joan's feet were numb with cold, which was just as well. Eber led the party without mishap to the peak in time for the sunrise. It was breathtakingly beautiful, seeing the first rays of the sun turn the whiteness to gold. She felt like a very small particle in the world—not because of human nature this time, but because of Mother Nature.

Then they had to make their way back again. Eber suggested a different route, a shorter but more difficult trail. Joan liked the idea of 'shorter' and agreed. Eber linked them together with a rope, handed out ice picks, and gave them brief instructions as to what to do if one of them fell down a crevasse. When Eber had said 'difficult' he meant 'dangerous'. The packed snow was hard to walk on—especially with painful feet—and the fissures were very frightening. Ironically it was Eber who fell into one, right up to his waist, and the others who hauled him out. Things were not helped when the Yugoslavs asked if they could search for a sprig of edelweiss. She didn't want to be a bad sport so she agreed. The diversion meant they left the track on the lower reaches and went looking for the bloom along perilous ledges. She spotted the flower first, much to everyone's relief, and they returned to the proper track. She staggered back to Hinterbichl in great discomfort, her pride intact but with no desire to do it again.

> I love to go a-wandering along the
> mountain track,
> And as I go, I love to sing,
> My knapsack on my back.
> Val-deri, val-dera,
> Val-deri, val-dera ha ha ha ha ha.
>
> 'The Happy Wanderer', Möller

SHE WORKED EXTREMELY HARD and learnt many operatic roles in a short time. In Hinterbichl alone she learnt the Countess in *The Marriage of Figaro*, Micaela in *Carmen*, Elisabeth in *Tannhäuser*, Elsa in *Lohengrin*, Agathe in *Der Freischutz*, and Pamina in *The Magic Flute*: six roles within two months—and she always studied the whole opera, not just her own part.

'Holiday' over, she went back to the palace.

Hunger was a preoccupation. Hunger to learn, certainly, but also hunger for food. The meals at the palace were never to her taste. She was saved in part by the guiding hand of her fairy godmother. Lady Gowrie had friends in Vienna and she prompted them to invite Joan to tea. One such friend was Lady Selby, the wife of the British Government Minister in Vienna. When Lady Selby heard Joan sing she resolved to do all she could to help her. Joan was invited to dinners, tea parties and large events such as the celebration of King Edward VIII's birthday—and was always given second helpings. It was very comforting to share the same language, customs and food; and of course the contacts she made at these functions were invaluable.

The palace lost its architectural charms when the autumn chill descended. A cruel draught rushed under every door and the heating was at best erratic. She decided she would be better placed living in Vienna and found lodgings with a kindly elderly couple. The food was better but the portions smaller.

The big bonus was that she could now go to the opera, ballet or drama at any time and without escort—and she feasted nearly every night. She could get cheap student tickets if she sat in the gods, and even cheaper tickets if she stood. In a single week she heard *Gotterdammerung*, *Tannhäuser*, *Elektra*, *Der Rosenkavalier* and *Don Giovanni*, and saw two ballets and Shaw's *St Joan*. She heard great singers on a regular basis: Lotte Lehmann, Kirsten Flagstad, Elisabeth Schumann, Richard Tauber. And witnessed an unforgettable performance of *Fidelio* conducted by Toscanini, and a wonderful concert conducted by Furtwängler. It was fabulous. She imagined herself on stage, singing a duet with Tauber, or being conducted by Furtwängler . . . but the fantasy was hard to sustain. Things took on a new light when she descended from the gods and caught the tram back to her digs.

The red and white trams were not so unlike the trams back home. They rattled and screeched as trams do, but the cityscape was a world away from what she knew. Vienna's streets and buildings were steeped in history, but she found it difficult to warm to the city as a whole. Vienna was like an eccentric old dowager: aristocratic, imperious, and difficult to get to know. Yet she did manage to form three good friendships with Viennese locals: Eber, the senior boy, Dr Alfred Komma, a dentist, and Grace Palotta, a retired actress who'd once been popular in Australia.

She met Dr Alfred Komma when she went to his clinic with a dental problem. A gentleman of the old style, he happily escorted her to various places of interest in his city, not least the beer and wine 'gardens' which had a relaxed atmosphere that Joan enjoyed. She met Grace Palotta through one of Lady Gowrie's friends and found her warm, generous and easy to be with. Grace Palotta took her to the theatre and always gave her a good meal afterwards.

Grace Palotta also rescued Joan when she was broke and in a panic. She gave Joan the 19 schillings required to send a cable to Miss Wray in Sydney asking that her next payment be sent immediately. It arrived a week later, much to Joan's relief. Grace Palotta advised her to buy a cheap fur coat to combat the winter cold, and she knew a furrier who had one that she could afford—an odd sort of thing made of 'skins unknown', but which kept her warm.

Christmas was strange. She saw snow falling in the city for the first time and marvelled at the transformation. People were kind: she sang with the British Embassy choir on Christmas Day as a favour to Lady Selby and attended a reception at the Embassy in the afternoon; Grace Palotta invited her to Christmas dinner; and she spent New Year's Eve with the son and daughter of her singing teacher. Yes, people were kind, but she found new meaning in the lyrics of an old song:

'Mid pleasures and palaces, wherever we may roam
Be it ever so humble, there's no place like home.

JOAN SUDDENLY FELT like Cinderella before the ball. She was to
sing at the British Embassy before British royalty at a special function
organised by Lady Selby and her husband. It was to be her European
debut concert and Lady Selby wanted her to look stylish. She took
her to the most exclusive couturier in Vienna and said she could have
whatever she wanted. Joan was so out of her depth and so intimidated
by the salon owner that she accepted the first thing offered—but Lady
Selby knew better. It took hours, but the end result was fabulous.

The grand occasion was a reception for the Duke of Windsor,
formerly King Edward VIII. His Royal Highness and, one presumes,
Mrs Simpson (the cause of his abdication), visited Vienna quite
frequently and it was Sir Selby's job to entertain.

Joan felt especially confident in her lovely gown, and the whole
evening was a glittering success. She chose a program of songs to
suit all tastes, especially the Duke's, and sang to a packed Embassy.
Oddly enough, the most popular of her English group of songs was
'The Green Hills o' Somerset'. Lady Selby introduced her to the Duke
afterwards and they had a long talk about Sydney, the Gowries, and
golf. It was the cream on the cake as far as Joan was concerned, and
she went to sleep in a bubble of happiness.

The enchantment disappeared next morning. She walked to the
bank in her worn-down shoes and 'bitsa' fur coat to find that her
monthly allowance was still overdue. She trudged back to her room
and emptied her purse to see what was left: 2 schillings exactly. Her
rent was 248 schillings a month, her coaching fee 237 schillings,
and there was also her singing teacher's fee. On days like these she
loathed being in Vienna. The aggressive beggars with their terrible
amputations, the shop assistants who always tried to overcharge

foreigners, the tarnished grandeur of the dominating architecture—
even the lack of sea and shore got her down. Glittering highs, dreary
lows, it was all part of the Vienna experience.

SHE DISCOVERED THROUGH the student grapevine that her 'nice
elderly landlady' had been overcharging. Grace Palotta came to the
rescue again. She had a friend, a Baroness, who could give her a much
better arrangement at a cheaper price. Joan moved in. The Baroness
had a daughter known only as 'V' and this young woman had many
young friends who visited the apartment. 'V' would invite Joan to
join them in the back room, away from the other guests. She would
sit with an interesting mix of people which included Hungarians,
Yugoslavs and Greeks, and try to follow their conversation. Their
main topic was politics. Her ability to converse with them in German
was limited, yet she picked up enough to know that this group was
strongly anti-Hitler. Some of them seemed to be posturing rather than
genuine, but she couldn't reason why.

She was too immersed in her studies and too cut off from British
newspapers to be aware of European politics. Small things she noticed
as 'odd' only made sense in retrospect. Karl Eibenschütz, her singing
teacher's son, was an example. She would sometimes see him wearing
army uniform, complete with swastika armband. He was quite a
friendly young man, yet vehemently anti-Jewish. It didn't make sense
to Joan because part of his family *was* Jewish.

She'd made good progress under Frau Eibenschütz's guidance: her
high tones had been brought forward, her upper registers made even.
Then progress slowed. Frau Eibenschütz had been very kind, but Joan
knew the extensions of her voice weren't developing as they should.
It took a while to work up to it, but she eventually announced that
she needed a different teacher. Frau Eibenschütz responded with an
emotional storm of considerable magnitude, but Joan held firm.

She eventually found a much better teacher, a Polish woman who immediately pinpointed her weakness: a lack of vocal agility. Initial lessons proved very positive but there was an unfortunate drawback. Her new teacher was unreliable. Joan spent many an hour waiting for a lesson that didn't eventuate. She put up with it for a while, then looked for someone else. That person didn't appear for some time, so she relied on herself plus the guidance of her new coach, a repetiteur at the State Opera House. These changes signalled a growing confidence. She was like a fledgeling ready for take-off, and her first flight proved surprisingly successful.

She auditioned for Vienna Radio and was immediately booked for two performances. This was especially surprising because Vienna Radio tended to be a closed shop to foreigners. Luck as well as talent played its part at the audition. She sang only German songs with an impeccable German accent, but the clincher was her handwriting. When she'd filled in the audition form she'd written 'Australia' as her country of origin, but officials had misread this as 'Austria'. She was booked to sing a series of guest recitals, in off-peak time slots, but it was a marvellous 'in'—and the income was *very* useful.

Next she found an agent who immediately arranged various auditions. She sang for the Director of the Aussig Opera House in April and was offered a six-month contract to sing lead roles starting in October. It was a wonderful opportunity and she accepted immediately, fully aware that Aussig was a town in North Bohemia, Czechoslovakia. She understood that the Aussig Opera House maintained a high musical standard and that German was the dominant language—so much so that only one of her roles would be sung in Czech, all the rest in German. It was her first definite step towards an international career.

Fate, luck and Lady Gowrie offered yet another glittering chance. Lady Gowrie had been in Britain since January and would remain till the end of May. Her private purpose was to see her son Patrick, her public purpose was to attend the Coronation of George VI (so suddenly thrust into the spotlight following Edward's abdication). It was a phenomenally prestigious occasion and Lady Gowrie wanted Joan to be there. She sent word via Lady Selby that she'd arranged for her to have a seat in the Mall so she could watch the Coronation procession in style. It was an extraordinarily thoughtful offer and Joan was overjoyed. Lady Gowrie had also arranged for her to stay with some friends in Chelsea until she found her own accommodation, and sent some travel money. It was only a matter of weeks before she was on her way.

She left Vienna by train on 9 May 1937, knowing she had a job to come back to in October. Even so, she travelled with almost every item in her possession. She took her golf clubs, violin, portable typewriter, metronome, wind-up gramophone and gramophone records. It was a ridiculous amount, yet she could not bring herself to leave any of it behind. These things had been with her since Sydney, old familiars in an unfamiliar world, and she was not to be parted from them. She travelled third class and her luggage cost as much as she did.

Central Austria, southern Germany, northern France; the country-side changed and changed again as the hours passed and the borders were crossed. And then she reached the coast. The sea! Green, white-crested waves, taking her towards the white cliffs of Dover. Such a short journey across the English Channel, such a brisk transfer from ship to train (despite luggage), such a delightful stretch of countryside, the spring flowers, the little cottages, the orchards of Kent, the outer suburbs, then the inner suburbs of London. London! The houses built so close, the backyards so small, so Dickensian; then a bridge over a river. The Thames! Then the gloom and boom of Victoria Station. This was London. This was where her parents used to live, where her two elder brothers were born, where she herself was conceived. This was also a very crowded place, filled to overflowing with people come to see the Coronation of their new king.

She didn't like to impose on Lady Gowrie's friends in Chelsea—

very pleasant though their house was—and quickly found digs with the help of a friend, a Scottish tenor she'd met in Sydney and kept in touch with. She moved into the front parlour of Mr and Mrs Jones in a modest terraced house in Earl's Court. They were very friendly, perhaps because they were only letting their front room for the period of the Coronation. Best of all, the room had an upright piano (out of tune) and Mrs Jones said she could do her singing practice as much as she liked. A unique offer, for she was never allowed to do this in any other digs, anywhere, before or subsequently.

The Coronation procession was an amazing experience. The uniforms, the horses, the carriages, the whole cavalcade. It was theatre on an epic scale and she never forgot it.

Lady Gowrie returned to Australia shortly after the Coronation, but she made sure that Joan was looked after. Some of her friends and relatives 'stood in' in various ways on her behalf.

Of course Lady Gowrie belonged to another realm entirely. Her friends and relatives were upper class, the *real* upper class: they had castles and country houses and fine city residences. Joan led a peculiar existence as a consequence. On most days she lived as frugally and studiously as she could, while on other days she was invited by these friends and relations to wonderful places to have extraordinary experiences. She was taken to the theatre, the opera, to Glyndebourne, to dinner, to lunch, to the races, to the tennis at Wimbledon; she even managed to play some golf at a big event at Beaconsfield Golf Club— and earned herself a prize while she was at it.

All in all there were numerous wealthy women ready and willing to give her a good time. Some she'd met before in Australia through Lady Gowrie, or through golf (the British golf team visited Australia in 1935); others were new introductions. All were very kind and many were influential.

Mrs Fleischmann, Lady Gowrie's sister, offered Joan ongoing use of her fabulously furnished drawing room complete with concert grand

Lady Gowrie

piano for daily singing practice. The Dowager Viscountess Hambledon arranged for her to audition for Lilian Baylis, administrator of the Old Vic and Sadler's Wells theatres, and sent her a chauffeur-driven car for the purpose. Lilian Baylis was impressed enough to offer Joan a contract, but the dates clashed with her commitment in Aussig. The well-travelled Mrs Fred Payne, who'd been one of the first to put money into the Joan Hammond Fund in Sydney, and who'd introduced Joan to Grace Palotta in Vienna, also helped her in numerous ways in London.

Mrs Payne became a key mover and shaper during the next few months of Joan's life. It was well meant and probably invaluable but it came with 'strings attached'. Joan had become Mrs Payne's pet project. She arranged a meeting between Joan and Dino Borgioli, the well-known Italian tenor. Dino Borgioli had sung in Australia with Melba, and married Pat, an Australian soprano and friend of Mrs Payne. Perhaps Mrs Payne had a prearranged plan, for when Joan met Borgioli he asked her to sing for him. His response was so enthusiastic that he immediately offered to become her teacher, having never taught before. Joan discussed it with Mrs Payne, who offered to broker the fee arrangement with Pat, who managed her husband's financial affairs. Joan was happy with all this until she learnt the figure they'd agreed — excessively high in her opinion. Yet the deal was struck: she had a new teacher.

She had doubts about Dino Borgioli's teaching later on, especially in relation to his breathing technique, but on the whole it was a fortuitous move. The Italian influence was exactly what she needed. Lessons started immediately.

She began to see some of the English countryside via various invitations from friends and relations of Lady Gowrie. The Scott family invited her for a weekend in their house-cum-castle in the Cotswolds. She had a wonderful time doing all the things one does on a weekend in the country, though she had a memorable problem with etiquette. She was surprised to find that her travel bag and its meagre contents had been whisked away and unpacked before she'd even reached her room. When she went back to her room later in the day she found that the maid, whom she never saw, had put out her evening dress. She thought this curious, very curious, and ignored it. When she went down to dinner in her best and nicest frock she saw everyone else wearing formal evening attire. The same thing happened the following evening in reverse. The maid laid out her frock, but Joan wore her evening dress. No one batted an eyelid, but she never made the mistake again.

Mrs Payne arranged for Joan to audition for Harold Holt, a leading concert manager and producer. He added her name to his books but warned her that he generally used only established artists. An affable man, he gave her complimentary tickets to his concerts, and introduced her to several musicians. 'Connections' also won Joan the chance to audition for Sir Thomas Beecham, Chief Conductor and Artistic Director of Covent Garden. Her hopes were high beforehand but Sir Thomas made no comment afterwards. Joan took the great man's silence to mean rejection and berated herself for giving a poor audition. She'd desperately wanted his approval. Dashed but undeterred, she resolved to work even harder.

She tried to be careful with her money but was always running short. There came a day when she only had sixpence left in her purse. The rent for her new digs (still in the Earl's Court area) was £1 10s a week and payment was overdue. She was rescued in this instance by Andrew Reid, a Sydney businessman who'd supported her fund and who was currently in London. He'd taken her aside one day and said most earnestly that if she was ever desperate for money she was to go to his bank and ask to draw on his account, and he gave her a signed letter to this effect. She spent her sixpence on the bus fare to his bank in the City and presented the letter to the cashier. Ten pounds was handed over without question.

She may or may not have taken the time to explore Cannon Street while she was in the City area. Cannon Street connected St Paul's Cathedral to London Bridge and was where her father once had his electrical business. It even had a Walbrook Street leading off it. Walbrook, the name of the Hammond family home.

One of the highlights of being in London was catching up with Australian friends, especially the McCay family. She felt a huge wave of emotion when she saw their happy faces. So much had happened since she'd seen them last, yet they picked up the threads easily. It was comforting to hear all the news and gossip. Comforting and just a little sad—homesickness would still wash over her at various times. The McCays were staying in London for some months and she spent as much time as she could with them.

She also met Miss Ivie Price, a relative and occasional aide to Lady Gowrie who had helped set up the Joan Hammond Fund. Ivie Price took Joan to lunch or dinner (everyone noticed how thin she was) and invited her and the Borgiolis to Buckinghamshire for a long weekend. Ivie described her country home as a 'cottage' but when Joan arrived she saw a very large old house complete with tennis court and stables, and the same silent procedure with the unseen maid. She went horse riding, played golf, had a tremendous time—and wore exactly what the maid left out for her.

DINO BORGIOLI WAS due to sing in Salzburg and the Borgiolis thought it would be a good idea if they drove to Austria in their car, and that Joan went with them. She could share the driving and keep up with her lessons. Joan agreed.

A letter to Bertie Lloyd in Sydney reveals much about her mood, enthusiasms and criticisms at this time:

11th August [1937] Salzburg.

I am back in this dismal country again . . . I hated leaving
London! It is a marvellous place. I am again finding the food
very distasteful after two months of our good English dishes . . .
it was wonderful seeing Mrs McCay again. I drove her car down
to Brighton & back. I have my continental licence as well as the
English & I drive Mr & Mrs Borgioli's a bit—She is a dear &
Dino also—really a marvellous couple. We motored over from
England together—through France & Germany. It was glorious.
I am quite used to driving on the right hand side of the road now
. . . Stayed the night at Rheims & saw the wonderful Cathedral
& many war ruins . . .

I spend my time going to the rehearsals at the Festspiel Haus
& to the performances. Dino Borgioli gets tickets for his wife &
me . . . I have been to the rehearsals and performances of 'Falstaff'
(simply marvellous with Toscanini conducting), 'Don Giovani',
Bruno Walter conducting—not very good, I must say Dino was the
only good voice & artist in it. Rethberg was most disappointing
in the role of Donna Anna & Pinza was too much the peasant &
not the graceful 'Don'. 'Die Lauberflati' (Toscanini conducting)
was good but not brilliant—the bass—Alexander Kifnis was very
good but the others very mediocre. There is no one outstanding
here this season except Stabile as Falstaff—in that he is simply
wonderful—the voice is perhaps not so beautiful but what an
artist—he is also excellent as the Count in Figaro.

I am going to Italy with the Borgiolis at the end of this
month—I would really like to stay there for 8 months or more.
Tell Miss [Lute] Drummond that 'Traviata' & 'Rigoletto' in Italian
are now two of my best roles & thank heavens I came away from
the Austrian teachers—The Italian School is the only one.

SHE WORKED WITH two excellent coaches while in Salzburg, one Italian, the other Austrian, and learnt an enormous amount in a short time. She also sang for an Italian agent who said he'd put her on his books.

Dino's next singing commitment was in Florence, his home town. The trio had a brief stay in Venice en route, then Joan was settled into a pension run by Dino's family. She studied with a coach but singing lessons with Dino were spasmodic due to his workload. One of her tasks was to restudy the Italian operas she'd learnt in German so she could sing them in Italian.

Ah Florence! The language, the people, the art, the food.

Her honeymoon with the Borgiolis came to an abrupt end the following month. She was due to leave for Aussig but when she mentioned it to Dino he flew into a rage—it was out of the question. She was appalled by his attitude. A contract was a contract and she felt duty-bound—it was also a good opportunity. She told Dino she *would* go. There was an almighty row which upset her so much she became ill and took to her bed. Letters crossed back and forth between London and Florence with opinions about what was best for her. Mrs Payne had the final word. She said Joan must return to London and continue her studies with Dino—London being Dino's home base. Joan obeyed.

They left the car in Florence and travelled back to London by train, Joan in third-class, the Borgiolis in first. Everything had become messy. Even Lady Selby, in London at this time, was having her say about what Joan should do. She felt like a rag doll being pulled in all directions except her own.

IT'S BEEN POSSIBLE to track Joan's movements during this time due to her own account given in her autobiography, *A Voice, A Life*, written with the help of her five-year diaries. Autobiographies can

Hilda and Joan sightseeing
with friends in England

be interesting for what they leave out as much as in and Joan's is no exception. She listed many names and details but failed to mention a vital element: her mother was in London during this phase of her life. Why she omitted this detail is unclear. Other sources prove that she'd missed her mother and was pleased to see her—*at the time.*

Joan and Hilda appear to have stayed in the same place in London, but it's unlikely Hilda accompanied her when in Europe. Perhaps Hilda's presence became problematic in retrospect, when their relationship deteriorated. Or perhaps money was the sensitive factor? It was generally understood that Joan's parents couldn't afford to assist their daughter with her overseas studies, so it's curious that Hilda was able to afford such an extended overseas trip—she was away for about two years.

So Joan saw her mother in London—but very briefly on this occasion. Bizarrely, Mrs Payne, and all the other people organising her life, ordered her back to Florence to continue her Italian studies and her singing lessons with Dino. This would have made more sense if Dino were there, but he was away on tour. She resented the interference but felt obliged to do as she was told. Mrs Payne's influence extended all the way back to her funding committee in Sydney.

Winter in Florence was surprisingly cold. Her arm ached, her voice didn't feel right, and she missed everyone—especially on Christmas Day.

February brought good news in the form of a contract to sing at Glyndebourne. It came via Harold Holt, the concert manager who'd put her on his books. Yet Joan was suspicious: the contract was vague. She wrote to Holt and Glyndebourne asking for more details: was she to understudy or play small roles or what? Yes, she was to understudy one or two roles but her main job would be to sing in the chorus. She refused.

A barrage of letters arrived. Pat Borgioli in particular demanded that she accept this fabulous offer (perhaps engineered by the Borgiolis). But Joan stood her ground. Chorus work was not her idea of progress. She packed up her things and returned to Vienna.

It was almost a year since she'd left Vienna, and she returned to that city a much tougher woman. She signed a two-year contract with the Volksoper (People's Opera) and started work immediately, rehearsing leading roles.

This remarkable step forward was overshadowed by political events that would one day affect her career. Hitler's army had rolled into Austria in early March 1938, just a week or so before her return. The occupation was called the *Anschluss* (annexation) and on the face of it the majority of Austrians welcomed Hitler without resistance. If she'd kept her eye on these developments via British newspapers—which she rarely saw and could ill afford—she would have read that the international response to this move was moderate rather than agitated. Neville Chamberlain, the British Prime Minister, made a speech of protest in Parliament, but otherwise he held to his policy of appeasement.

She could not help but notice at least some of the changes that had occurred in Vienna in her absence. City buildings were bedecked with long red banners bearing the swastika, and Hitler's photograph was everywhere, as were German soldiers. The most disturbing change within the opera world was that Bruno Walter, conductor and music director of the State Opera, had left the country immediately because of the Nazi Race Laws, as had some other Jewish musicians. The most direct effect as far as she was concerned was the notice on the stage door of the Volksoper. It commanded that everyone was to use the new greeting 'Heil Hitler' instead of the traditional 'Gruss Gott'. She soon noticed that her colleagues ignored this ruling unless there was a Nazi (or a stranger who might be a Nazi) within earshot.

She didn't know what was going on. Austrian newspapers were

positive about developments and she accepted this as true. Had Lady Selby still been in Vienna she might have told Joan it was all Nazi propaganda, but the Selbys had left Vienna for a new posting in Lisbon.

Music, singing, performing: this was her focus and she refused to be distracted from her path. She put her head down and worked harder than she'd ever worked before. The hours were long, the pay was poor, but the experience was as rich as it could be.

She made her operatic debut in the dramatic role of Nedda in *I Pagliacci* (*The Strolling Players*) and performed very well. Good contrasting roles followed: she played Lady Harriet in the light opera *Martha* and Constanze in Mozart's *Die Entführung aus dem Serail* (*The Abduction from the Seraglio*) — all sung in German. Her days were filled with rehearsals and the evenings taken up with performances — her own or watching colleagues. She worked, she observed, she learnt; if she had a Sunday off she'd spend it with her dentist friend, Alfred Komma. That was life in Vienna. It wasn't comfortable but she was getting the first-class experience she needed.

No one doubted she would progress to the State Opera in due course. Yet Joan wasn't satisfied: she also wanted a London debut.

Her contract with the Volksoper allowed her to go elsewhere for auditions or performances as long as she returned within three weeks. She made good use of this option; in fact she stretched it to the limit and made at least four trips to London over the next twelve months.

Her first trip was in answer to the call of Lady Gowrie who was in London for an extended visit. The Joan Hammond Fund was almost empty and Lady Gowrie wanted to replenish the coffers by way of a fundraising party. She was staying with relatives in an elegant house on Berkeley Square and this became the venue for the gathering. Lady Gowrie sent Joan the cost of her train ticket, Ivie Price organised the invitations, and Joan arrived in London to sing before a select group of wealthy Australians. It was a wonderful moment for her. The 'peerless voice' that had woken Lady Gowrie from her slumbers one hot afternoon in Sydney was now sounding more beautiful than ever. Lady Gowrie's faith had been vindicated. Donations were generous and Joan was deeply grateful. She boarded the train back to Vienna knowing that her fund would sustain her for a while longer.

Her next trip to London was in answer to the call of Harold Holt. He'd arranged for her to audition for Covent Garden, the BBC, and two recording companies. Through the BBC audition she managed to impress two influential people: Ivor Newton, the accompanist, and Stanford Robinson, conductor of the BBC Theatre Orchestra. Both men responded to Joan's musicianship and direct manner. They also liked her lack of affectation—most unusual in a young soprano.

Nothing came of the Covent Garden or record company auditions but the BBC gave her a contract to sing two arias with Stanford Robinson's orchestra. It was a fantastic breakthrough; but then something even more wonderful happened. She received a contract to sing in *Messiah* at Queen's Hall with Sir Thomas Beecham conducting. She was flabbergasted. Beecham's apparent reticence at her audition hadn't signified rejection after all.

She began to prepare for both performances and delayed her return to Vienna. This was in September 1938 when the possibility of war with Germany seemed imminent. She couldn't believe that the situation had deteriorated so quickly. War would ruin all her plans— just as she was getting started. Her friends thought things looked bad and advised her to remain in London. Everyone felt sure war would be announced when Neville Chamberlain came back from his meeting with Hitler and Mussolini, so much so that London put on an anti-aircraft and searchlight display the night before his return. But then Chamberlain held up his piece of paper signed by Hitler and said it represented 'Peace in our time'. Appeasement had won the day. She could stick to her path.

The BBC performance, with Stanford Robinson conducting, went

QUEEN'S HALL

Sole Lessees   Messrs. Chappell & Co. Ltd

UNDER THE AUSPICES OF ORCHESTRAL CONCERTS SOCIETY, LTD.

HAROLD HOLT presents the

BEECHAM SUNDAY CONCERTS

Eighth Concert of the Season

Saturday, DEC. 17 at 3

HANDEL'S

"Messiah"

LONDON PHILHARMONIC ORCHESTRA

| JOAN HAMMOND | MURIEL BRUNSKILL |
| WEBSTER BOOTH | NORMAN WALKER |

ROYAL OPERA CHOIR

Choirmaster   -   -   EUSTACE PETT

CONDUCTOR:

SIR THOMAS BEECHAM, Bart.

POPULAR PRICES   2/6   3/6   5/-   7/6

ALL RESERVED AND BOOKABLE IN ADVANCE

From Chappell's, 50 New Bond Street, Queen's Hall and Usual Agents so well that fan mail arrived at Broadcasting House. There was something in her voice that had touched the British listening public and the BBC took note.

Things were progressing wonderfully. The BBC booked her for further engagements and the Dowager Viscountess Hambledon (who had arranged for Joan to audition for Lilian Baylis) said she would sponsor her in a solo recital if Harold Holt would produce it. The deal was done. She was to give her debut recital on 15 November at Aeolian Hall with Gerald Moore (second-best accompanist after Ivor Newton) at the piano.

She was disappointed that Ivor Newton was too busy to play, but found that Gerald Moore was just as marvellous. Nothing seemed to rattle Gerald and he was always ready with some gentle joke to put her at ease—and 'ease' was what she needed most. She had the talent; she just had to be relaxed enough to allow her natural warmth to shine through. Not easy at one's debut performance in a prestigious venue with high-profile people in the audience. Dowager Hambledon's invitation list read like the *Who's Who* of London. Expectations were very high and she was extremely nervous.

A poster was prepared showing Joan's surname in large bold letters: 'Harold Holt presents Joan Hammond soprano'. Ticket prices ranged from 10s 6d to 2s 6d, bookings via the usual agents, starting time 8.30 p.m., patrons requested not to smoke. There was also a photo of Joan on the poster. A head shot of a smiling wholesome young woman with good teeth, bright eyes and a plain hairstyle—the same hairstyle she'd had since leaving school (straightened hair down to earlobe level with an off-centre parting). She'd bought an 'off the peg' dress for the occasion, possibly because her better gowns were still in Vienna.

She arrived at the Aeolian Hall well before time on the evening of the performance and was reasonably composed until Harold Holt came into the dressing-room smoking a cigarette, very excited because the hall was packed, absolutely *packed*. Then he looked at her dress and hair and frowned with obvious disappointment. Didn't she have any jewellery to brighten things up a bit? No, she did not. He shrugged and said she'd be fine and made a quick exit. Joan looked at herself in the mirror. What was wrong with her nice new dress? It was pale blue, a colour that was supposed to suit her. Her heart was thumping, her hands were trembling and Harold Holt had criticised her appearance—and left her with a cloud of cigarette smoke. Not a good start! Then the call came to go onstage.

No one seemed to care what she looked like. Friends and associates crowded backstage afterwards and showered her with compliments. She smiled and smiled and thanked and thanked and quietly worried about the press notices. It was a 'make or break' moment.

The verdict was good. One quote from *The Times* gives an example:

Miss Joan Hammond included two very difficult arias in her recital at Aeolian Hall on Tuesday: Elvira's "Mi Tradi" from Don Giovanni and "Casta Diva" from Bellini's Norma. One requires exceptional agility, the other a flawless legato style. In both cases the young singer passed the test with credit. Her's is a fine and generous soprano voice (Not a made up one), and it was well used. The tone is clear, true, and properly concentrated. In both arias the flow of tone was confidently and artistically controlled, and the management of the long phrases and the climax of the second suggested thorough training and an awakening sense of style.

The general response was that her voice had a remarkable purity of tone, and range of register, and that it was supported by a keen intelligence.

Harold Holt was so delighted he decided to produce a second recital for the following February. Holt also procured a 'filler' engagement to

help things along in the meantime. The filler happened to be a Press and Advertising Dinner at the Connaught Rooms in the Waldorf Hotel, and she shared the billing with none other than Paul Robeson.

Everything was going like a dream. Her performance in *Messiah* went well and seemed to please Beecham. The BBC engaged her to sing Nedda in *I Pagliacci*—a live broadcast conducted by Stanford Robinson who obviously liked her work—and there were more BBC engagements in the pipeline. The only dampener was that the Volksoper was losing patience and wanted her to return. She told them she'd definitely return by mid February, after her second recital—and somewhat surprisingly the Volksoper accepted this date. Her short leave of absence had now stretched to several months.

She had a terrific Christmas and New Year. Ivor Newton was thoughtful enough to invite her to share the festivities with some of his friends. His friends included the Howard de Waldens, top-drawer patrons of the arts who had a castle in North Wales. She travelled there with Ivor and was feted and well fed and thoroughly spoilt. Her bedroom was in one of the castle turrets and her bedside table was stocked with Scotch and brandy (constantly topped up by the unseen maid). She sang at a charity concert in the village hall, enjoyed some choral singing with the local villagers, and played golf in the snow with a red golf ball.

Ivor Newton was a single man in his mid-forties; elegant and amusing, he knew absolutely everyone in 'Society'. Joan enjoyed Ivor's company and felt comfortable with him, and vice versa.

Ivor was homosexual, though how apparent this was to Joan is uncertain. Sex and sexuality didn't seem to interest her, so her experience and awareness were limited. Music was her obsession and as far as one can tell she had neither time nor inclination for anything deeper than loving friendship.

The poster that promoted Joan's second recital was bigger and bolder than the first—and her new photo showed a very different looking young woman. The fresh innocence was still there, but her hair had some gentle styling, her eyes and lips were skilfully highlighted, and she wore a classy white fur jacket with a high collar. The overall effect made her look uncannily like the Disney version of Snow White: pure, fresh and lovely. And this is how she looked when she walked on stage, this time with Ivor Newton at the piano. She sang well and proved that she wasn't a one-hit wonder. Reviews were positive:

She confirmed the earlier impression that she is a singer likely to gain a considerable place . . . Her sphere will probably be opera. Her brilliancy of voice on the stage, coupled with her handsome appearance, will compensate for a certain want of serenity of style. Miss Hammond can handsomely answer Puccini's demands, and was successful, too, in some of the Joseph Marx songs.

Daily Telegraph

She commands a wide range of modulations and praise is also due for her German articulation which could be mistaken for that of German natives. Her handling of English displayed a mastery which many English singers lack.

The Times

Then 'Snow White' had to return to the hard graft of Vienna.

SHE FOUND VIENNA remarkably changed. The coffee houses were empty and a great many shops had large ugly notices proclaiming they were owned by Jews.

She was disturbed by what she saw but the fact remained that the Prime Minister of Britain had said there was to be no war, and the Austrian newspapers said the same, or didn't mention the subject at all. What could she do but believe them? She picked up her things from Alfred Komma and moved into her old digs with the Baroness.

There was a backlog of commitments to fulfil at the Volksoper, and she was delighted to find that the State Opera had scheduled her to sing Mimi in *La Boheme* and Violetta in *La Traviata*. So the workload was big. She also intended to fulfil her long-delayed commitment in Czechoslovakia. She was ambitious and determined: if she kept up the pace, success would surely be her reward.

One day the Intendant (manager) at the State Opera called her to his office. He said she had to produce certificates that proved she was Aryan. He required certificates concerning herself, her parents and grandparents. Joan was surprised and mystified—she was Australian after all—but dutifully wrote to Somerset House for the documentation. She was probably equally surprised to see the results of the Somerset House research: yes she was Aryan, and she was born illegitimate. Perhaps Joan's difficulties with her mother stem from this point.

On 28 April 1939 the entire staff of the State Opera was ordered to attend the broadcast of a speech to be given by Hitler. No one was exempt. Audio speakers were rigged in the theatre for the purpose and everyone gathered at the due time. Hitler spoke long and loud about the glories of the Fatherland and peppered his speech with insults against the British. Her colleagues, some of them in rapture, looked at Joan for signs of reaction so she kept her face as still as she could. Then it was over and everyone got back to their work.

Things were strangely reversed at her digs. People were still meeting privately in the back room and the Baroness's daughter 'V' was still encouraging Joan to join them. Joan was fond of the thick sweet Turkish coffee that was served at these gatherings so she often accepted the invitation. She met an extraordinary mix of people in this room and they all spoke against Hitler with great passion. There were princes and counts from different parts of Europe, a determined activist called Yasha, and a very attractive woman called Maidi whom Joan liked. Maidi could speak seven languages and showed a particular interest in Australia. Joan sipped her coffee and said little about politics but happily answered Maidi's questions about Melbourne and Sydney. Joan thought it was odd that these people were so obviously anti-Hitler, even in a private back room, for people were hauled away in the night for speaking against the regime.

She was determined to make her way up the ranks of the State Opera but she was always interested in what Harold Holt had to offer, and he managed to entice her back to London with a cluster of engagements she couldn't resist. There was the chance to sing a duet with Richard Tauber at a concert in June—Richard Tauber, the famous tenor she'd watched from the gods not so many months ago—and there was an irresistible contract to sing at the opening night of the Promenade Concert Season with Sir Henry Wood in August. She made a quick visit to London in June and made arrangements to be back in August.

Each time she returned to Vienna she found the atmosphere more strained, more suspicious, more threatening. Many of her friends were leaving, or trying to leave. Alfred Komma saw no reason to leave but English friends kept sending her letters telling her to get out. She dismissed their concerns and refused to believe she was in danger.

Fritz Berens, a Jewish opera coach, heard that Joan was going to London in August and asked if she'd take his father's gold watch to a place in Hampstead for him. It was of sentimental value and he felt sure that the authorities would confiscate it if he ever managed to get a pass to leave Austria. Joan agreed.

She travelled back to London at the beginning of August and delivered the watch the day after she arrived. She knocked at the appointed door and someone opened it a fraction. She explained why she was there and held out the package and a hand took it from her and closed the door.

Then a strange thing happened a couple of days later. Joan got off the bus at Hyde Park Corner and saw 'V' crossing the road. She waved and called and finally attracted her attention, but instead of coming over 'V' ran off in the opposite direction, and kept moving until she could jump on a passing bus. It was perplexing. Why had she run away? And why hadn't she said she'd be in London at the same time? And how had she got a travel pass when Austrians were banned from leaving the country? It was very odd, but she let the matter go. She had the first night of the Proms to think about.

There was only one orchestral rehearsal for the concert, but she coped with the pressure very well. She liked Sir Henry Wood's sympathetic and straightforward approach to conducting, and he seemed to like her. Once again she was a success.

There was so much talk about war, and such an air of expectation, that she had to concede war might be imminent. It worried her that her money and half her possessions were still in Vienna: what if she couldn't retrieve them? She was due to start work again in Vienna on 1 September and dithered about whether to return or delay. Everyone advised delay—and that's what she did. It was a good decision. Germany attacked Poland on 1 September and war was declared two days later.

Her dream run had come to an end: the concert halls closed, the theatres closed, the opera houses closed.

CHAPTER 4

BLOOD, SWEAT
AND TEARS—THE
WAR YEARS

TEN DAYS AFTER the declaration of war Joan was at Chelsea Barracks singing to 500 soldiers. It was a rude awakening. The Barracks was cold, smoky, noisy and acoustically dreadful. The *Daily Telegraph* ran a photograph showing 'the Australian soprano' in a long pale dress singing cheerily to an expanse of smiling if somewhat bemused faces—arias and classical songs not being the usual fare for young soldiers.

She was one of the first Australian artists to volunteer for entertainments like these, Florence Austral being another. Volunteer work was important but earning a living was a necessity. How was she going to survive? Harold Holt said classical music was doomed—the Opera House at Covent Garden was already a dance hall—and he suggested she learn popular songs like 'Roll out the barrel'. Joan was appalled and turned to her second agent, Mr Tillett (of Ibbs and Tillett), but he too said prospects were grim.

Then hope appeared in the form of a booking to sing at a festival in the north of England with Sir Thomas Beecham conducting. It was especially exciting as there were new works to learn—a time-consuming challenge that took her mind off general worries. But a few weeks later she was told the festival couldn't go ahead.

THE MOST TANGIBLE SIGN that war had begun was the blackout. Street lamps, windows, train stations, vehicle lights—not even torches were allowed to shine. Ration books appeared, as did identity cards, gasmasks, bomb shelters, sandbags, military movement, air balloons, sirens, searchlights; everything changed and everyone was affected.

Joan's desperation was such that she put her name down to join the Women's Auxiliary Air Force (WAAF). If she couldn't sing beautiful music she'd rather not sing at all. It was an impetuous move. She had visions of learning to fly, so maybe hadn't read the small print regarding the less glamorous duties women were really needed for (caterer, driver, teleprinter operator). In any event it came to nothing. She was in and out of the interview room in seconds—rejected because of her left arm.

The good news was that Germany didn't attack Britain in the first few weeks or months of the war. The anticlimax was such that people started calling it the 'phoney war' or 'bore war'. Cinemas opened again and restricted lighting could be used. Life continued as semi-normal so there were work opportunities. Stanford Robinson threw the first rescue line in the form of two bookings with the BBC Theatre Orchestra, and there was talk of concerts starting up with Beecham.

She sang in charity concerts, training camps, barracks and hospital wards. It was useful experience but there was little or no remuneration beyond travel costs. Such performances were challenging and strenuous, partly because of the ad hoc conditions but also because audiences were there for the wrong reasons. It was imposed entertainment rather than free choice. Joan found it difficult to win these audiences over, yet refused to compromise on quality or repertoire. She'd sing with the same commitment whether she was in a hangar, hospital, or BBC studio.

An offer arrived out of the blue from the ABC in Australia. It was a contract for an extensive tour beginning in Sydney in a few weeks. It was her ticket home—but she refused to take it. Not because the money and conditions were dreadful (which they were) but because there was nothing about the offer that would advance her career. She could see no reason to go home.

Her refusal caused a stir, not with the ABC but with members of the Joan Hammond Fund committee. They'd moved mountains to persuade the ABC to make the offer. It was a horrible situation. The rift intensified when they discovered she'd curtailed her lessons with Dino Borgioli because she didn't like his breathing method. She appeased them by saying she would have the occasional lesson, but remained steadfast about staying in London.

Interestingly, Hilda Hammond was still in London in December 1939; they spent Christmas together. Joan's feelings about her mother's presence were unequivocal: she pressed her to go home. It's unclear whether Hilda went willingly, or who paid the fare, but she was back in Sydney by the end of January 1940.

JOAN RECEIVED AN extraordinary invitation: would she come and sing at La Scala, Milan? La Scala, Milan! The most famous opera house in the world wanted her for three performances: two Mimis (*La Bohème*) and one Violetta (*La Traviata*). The second part of the offer was a tour to Madrid and Barcelona with an Italian company, the whole engagement to be completed within the month of February. It was a dream come true; 'all' she had to do was gain the necessary travel permit.

A passport was irrelevant if it didn't have a travel permit, and gaining one was very difficult. Joan laid siege to the Passport Office, returning again and again with extra letters, contracts and cables of confirmation until the permit was granted.

She went to Victoria Station as she'd done so many times before to catch the early evening train to Folkestone, but found it too crowded to get on so had to wait for the later train. She'd just come back from South Wales, where she had performed in a concert at a vast RAF hangar, and was extremely tired. So tired that the rhythm of the train and the stuffiness of the carriage sent her to sleep . . . and she missed her station. She woke up in Dover and found it impossible to get back, despite the help of some friendly soldiers. She had to spend the night in a hotel and eventually managed to get back to Folkestone in time to catch a cross-channel steamer next morning.

The channel crossing was made in convoy with aeroplanes overhead and destroyers close by. Only then did she question the wisdom of her expedition. La Scala, Milan, La Scala, Milan—how many sopranos would have declined La Scala, Milan? After all, it was Germany, not Italy, that was at war.

She had a few hours to spend in Paris and found the general atmosphere strained and apprehensive. The train officials were especially edgy. The Italian officials were more courteous, but Milan displayed none of the characteristic Italian warmth she'd so enjoyed when in Florence.

Rehearsals began immediately and progressed well. Her digs were fine but the food was surprisingly poor. The Italian agent was enthusiastic and assured her that work prospects were good.

She sensed some disquieting undercurrents, not only in the theatre but in the streets and eating houses. People huddled together in furtive albeit animated discussion, just as they'd done in Vienna. Yet she refused to be put off. She went to the opera almost every evening and soaked up the atmosphere from the gods. Teatro alla Scala was everything it was supposed to be. The horseshoe-shaped auditorium was plush and the acoustics glorious. She cast a critical eye over performances and especially enjoyed Puccini's lesser-known *La Rondine*. She worked hard and looked forward to her debut in *La Bohème*.

Three days before opening she received a message calling her to the Director's office. When she arrived she could see he was extremely tense. He spoke in veiled terms but the underlying theme was that a major 'declaration' would soon be made concerning Italy's alliance with Germany and it would be best if she left the country immediately, if she valued her safety. There was a long silence while he watched the young Australian process what he'd said. It was a terrible moment, an operatic moment: swift departure or delay?

Twelve hours later she was on the train.

The French Customs officials examined every item of luggage and questioned her movements in detail — where had she been in Italy and why? It took a long time. She'd seen nothing specific in the Italian newspapers but things certainly seemed to have deteriorated in France, even in that short time. People's faces looked different, interaction was different. It was fear she was observing, fear and desperation. It was a very uncomfortable journey but she at last reached Calais, and eventually crossed the channel to Folkestone, and caught the train back to Victoria Station. Home.

London seemed just the same. The 'phoney war' was still phoney and it was still only February. Italy entered the war three months later.

SHE DIDN'T HAVE TIME to feel sorry for herself. She received a call to do a recording test for a gramophone record. It was a two-hour, in-depth, rigorous test. She passed and was signed to sing under the Columbia label (part of the EMI group). The other great news was that Thomas Beecham wanted her to sing at a concert at the Queen's

Hall in mid-March. Orchestral concerts were running again. It was a fantastic boost.

Then an offer came from the Dublin Operatic Society. They wanted her to sing two Paminas in *The Magic Flute* and two Mimis in *La Bohème* in early April. It meant four performances within six days. Joan knew her voice wasn't ready for that amount of strain, so she refused the offer. Harold Holt was staggered, and somewhat annoyed, but she was adamant. She wasn't prepared to risk vocal damage.

A great voice was useless if it couldn't last the distance. Progressing her career meant future planning. It was a tactical exercise involving choice, strategy and patience; it was also about judging the fine line between risk and reward (elements that could be applied to championship golf). Self-promotion and networking also played their part. And then there was good luck: fortune favours the brave. Joan had nerves of steel when it came to looking after her career. She knew her potential and was determined to protect it at all costs.

The Dublin Operatic Society rethought their offer and came around to her point of view. They offered her two Paminas without any Mimis and the contract was signed.

March and April suddenly looked very positive. Work started to flow in from all directions and there was an enormous amount to learn. There was *The Creation* for South Wales, *The Magic Flute* in English for Dublin, a little-known aria that Thomas Beecham wanted her to sing for the Queen's Hall concert—an aria called '*Mi restano le lagrime*' ('Only tears remain to me') from Handel's *Alcina*—plus performances of *Elijah*, *Hiawatha*, the demanding soprano part in Beethoven's Ninth Symphony, and Sullivan's *Golden Legend*—all within a few weeks. Life was good.

THE QUEEN'S HALL CONCERT was especially successful, and *The Creation* was much appreciated by the Welsh. One reviewer wrote:

Joan Hammond's soprano has a pure joy of youth—round and pure in all its register, and of a timbre that recalls a quality present in all the greatest sopranos. Her singing of the air, 'The Marv'llous Work,' and its continuation with the choir in the chorus, 'And to the Ethereal Vaults Resound,' was too much for the audience, who broke the no-applause rule in their surprised delight.

Dublin was a very different experience. Joan could hardly believe the amount of chaos when she arrived for rehearsals. The principals didn't know their roles, the amateur chorus was unspeakably bad, and there were four different operas to be rehearsed *and* staged within five days. She was used to the rigid discipline of the German tradition and was appalled by the shambles that called itself the Dublin Operatic Society. She thought the Irish must be mad. Mad, but also seductively charming. She began to see the funny side. The Irish were 'creatively spontaneous', a quality that seemed to sit well with Mozart's magic.

Performing *The Magic Flute* stretched her in new ways. She found she could think on her feet and deal with oddities and surprises. The music stopped for no one but there were ways of helping people out when fear or some mishap caused a problem mid-scene. A forgotten prop, a missed cue, she could find a way—and enjoy the challenge. She discovered that the solidity of her preparation gave her the security to release. She had the power to 'take flight'. Pamina and Tamino's duet towards the end of the opera was particularly evocative—the magic flute casting its protective spell:

We walk by the power of its music
Joyously through death's dark night.

The Magic Flute, Act 2

The mood was captured by audience and critics alike: 'Joan Hammond was in brilliant form as Pamina. She took the music in the happiest style and thrilled the audience with its exquisite quality and fluent delivery. She was a distinct success.'

There was something about the Irish Joan really liked, and there was one Irishman in particular who may even have won her heart—or as much of her heart as she was able to give.

The man in question was Ian Blacker. Joan met him because he was the nephew of Lady Gowrie (herself Irish). The Blacker family lived at Castle Martin in the Curragh, west of Dublin, and they invited her to stay for a few days. Ian Blacker picked her up after her final performance and they set off in his car. It wasn't a great distance to Castle Martin but the journey was full of incident. Ian's car was as eccentric as its owner and all kinds of mechanical faults and bizarre solutions delayed their arrival. She could have become annoyed but once again she saw the funny side.

The Blacker family had been at Castle Martin since 1730. The area had once been the scene of battle but now the land was given over to horse breeding. The countryside was beautiful and Ian took her to as many places of interest as possible during her 4-day stay—eccentric car and all. They kept in touch thereafter and saw each other again.

Joan had a great many friends, and the connection with Ian wouldn't have been especially noticeable except that she went out of her way to mention him in her autobiography. She chose her words very carefully (as always) by saying: 'Friendship with Ian grew into a very happy relationship'. It's a significant comment because it's the only time she mentions a relationship of any kind in the whole book. Friends aplenty, relationships never. 'Relationship' is open to myriad interpretations, but some kind of attachment is implied. It would have been a fairytale partnership given the Lady Gowrie connection.

Joan had tunnel vision as far as her career was concerned, but she wasn't immune to 'relationships'. The war intensified everyone's emotions; love, honour, romance, sex; people were living in a heightened state, they took more risks. Ian Blacker became a Captain with the Rifle Brigade and went to the Middle East in 1942, visiting Joan in London before he went.

THE WAR BEGAN in earnest in May 1940. Germany invaded the Netherlands, Belgium and Luxemburg. British and French troops advanced through Belgium to defend the Channel ports but the Germans broke through the front line, trapping allied troops on the coast at Dunkirk. A valiant rescue took place but it meant that German tanks had reached the English Channel. Paris fell on 14 June and France surrendered a week later. Winston Churchill roused the British people with stirring sentiments: 'We shall fight them on the beaches . . . We shall never surrender'.

Dino Borgioli was interned as an enemy alien when Italy entered the war. It was a horrible time for Dino but there was a silver lining for Joan; three of his pupils asked if she'd teach them. Work had slumped to an all-time low so it was useful as well as a stimulating.

Work prospects looked so bad that she made a concerted effort to be accepted into the Wrens, damaged arm or no. She went to the top this time and saw Lady Cholmondeley, head of the Women's Royal Naval Service (and perhaps a friend of Lady Gowrie?). But the lady said no, not because of Joan's arm but because of her voice. She told Joan to 'hang on'—classical music would surely play its part in the war in due course. And she gave her an egg by way of consolation (eggs, of course, being precious by this time).

Her ability to 'hang on' was helped enormously by a friend who was getting married and moving out of London. The friend offered Joan her Eaton Mews house—a marvellous gesture in every way. She'd moved digs so many times that people complained they'd run out of Hs in their address books. Eaton Mews was between Sloane Square and Belgrave Square. Hyde Park was to the north and Chelsea

Bridge to the south, so it was conveniently close to the West End. The house was furnished and even had a 'Minipiano' (a miniature grand). It was a wonderful opportunity except for one drawback: the friend also wanted her to accept a puppy. Joan had always loved dogs but couldn't see how she could look after one, especially a puppy; she had trouble enough looking after herself. The puppy was a black standard poodle (the large variety); he had a thin white stripe down his chest, rather as if he'd forgotten to do up his jacket. Last of the litter, he was in need of a good home. Joan had no intention of accepting him but when she saw his fluffy black curls and knowing dark eyes it was love at first sight. She called him Pippo.

She settled into her new home at the beginning of August, and Pippo settled in too. She couldn't bear to think of him left on his own, especially when the bombing started, so she took him with her as much as possible. Pippo became accustomed to the daily walk to Mrs Fleischmann's house and sat quietly under the grand piano while she did her singing practice. Pippo also went to rehearsal and coaching sessions—in fact anywhere that was dog-friendly. He became so attuned to Joan's voice that he recognised it when she sang on the radio, and looked behind the radiogram to see where she was. 'HMV' took on new meaning: His Mistress's Voice.

MAKING A GRAMOPHONE RECORD was Joan's next important step, and she made it at the prestigious Abbey Road recording studios with the well-regarded Walter Legge, who had been the Assistant Artistic Director of Covent Garden before the war, and was already recognised as a talented record producer. He was in charge of EMI's Columbia and HMV record labels (both part of the EMI group), and he managed ENSA's classical music tours. He was overseeing so many areas because most of his colleagues had been called up (he was unfit for war service due to poor eyesight). Joan was reticent about Walter

Legge because she thought he'd rejected her after a perfunctory test the year before. Perhaps she didn't know he'd sent a memo to his superiors in the interim saying: 'She is the best of the younger generation of English-singing sopranos. I would like to put her under contract'—which is how she came to be signed with Columbia, the label that served the classier end of the classical music market.

It was a daunting experience to be in the Abbey Road studio, scene of so many magnificent recordings. Gerald Moore was her accompanist. Gerald spent half his time in recording studios so he was calm and confident, a good contrast to Joan's jitters. Gerald didn't play for 'just anyone', so it was a terrific endorsement to have his name linked to hers on her first record. She had about two hours of studio time to record two songs: the Bach–Gounod 'Ave Maria' (with Alfred Campoli on violin) and 'On wings of song' by Mendelssohn. The selection was made in consultation with Walter Legge but the overriding factor about the process was the technology.

A 78 rpm ten inch gramophone record could only hold one or maybe two songs per side. The sound was cut into a wax master and each side of the record had to be made in one take. One technical or musical blemish and the whole side had to be done again. The large and somewhat imposing microphone was unkind to high notes, especially those of sopranos, and the higher and louder the note the more distorted the sound could be—depending on the voice, for the microphone loved some voices and hated others. The microphone also picked up every vocal deviance, every little catch in the throat, every over-enunciated consonant, every extraneous bit of noise—and magnified it. Joan's anxiety was also magnified with fears of breathing too loudly or holding a breath too long or getting a dry throat or a 'sticky' sound. A momentary roughness in the voice could sound like a foot scraping on gravel; and of course feet, hands, clothing, jewellery, page-turning all had to be kept from making any noise. If there was an error, or problem, it meant a lengthy process of resetting before everyone could start again, and it was the resetting that often took much of the studio time. A good sound engineer helped enormously but it was a cruel business. Stamina, patience and exceptional technique was the key.

It was a nerve-racking initiation but Walter Legge and the engineer seemed happy with the result. Joan and Gerald skipped away from Abbey Road and celebrated with a stiff drink.

BOMBS STARTED TO SHOWER down on London by the beginning of September 1940. Initial attacks were aimed at the East End but nowhere was safe. Joan and Pippo were at home when a bomb dropped very close to Eaton Mews. There was a colossal noise and the whole house shook. Then a second bomb fell even closer, and a third and a fourth. A direct hit seemed certain. Joan held Pippo and prepared to die; there was no time for anything else. Then there was an eerie quietness, no fifth bomb, no direct hit. Then wardens came shouting that there was a time bomb and everyone must get out. She put Pippo on his lead, grabbed a couple of things and headed for the nearest air-raid shelter. She huddled down with other Eaton Mews residents and waited for the big bang. After a while she became conscious of how she was sitting. She had Pippo between her feet, a toothbrush clutched in her left hand, her gasmask slung over one shoulder and golf clubs over the other—and no handbag. She'd left it behind in the house. The absurdity made her laugh.

When the all-clear came she walked back to a windowless house— but at least it was still there. Two days later a German airman floated into the Mews on the end of a parachute. He was alive and duly arrested. A week after that a large piece of shrapnel crashed through her bathroom skylight and embedded itself in the bath, just ten minutes after she'd been in it. A couple of days later Walter Legge rang to say that both the wax master and back-up copies of her recording had been damaged during an air raid so her debut record couldn't be made.

This was nothing compared to future shocks. London endured fifty-seven consecutive nights of bombing from early September to mid-November, with more to follow. One of Joan's new pupils, a promising young tenor, died in an air raid. A family she knew (friends of Hilda's) had a direct hit—all of them killed. She'd known these people, laughed and chatted with them just days before. Now they were gone, and she felt shocked and numb.

THE SIRENS HOWLED, the searchlights crisscrossed, the aeroplanes roared, the bombs thundered, pounded, destroyed. The morning after would reveal yet another changed landscape. There would be rubble and glass and the hollowed-out carcasses of shattered buildings, shattered lives. Smoke and brick-dust would mix with the acrid smell of high explosive and domestic gas. Joan's walk to Mrs Fleischmann's house to do her singing practice would reveal the changes: a hospital gone, a Christopher Wren church gone, and a large crater where some-one's vegetable garden had been, the odd yet strangely pleasant smell of fried onions still apparent . . . One morning even Mrs Fleischmann's house was gone: direct hit. Fortunately no one had been at home.

People adapted as best they could and a stubborn fighting spirit was born. A spirit that impressed Joan and helped her find the strength to 'hang on'.

Persistence was rewarded with a couple of good contracts from Stanford Robinson and the BBC. The BBC Theatre Orchestra had been moved to a country house near Evesham, south of Stratford-upon-Avon, so she was required to attend rehearsals and broadcast sessions there. It was a pleasant respite to be in a large country house with fellow musicians but the train journey was fraught with difficulty. Trains and railway lines were frequent targets, yet carriages were always packed with servicemen and civilians. She'd be lucky to find a place to stand, let alone sit. The blackout meant that night travel was very much in the dark. If there was an air raid the dimmed lights went out completely and the train stopped wherever it was. Hours could be spent just waiting in the darkness, too squashed to move, the air too stuffy to breathe properly.

She had to rely on friends to look after Pippo when she worked away from home and one of the best of these was Estrées Walker. Estrées, or 'Essie' as she was known, was a gentle, loving and gifted person, a talented pianist and first-class cook. She came to know Joan through her aunt, Oenone Palmer. Mrs Palmer had been kind to Joan in Vienna and later in London, and had asked a favour in return. Her niece needed 'bringing out' and she hoped Joan could introduce Essie to some musician-type friends. Essie was four years younger, overly plump, taller than average and acutely shy. Joan was happy to oblige, especially when she discovered how excellent Essie's musicianship was—she could sight-read and had perfect pitch. There were times when Joan couldn't afford a professional accompanist so it was marvellous to find that Essie could fill the breach. Essie also liked dogs, so it was easy to become friends.

Among Joan's wide circle of friends were musicians, actors, law and medical students, golfers, and the friends she'd made through Lady Gowrie. She was good at keeping in touch but the circle gradually dwindled as the war intensified. Some friends moved out of London, some joined up, and some took on war work. Essie Walker was a genteel, well-educated woman of modestly independent means. She could have left London but chose to stay, possibly because of her family's distinguished military background. Her father, Major General Walker, had won the Victoria Cross at the Battle of Daratoleh in 1903; and her brother was serving in Singapore. Essie was calm, secretive, gentle and giving. Her presence in Joan's life became more and more important as time went on.

A CONTRACT CAME for some concert tours to Wales. Four singers were in the touring party, Joan and three established artists: Mary Jarred, a big-hearted big-bodied mezzo-soprano from Yorkshire, Trevor Jones, a Welsh tenor, and Roy Henderson, a Scottish baritone and singing teacher, later to become well known as the teacher of the contralto Kathleen Ferrier. These three singers were in their early forties, well-seasoned travellers, used to the joys and sorrows of touring the provinces — unlike Joan, the 'baby' of the party.

The contract included 'accommodation' but it was pot luck as to how that word was interpreted. On their first evening away Joan and Mary were billeted with a cheery Welshwoman whose house smelt of boiled cabbage. The woman led them up a narrow dark staircase, chatting all the while, then showed them into a drab little bedroom with a three-quarter bed. She said they'd be 'warm and cosy in the one bed' and left them to it. Mary was a *very* large woman, and when she sat on the bed it groaned. It was a groan that seemed to speak for all of them. Mary didn't want to share a bed any more than Joan, and had an easy solution. She tossed a coin to see which of them would go to a hotel. Joan won the dubious right to remain and offered to share the hotel expenses but Mary wouldn't hear of it. When she got to the hotel she found Roy Henderson had been in exactly the same predicament.

'Accommodation' could also mean a lovely room with a coal fire and a place to put your suitcase. But these rooms often came with 'chatty families'. The hosts would want Joan to sit and talk when what she really wanted was to conserve her energies — and voice. Hotels weren't necessarily better. On one occasion she woke to find herself cold and clammy and realised the sheets must be damp. She caught a chill soon afterwards which led to something like pneumonia. It was a hard way to learn about 'the mirror test': place a mirror between the sheets to check for condensation.

She soon saw that these touring difficulties were part of a singer's life. She didn't always like it but she found ways of dealing with it. The concerts were the main thing and they were usually uplifting. The Welsh knew their music and if they liked what they heard they showed their appreciation with much warmth and many calls for encores, making the evenings rather long and unwieldy as a consequence. The Welsh were also very generous with after-concert 'bouquets'. She was often given a flower-decked box with the instruction to keep it unopened until she got home. These boxes contained the best treasure imaginable: food. Rare and severely rationed items such as eggs, ham, butter, jam, tinned meat, sugar, cheese and chocolates. It was heaven, and almost certainly illegal. Such things could only have come via the black market.

Art thou troubled?
Music will calm thee,
Art thou weary?
Rest shall be thine.
Music, source of all gladness,
Heals thy sadness.

Rodelinda, Handel

THE WORSE THINGS BECAME the more people pulled together—and things were definitely getting worse. Government propaganda kept the bad news to a minimum but it was obvious that Hitler's forces were winning the war. Morale had to be kept buoyant somehow, and classical music played its part.

Joan started singing with ENSA (Entertainments National Service Association) and CEMA (Council for the Encouragement of Music and the Arts) towards the end of 1940. This meant that she could be sent to unpredictable locations. Performances might take place in troop camps, factory canteens, in the crypts of churches or on the platforms of Underground stations filled with men, women and children in the process of bedding down for the night.

Important and even lucrative engagements began to flow in towards the end of 1940. The BBC gave her various bookings over the Christmas period which included two complete performances of *La Traviata*.

She sang a *Messiah* in Bradford with Malcolm Sargent, an occasion that marked the beginning of a very fruitful and long-term association. She particularly liked his sensitivity to a singer's needs. She also liked his meticulousness: if he said he wanted her to rehearse a certain passage at a certain time then that is exactly what happened. There were also numerous concert bookings in the new year, one with Sir Adrian Boult at Colston Hall in Bristol — another conductor she liked and would work with again.

The next big step was to make another attempt at a debut gramophone recording. This was done in the Birmingham Town Hall with the Birmingham Symphony Orchestra. Leslie Heward was the conductor and Joan liked him immediately. He was 43, energetic and on the ball. It was a long session and a number of recordings were committed to wax. Some were solo, and some were duets with the Welsh tenor David Lloyd. All were issued eventually but two popular Puccini arias were selected for initial release.

Her debut recording announced her intention to make her mark as the new English-singing soprano of note. 'English-singing' because there was a government ban on non-English language recordings. All those German, Italian and even French arias had to be re-expressed in English translations, that rarely rolled off the tongue and barely made sense. Joan's special talent was to make those translations work. She did this by using her excellent interpretative powers and by occasionally altering phrases to give her the best vowel sound, articulation, and sense.

For example, here's a line from *Manon Lescaut*:

Italian:

> Il mio fa – to si chia – ma: Vo – ler del pa – dr mi – o.

English translation:

> My sad fate is de – ci – ded: Al – las! by will pa – ter – nal.

Joan's adaptation:

> But my fate is de – cided, be – cause my father wished it.

Joan was entering a new league, a tougher league, where the critic's knife could be very sharp. One who had the potential to cut deepest was Alec Robertson, contributor to *The Gramophone*, an influential and somewhat élitist magazine established by Compton Mackenzie in 1923. Alec Robertson (or 'A.R.') was the doyen of *The Gramophone* reviewers. He had extensive knowledge, very high standards and was hard to please.

Robertson's review of the debut recording examined the producer as much as the singer and is quoted in full:

Joan Hammond (soprano) : with orchestra : **One Fine Day** :
They Call Me Mimi (Puccini). Columbia DX1003
(12 in., 4s. 10½d.).
There are several new things to be said about this recording of
very well-worn material. It achieves a better balance between
voice and orchestra than I ever remember to have heard before.
At the climax of "One Fine Day" the merging of both elements
is genuinely thrilling. Then Mimi's question "do you hear me?"
is answered for the first time in gramophone history, so far as the
separate recording of the aria is concerned. Is this, perhaps, Walter
Legge's first appearance in opera? if so it is most promising!
    To come to a more serious matter, Joan Hammond sings
English as if it was both natural and easy so to do. Her voice has
ample power, but could do with more forward tone on the high

notes. It is of consistently good quality throughout its compass and has the sensuous appeal so necessary to the singing of Italian opera. Miss Hammond evidently has a strong dramatic sense, and in every way I regard this as a most promising gramophone *debut*. There is a pleasant sense of space about the recording which will not escape the notice of our connoisseurs.

Plans went ahead for several more recordings that year.

Yet it was a strange dual reality. A career was in the making at the same time as the country was being battered by air raids day and night. From February 1941 the Luftwaffe targeted major seaports and cities as well as keeping up its attacks on London. One of the strongest fears was that the Germans would drop poison gas. Everyone had been issued with a gasmask at the beginning of the war but Joan was increasingly worried about Pippo. A gasmask for dogs may seem a novel idea but they were readily available to the dog-loving British public. They came in three sizes and cost a rather expensive £9. Joan purchased the large size, Pippo having grown apace, and thought it worth every penny. Pippo was her mate and her comfort. He was also her early-warning air-raid alarm. He could hear the Luftwaffe coming long before the sirens started wailing and would bark with a particular kind of urgency which gave her the signal to collect some things and be ready for the off—gasmasks and all.

Living in Eaton Mews was a revelation. It was the first time she'd 'kept house' or lived on her own. Some time in the early months of 1941 she cooked the first meal of her life. It took her a very long time to prepare but the result was particularly bland: sprouts and potatoes followed by stewed apples. Food rationing helped to simplify things, especially the meat issue; she preferred vegetables to meat in any case. Her culinary efforts would remain on the simple or non-existent side for the rest of her life, which was another reason to enjoy the company of Essie Walker. Essie had studied gastronomy to a cordon bleu level. She could create a wonderful meal, despite the limitations of rationing, and was happy to cook for Joan on occasion. Such occasions were particularly welcomed by Pippo.

House cleaning was another novel aspect of living at Eaton Mews. Dirt and untidiness made her feel uncomfortable. She had to have a clean and orderly environment before she could practise, study or relax—not that there was much time for relaxing.

JOAN'S SECOND RECORD came out in June 1941. It was her old favourite 'The Green Hills o' Somerset' with 'By the waters of Minnetonka' on the B side, Gerald Moore accompanying. Alec Robertson's review gave praise but also cut her down to size:

> There is no question at all that Joan Hammond has got the quality of tone in her voice that can thrill.
> I hear there a potential Marschallin, a Tosca, a Desdemona: but she will not be ready for such roles without many tears and much sweat, perhaps even some blood! I hope she is ruthlessly ambitious. Meanwhile one can accept these prettily-sung trifles for what they are worth, but I beg her to leave Somerset, abjure Minnetonka, and soak herself in the music of great opera writers and—excuse mixed metaphors—in the records of great singers.

Ruthlessly ambitious?—Very probably. Blood, sweat and tears?— Part of the process. Listen to the records of great singers?—No!

Joan refused to be guided by the definitive performances of famous prima donnas, so she rarely listened to their recordings. She studied a score in great detail, asked herself why it was written that way, and created her interpretation accordingly. Well-known pieces needed an individual stamp, one that people would remember, and (hopefully) purchase in the form of a gramophone record.

Joan had a good intuitive sense when it came to choosing what pieces to record. She backed this sense against Walter Legge's greater experience when they disagreed about what to put on the B side of her next record. The A side was to be the ever-popular 'Love and Music' ('*Vissi d'arte*') from *Tosca*. Legge wanted something equally popular for the flip side but Joan held out for a piece he didn't know or want. It was an aria from Puccini's one-act comic opera *Gianni Schicchi*. She'd learnt the role of Lauretta while in Florence and found the little aria poignant and appealing. It could go for nothing without due care, or it could shine out as a strong cameo if given the right kind of delivery. It was called '*O mio Babbino caro*'—'O my beloved father' (sometimes known as 'Oh my beloved Daddy').

Walter Legge's knowledge of music was vast but this (now very popular) aria had passed him by. Legge had much power within the EMI organisation and Joan was pushing her luck to argue with him. He made several suggestions but she clung to 'O my beloved father' with surprising tenacity. He eventually agreed and the aria was recorded with 'Love and Music' with the Halle Orchestra under Leslie Heward in Manchester in September 1941.

Alec Robertson's review, or at least the latter part of it, must have made her chuckle:

> Miss Hammond sings these arias so well that I am sure she
> could sing them better! A greater sense of style, a more forward
> production of the high notes, strict attention to diction, would
> increase her artistic stature. With such a fine voice and so much

of the grand manner she must not, as so many English artists tend to do, rest on her laurels.

Meanwhile one particularly welcomes the aria from *Gianni Schichi* [sic] which, though sniffed at by the superior, is, I think, enchanting. We needed a new recording of it.

Two recordings of 'O *mio Babbino caro*' had been made several years earlier but this was the first time in English. Joan's rendition was rich, round and fruity. A powerful yet sensual experience lasting two-and-a-half minutes. People listening to it for the first time heard a melody that was immediately appealing: it was one of those tunes that stayed in your head. There was a lyrical sense of joy tinged with yearning: 'O my beloved father, I love him yes I love him. . .' It didn't really matter what the lyrics were about; people made their own meaning. The subliminal connection was to one's own father or to God, a compelling connection given it was wartime.

An English version of Tosca's famous aria had its own special novelty too. The initial phrases: 'Love and music, these have I lived for. . .' were appealing, and the melody looked after itself. The result was a recording that the housewife could 'la la' to and the milkman could whistle while on his rounds. The disc was a 'ten-inch' and cost 3s 8d—a reasonable price, though records were still a luxury and the materials to make them were becoming scarce. The 'wireless' was the cheaper alternative so it was often through the airwaves that Joan's recordings first found their way into people's living rooms.

JOAN WAS IN a strange situation. The war had scuttled her operatic career in Europe but it had also kept the new generation of European sopranos at bay: there was less competition but there was also less opportunity. The not-so-young Isobel Baillie, Lisa Perli and Maggie Teyte were among the very few British sopranos making new recordings, so Joan's records shone out as exciting new talent. She was twenty-nine and ready for prima donna roles, should there be any in the offing.

Opera had been kept alive through radio broadcasts, but the two main opera houses were closed for the duration of the war. Covent Garden was still a dance hall and Sadler's Wells was a hostel for the newly homeless. 'Live' opera might have disappeared but for the efforts of two key people, Joan Cross and H. B. Phillips.

Joan Cross was a soprano with Sadler's Wells. She put her singing career on hold and kept that company going by organising scaled-down productions in other theatres. H. B. Phillips was the owner of the long-established Carl Rosa touring company. Touring had ceased at the beginning of the war, but he put his troupe back on the road in early 1942. H. B. Phillips asked Joan to open his Glasgow season as a guest artist and offered two plum roles: Cho-Cho-San in *Madam Butterfly* and Violetta in *La Traviata* (sung in English). It was through Carl Rosa that Joan first performed her key diva roles.

H. B. Phillips had taken control of Carl Rosa in the 1920s. He'd made a success of it on the whole but the company was always on shaky financial ground. Carl Rosa was a touring company only, it did the rounds of the provinces, with occasional London seasons, and didn't have a home base. The permanent members of the company were experienced professionals, capable of carrying any production. Many of the singers were in their forties, troupers to the core. There were some younger artists and these included Ruth Packer, a lead soprano. Ruth Packer was the closest to Joan in age and experience and is an example of the 'competition' that Joan had to outshine if she was to get ahead. Ruth had studied in Leipzig and Vienna and sung minor roles at Covent Garden before the war intervened. Ruth would have sung the lead role if a guest soprano wasn't present, but clearly Joan surpassed her as an up-and-coming talent as far as H. B. Phillips was concerned. Regular guest artists with the Carl Rosa included Heddle Nash (tenor), Dennis Noble (baritone), Edith Coates (mezzo-soprano), Gwen Catley and Lisa Perli (sopranos)—and the newcomer, Joan Hammond.

> One fine day . . .
> From out the crowded city there is coming
> a man, a little speck in
> the distance, climbing the hillock.
> Can you guess who it is?
> And when he's reached the summit,
> Can you guess what he'll say?
> He will call: 'Butterfly'. . .
>
> *Madam Butterfly*, Puccini

Joan hugged Pippo, kissed Essie, and climbed into the taxi. Quick goodbyes were best because Pippo was apt to jump in with her, especially when suitcases were involved. Essie waved and Pippo looked mournful as the taxi left Eaton Mews bound for King's Cross station. Joan's destination was the Theatre Royal in Hope Street, Glasgow, hope being the operative word.

The train journey was long and arduous but not especially frightening. There were delays but nothing due to air raids. She'd never been to Scotland but had long wanted to go there, mainly to see the famous golf course at St Andrews. She'd been tempted to pack her golf clubs but decided there wouldn't be time for a game. Golf was the last thing on her mind as she arrived at Glasgow Central. She caught a taxi to the hotel she'd been booked into and found it was a pub with rooms above.

Madam Butterfly was her first opera in the season and she had four days before opening night. The company had been on the road so there'd been no chance to meet for preliminary rehearsal in London.

The other difficulty was that another show was running in the theatre so she wasn't able to rehearse on the stage till the day *Butterfly* opened. The core members of the company had done the production many times so there was little rehearsal needed, except for the guest artist. Joan knew the opera inside out but it was a tough way to bring her first Cho-Cho-San to life.

Carl Rosa was a tight-knit company, and its members had known each other for a long time so Joan was at a disadvantage initially. Everyone was friendly and H. B. Phillips was fatherly but there was no time for 'getting to know you' pleasantries. Rehearsals took place in a church hall. There was a blueprint to follow and everyone got on with the job. The outline of the scenery was marked on the floor, the stage directions were laid out in the score, a stage director guided proceedings and an upright piano served as orchestration. The chaos began when they moved into the theatre for the dress rehearsal before the evening performance.

The set, props and costumes had been in storage in London and unfortunately the storehouse had been bombed. Much of the scenery and props were damaged or missing. The Japanese setting — the house in Nagasaki with its dainty screens and cherry blossom garden — looked shabby as a consequence. Rose-coloured stage lighting softened the effect but only to a degree. The orchestra was adequate, the conductor likewise. The theatre itself had a good feeling: the bell-shaped auditorium was acoustically excellent and had been designed with opera in mind. That, and the fact that Joan had brought her own costume, were the only comforters.

All the practical aspects of the production were in disarray. The opening night performance was the first time that Joan had a complete run-through with everything and everyone present — or as present as possible. Her saviour on that night was Gladys Parr, a mezzo-soprano with a good voice and fine acting skills. Gladys was twenty years older than Joan and had worked with Carl Rosa and the other major companies for many years. She played Suzuki, Butterfly's maid, which meant she was on stage with Joan for much of the time. Gladys guided her through the whole performance, solving problems as they came. A missing prop would be brought at the first opportunity, a discreet gesture would indicate where she should be standing, and an encouraging word would be given after a tricky scene.

Cho-Cho-San is a mammoth role, even in the best of circumstances like the clockwork precision of the Viennese theatre tradition where Joan received her training. The real test, whatever the situation, is the singing. It's an exhausting challenge. Act One sets up Butterfly's arranged marriage with Lieutenant Pinkerton of the United States Navy. Butterfly has to charm Pinkerton with coquettish niceties while his main ambition is to get her to the bedroom. A series of luscious exchanges culminates in Butterfly's impassioned solo 'Love me a little', which ends on a high C. Night falls and the pair retire to the bedroom as the curtain slowly descends. Act Two brings the scene inside the house. Pinkerton has been away for three years with no sign of returning. Butterfly is desolate, poverty stricken, and she's the only one who believes her husband will come back to her. She explains how the scene will happen with her famous aria 'One fine day', and if this doesn't win the audience and earn her a round of applause then nothing will.

Joan won her round of applause but she didn't feel she'd earned it. She went from scene to scene in a kind of daze. She didn't feel she was connecting with the audience or with Butterfly. She just couldn't bring the strands together. She felt ghastly, scene after scene. She also felt herself tiring as the burden of the emotional anguish intensified, Butterfly's and her own. Worst of all, her voice was out of sorts; it had strayed from its relaxed centred position, and an unrelaxed un-centred voice is much harder to control. Then she reached the 'Flower Duet' with Suzuki (Gladys)—a joyful lyrical duet, perfectly placed within the structure of the opera to give vocal respite to the soprano before the massive demands of the final act. It was effortless, relaxing, enjoyable: she literally sang her voice back to strength. Act Three demands everything of Butterfly; it brings her to absolute despair. She must fall and break emotionally, yet rise up in a moment of great sacrifice: a noble tragic heroine. She sings a touching lullaby to her child, son of Pinkerton, knowing she must give him up to her husband and the 'real' Mrs Pinkerton. Her sense of honour leads her to the only possible conclusion. She recites the inscription on her father's dagger: 'Death with honour is better than life with dishonour'. Then the full force of the music swells as Butterfly cuts her throat and dies, her child nearby, the cowardly Pinkerton arriving too late. It's a massive emotional journey.

The applause was good when Joan took her bow but she couldn't be comforted. She'd had high expectations of herself and failed to come anywhere near them. She'd failed to capture Butterfly, vocally, emotionally, physically. She'd wanted to slit her throat in earnest by the time she'd reached Act Three. Taking a curtain call felt obscene; she couldn't wait to get offstage, couldn't wait to get out of the theatre and hide her shame. Inconsolable, wretched.

This forgettable performance happened on 16 March 1942. She had a second try two nights later, then a third straight after that, and it was the third when everything started to connect. She wasn't chasing Butterfly any more; she *was* Butterfly, and the audience responded. There were bravos, there was thunderous applause, and there was the demand that she come back again and again for a solo curtain call. Joan tried to share the praise with Gladys, who'd done a wonderful job, but Gladys refused: 'It's you they want, go on,' and she gently pushed Joan forward to receive her due.

Joan's Butterfly grew and blossomed as the season went on. The only thing to mar her joy was an uncomfortable moment after her final performance. In the best of all possible worlds she would have enjoyed some kind of party, but due to 'feast or famine' work

Butterfly

opportunities she had to return to London on the night train to fulfil an engagement next day. Catching the train was the problem. The *Butterfly* performance ended at about 9.30 p.m. (shows started early due to the blackout) and the last train to London left twenty minutes later. The stage manager said it was possible to get to the station in time, but it was tight. Minutes were saved by starting the performance promptly and keeping the intervals brisk. Joan took her final curtain call with apparent grace but the moment the curtain came down she rushed from the stage, through the wings, down the corridor, down the steps, out the stage door and into a waiting taxi, suitcase and make-up box already installed. The taxi sped to Glasgow Central Station with fearsome speed and arrived with about four minutes to spare. A sleeper had been booked and she had the ticket in her hand.

All she had to do was get to the platform, find her carriage, and get on the train. Her costume and luggage refused to let her make large strides so she trotted along with tiny steps as fast as she could go. When she got to the barrier she could see the train and many people on the platform saying their goodbyes. She smiled with relief at the ticket collector, but he didn't smile back. He looked puzzled, almost aggressive. She pressed on. The platform was very dimly lit due to the blackout and she had to push through various groups in the search for her carriage. It was like the parting of the waves. People looked at her and stepped back, but not out of politeness. She knew she looked odd but surely they could see it was just a costume and theatrical makeup. But they couldn't. Under normal lighting the image would have been absurd. The kimono and wig were authentic but the elaborate makeup would have verged on the grotesque if seen in daylight. White face, over-emphasised red lips, over-accentuated eyebrows and eyeliner, eyelashes so obviously false—extremes so necessary under the ruthless glare of stage lights, and yet strangely real in the dim light of the railway station. It could have been amusing, even camp— someone quite tall with broad shoulders in fancy dress—but people were sneering, not laughing.

Japan had bombed Pearl Harbor just three months before. The Japanese were the new enemy, and here was a 'geisha' tottering along the platform. If she'd had a free hand she would have removed her wig, but she didn't and she daren't stop. The word 'Jap' rippled down the line. Some people hissed, one spat, and another shouted something unintelligible but obviously abusive. A whistle blew, the steam engine puffed, a man in railway uniform beckoned her on. She recognised him. He was a sleep-car attendant she'd met on other northbound trips. He took her things, helped her up the steps and settled her in. He knew who she was, saw her distress. The train jerked forward and started its journey and the attendant said he'd bring her a 'nice cup of tea'. She caught sight of her reflection in the window: the shadowy outline of a Japanese woman, her eyes just catching the light. She would be haunted by the experience and draw upon it every time she played Butterfly, poor Butterfly, forever under siege.

JOAN SANG WITH Carl Rosa many times during the war: *Il Trovatore, La Bohème, Tosca, Faust, Madam Butterfly, La Traviata*. Audiences loved her. Carl Rosa went the extra mile under difficult conditions and the people in the provinces appreciated it. There was little else in terms of entertainment being brought to them, so people who'd never been to the opera bought a ticket and gave it a go. Confirmed opera buffs were also in attendance, of course. One such was the 18-year-old William Mann, later to become a renowned music critic with *The Times*. He was earnest about his opera and eager to see whatever he could:

> Birmingham 1942, and I was starved of opera. Then one Friday
> . . . the Carl Rosa was giving *Madama Butterfly*, so of course
> I went. The woman who sang Butterfly wasn't tiny, but from her
> entrance the purity of her voice and the clarity of her enunciation,
> and the nobility that welled out in the Triumph of Butterfly and
> in the arioso we call 'Che tua madre', all struck home very firmly.
> I became an admirer of Joan Hammond's singing that evening. . .

He wasn't alone. Her popularity grew considerably. There were concerts, oratorios, operas, broadcasts, gramophone recordings, and two more seasons in Dublin. Engagements flowed in from all directions, mostly paid, some voluntary. Work was unpredictable; there might be days of nothing then a host of engagements crammed together. One particular week began with an appearance at an afternoon tea party given by Mrs Churchill who was raising funds for the Russians by enlisting the help of the wives of top brass and dignitaries. Joan went straight from that to a BBC broadcast with Jack Payne and his band at the Criterion Theatre. Next day she did a *Messiah* in Huddersfield, the following night a recital at the Washington Club in London for American troops, then there was a *Bohème* and a *Traviata* for Carl Rosa in Wimbledon to round off the weekend.

THE USA HAD declared war on Japan; Germany and Italy had declared war on the USA—and Russia. It was total war, world war. Australia was fighting a double offensive: initially alongside her allies in Europe and North Africa, and latterly back home against the Japanese to her north. Tony, Joan's youngest brother, had joined the RAAF and was piloting Lancaster bombers. Essie Walker's younger and only brother had been captured in Singapore and held prisoner in Changi. Lady Gowrie's son, Patrick, was fighting in North Africa, as was his relative, Ian Blacker, Joan's young Irish friend. Almost everyone had a connection with someone who was in peril in a foreign land.

Civilians on the Home Front were pressed harder to take up war work. The upper age limit for conscription was extended to 51 for men, while unmarried women between the ages of 19 and 30 were conscripted for the first time. Women could choose to work in industry, the Land Army or in one of the auxiliary forces like the WAAF. The wise woman made her choice early, before she was pushed into something she didn't want—like an armaments factory in a town she'd never heard of. Essie chose to join the London County Council Auxiliary Ambulance Service, perhaps to ensure she stayed in London. Shy and gentle Essie excelled in the job.

Joan was working for ENSA and CEMA so was already doing her bit. Even so, she decided to make her life even busier by volunteering to join the Auxiliary Ambulance Service as a part-time driver. Essie's involvement in the service must have been an influence, but her motivation was patriotic: she wanted to serve as well as sing. She had an interview, passed the driving test and was measured for a uniform (navy jacket, trousers, cap and tin helmet). The understanding was that she'd be a driver only, with no stretcher-bearer duties. But when bombs were dropping and people dying it was pointless trying to say she wasn't supposed to carry stretchers because of her weak left arm. She worried about the possible damage, let alone pain, this caused, but she did it and remained an ambulance driver till the end of the war.

The regular ambulance service attended to routine casualties; the much larger auxiliary force dealt with war casualties and had makeshift stations all over London. It was known as the 'Cinderella force'. The ambulances were a hotchpotch of converted vans, such as laundry or carpet vans, fitted with four metal 'shelves' to take four canvas stretchers. The stations had garaging space plus a rudimentary building to house the control room and mess room. Joan was assigned to Clerkenwell station in East Central London, which was perhaps where Essie was based. Circumstances were unpredictable but her station manager was co-operative regarding her timetable. She worked night shifts which meant it was possible to arrive at Clerkenwell after a performance, do her stint, then go off duty at eight next morning in time to catch a train to Huddersfield, or wherever, if she had a performance to get to.

Air raids in London were intermittent by this time so it was possible to grab a few hours sleep while on duty. Joan opted to sleep alongside her ambulance rather than suffer the stuffy, overcrowded dormitory. The garage had a roof but no walls yet she preferred the 'healthier' open air, even in mid-winter. Sharing a room with people who might have colds or sore throats was the worst thing possible, so she'd doss down in her sleeping-bag ('flea bag'), as did some of the other drivers. There was a rule against sleeping inside the ambulance due to certain 'goings on'. It was an intense existence, and everyone coped in their own way. Some liked company; some needed space. Once a raid came over it was hell on earth for the next few hours, and it was fifty-fifty whether you made it back in one piece. Joan made no pretence about the fear she felt: 'I expected to leave this world at any minute'.

Joan saw corpses, body parts (decapitation was common), and horribly injured people on a regular basis. It was shocking at first, but after many, many nights of the same she got used to it, or at least 'dealt' with it.

One of her ways of coping was to have Pippo with her, which is perhaps how she managed to keep warm at night. Joan's method of transportation was a grocer's delivery bike—the type with a smaller front wheel and very large front basket. She'd seen a boy on one when waiting at a bus stop and realised it was the perfect mode of transport for 'two'. Pippo was happy in the front basket (suitably padded) and Joan was able to go anywhere that her legs could manage—and they certainly did manage. Essie was persuaded to get a bicycle also and they'd go for jaunts on their days off—to Kew or Wimbledon or up the meandering hills to Hampstead Heath, where Pippo could run mad. A newspaper photographer looking for interesting wartime scenes happened to see Joan and Pippo riding through Clerkenwell one morning and asked if he could take a photo. Her name was well known by this time but he didn't ask it and she didn't tell it. The photo was published in a daily newspaper a few days later. Pippo looked perky in his basket and Joan looked workmanlike in her ambulance uniform, but her face showed signs of strain. The background told its own story—bombed houses and heaps of rubble.

Most of the bombing raids came at night. A direct hit could bring down a house, start a fire, blow people up (literally into trees) or bury them alive. One of the most damaging side-effects was flying glass. People could be covered in cuts—like a diamante hedgehog—and the cuts would produce enormous quantities of blood. Talk of blood running down walls and into gutters was not exaggerated.

Joan and Pippo

People worked in teams: nurses, doctors, air raid wardens, firefighters and stretcher-bearers would be on the scene (or were supposed to be) before the ambulances arrived. Drivers worked in pairs. Joan's job was to transport the injured to a hospital, or the dead to a morgue. On some nights she'd have bombs exploding along the route she had to drive, and sometimes the hospital itself would be in flames when she got there. On one occasion a bomb exploded very close and she had to be treated for shock and minor injuries. She was supposed to sing at City Hall in Sheffield next day but was forced to cancel, which pained her greatly.

She was stoic under these pressures. She held her emotions in check, locked her personal pains away. Tears, for Joan, were a sign of weakness, and they were bad for the voice. Emotional release came second-hand, through her performances. She poured her feelings into the characters she portrayed, and her work matured as a consequence.

SHE MADE ONE OF HER finest recordings in October 1943: 'Tatiana's Letter Scene' from Tchaikovsky's *Eugene Onegin*. It was recorded under the usual difficult conditions—this time with the Liverpool Philharmonic Orchestra, Constant Lambert conducting, Walter Legge producing. Alec Robertson cast his judgement in *The Gramophone*:

> . . . This is a big, most testing aria—one of the very great things
> in opera; and it is sung in a big way and with more emotion than
> I knew resided in Miss Hammond. She makes us feel the changing
> emotional phases through which the love-struck girl, now taking
> so bold and courageous a step, passes. The singer puts a moving
> tenderness into her description of her dreams of Onegin . . . her
> wrestling with doubt. Then comes the fine climax, and in a torrent
> of passionate sound from the orchestra she finishes the letter.
> The high notes must not be less than bold and thrilling and they
> are so here . . .

Yet he took a strong dislike to the flip side: '*Louise Depuis le Jour*' by Charpentier:

. . . it is sung with very little understanding. No singer who cannot achieve *mezza voce* on her high notes should attempt an aria which calls for it repeatedly. *Je crois rêver*—the final syllable on a high A is marked p. The top B natural (*je suis hereuse* [sic]) is marked *pp*, *crescendo* to *forte*. All these are sung too loudly and though Miss Hammond makes a thrilling sound on her scooped-up-to double-forte top B, that is not what Charpentier wanted . . . No wonder Verdi put five pianissimos when he wanted some ordinarily soft singing. Anyone who heard Edvina or Miriam Licette sing this aria will decide that Miss Hammond is not really in the skin of the part of Louise.

Robertson was more lenient with the orchestra, particularly by not mentioning the horn player who fluffed some vital notes in the final section of 'Tatiana's Letter Scene'. A blemish that confirms how difficult it was to get everything right at the same time.

Robertson continued to be critical when Joan recorded two arias a couple of months later: 'Grant O Love' from *Marriage of Figaro* and 'Ah, 'Tis Gone' from *The Magic Flute*. His knife was particularly sharp:

I have an unfading memory of Claire Dux pouring out, with exquisite tone, Pamina's aria from "The Magic Flute." That was in one of the Joseph Beecham seasons at Drury Lane. She stressed nothing but let the great music, through the magic of her voice, make its own effect. The phrasing and the gradations of tone, the sheer loveliness of the interpretation, deeply moved the whole house.

It may be irritating when those of us of a past generation recall such things, but in these days of low standards it is necessary to do so. Miss Hammond has, of course, a standard, but she had not the musicianship to shape and mould her phrases with beauty, nor is her tone nearly disciplined enough. [*criticism of the orchestra follows*]

Opera in English must aim higher than this. And that means, does it not, incessant hard work and a study of the finest models.

Such a review must have hurt. Yet how could it be otherwise? Joan was pitching herself against the highest 'standard' in the world—as defined by Alec Robertson anyway—though one can be forgiven for saying 'who?' in relation to Claire Dux.

Joan's attention was diverted to more serious issues when she was transferred to Stepney ambulance station in the East End. She'd never had cause to travel so far east before and was shocked to see how the 'other half' lived. She'd known what it was like to be short of money, but that experience was relative. East Enders lived in slum conditions, they were *really* poor. Tenement houses had no plumbing, and people had to cart their water from a ground-floor tap that served a five-floor block. The East End, the docks area, had borne the brunt of the bombings and continued to do so. It was an eye-opener in every way and Joan was deeply affected by the experience.

In her darkest moments she drew strength from her faith. She didn't attend church but she did pray, especially in times of need. She could also draw on the rarefied experience of singing the great oratorios, Handel's *Messiah* for instance. Such occasions were very demanding in a practical sense, and gloriously uplifting in a spiritual sense. When she sang 'I know that my Redeemer liveth', she really meant it, so her message was really conveyed.

It was Joan's electrically 'alive' performances, her warmth of personality, her richness of voice that won people's hearts. And their warmth in return gave her strength.

JOAN HAD INHERITED a second dog by the summer of 1943. She had 'Mr Pippo' plus a white standard poodle called Jani (pronounced Yani). Jani belonged to a South African couple who needed to find him a home. He was given to Joan to look after 'for a few days', but the term extended to the end of his long life.

Essie and Joan were walking the two dogs down by the Thames near Chelsea Bridge. The ebb tide was low and they sat in the sun on a tiny patch of sand by the water. Jani hadn't learnt to swim at this stage but Pippo adored swimming. The tidal current was very strong that day so Joan kept him on the sand; but a boy threw a stick far into the river and Pippo dashed after it before Joan could stop him. He got the stick, but when he turned to swim back he was in trouble. He couldn't swim against the current and as he panicked he started to disappear under the water. Joan tore off her shoes, ran into the water and swam out to save him. Reaching him was fairly easy, but holding him while he struggled, and swimming against the strong current, was terribly difficult. She could feel an undercurrent pulling her down and was in danger of being dragged away. Her clothes were a dead weight and she had to use all her might to push forward. She was tiring and swallowing a lot of water. It was no use swimming straight ahead; she had to 'tack' in zigzags in order to gain ground, which confused Pippo and made him struggle even more. She knew she couldn't last much longer, then saw her chance. She shouted to Essie, stranded on the shore, to get to the wall downriver. Essie worked out what she meant and ran to the embankment wall, which had a corner that jutted out. She found a crevice to grip on to and leant out as far as she could. Joan, utterly exhausted, gave one last desperate push towards that corner and Essie, with what could be described as miraculous timing, managed to grab hold of Joan's hand. They stayed like that until a couple of men in a boat came across and helped them back on to the embankment. Joan lay there, in the Thames mud, gasping for breath, unable to move or speak for a considerable time.

O death, where is thy sting?
O grave, where is thy victory?

Messiah, Handel

DEATH WAS ALL AROUND: Lady Gowrie's son died after a commando raid; Essie's brother died in Changi; one of Joan's golfing friends was killed while on duty with the WAAF; and Ian Blacker, the eccentric Irishman, was killed in action.

Joan held the pain in and sang the emotion out.

The most bizarre twist in this series of tragedies was the death of someone she'd met at her digs in Vienna. A picture of a dead woman on the front page of a newspaper suddenly reminded her of 'V' and the back room in the Baroness's house where all kinds of exotic people used to gather to talk politics. 'V' had served Turkish coffee which Joan especially enjoyed. The picture in the newspaper was of Maidi, the attractive young woman who'd sat beside her and asked questions about Australia—questions which she'd been happy to answer. Maidi had been shot dead in a Paris nightclub; someone had discovered she was a Nazi spy! Joan stared at the photo and remembered the day she saw 'V' by chance in London not long before the war. She'd attracted her attention but 'V' had run away. She felt sick when she pieced two and two together: those gatherings in the back room of the Baroness's house must have been peppered with Nazi spies.

You had to laugh—or go under. There were many cheery moments to combat the gloom. One such occurred in a taxi when Joan and Dennis Noble were travelling to the Royal Albert Hall to take part in a charity concert. They'd had little time to rehearse so sang their duets as they travelled through the streets of London. Heads turned, people smiled, and the taxi driver waived the fare.

The charity concert was in celebration of the Russians. They'd forced the Germans to surrender at Stalingrad and were steadily

In the recording studio

pushing Hitler's forces back. The concert was organised by the BBC and was one of the biggest shows of the war. Military bands, the London Philharmonic, and various 'names' performed. Joan was now doing this kind of variety show on a regular basis. She rubbed shoulders with élite artists such as Laurence Olivier, Ralph Richardson, Sybil Thorndike, Jack Buchanan and Australia's actor/dancer Robert Helpmann. She'd be on the same bill as Bing Crosby and Fred Astaire, and was often accompanied by top dance bands led by the likes of Jack Payne, Carrol Gibbons and Geraldo. She found that Geraldo's swing band accompanied her arias with more sensitivity and indeed 'swing' than some of the more rigid classical orchestras and conductors. She liked making use of *rubato* (a hurrying or slowing of the pace for expressive effect), and the swing bands understood that freedom. The chemistry was so good that Geraldo invited her to go on tour with him. She declined.

Joan's warm rapport, her robust appearance, her endearing Australian accent, all combined to win the hearts of the people, and broadcasts and gramophone recordings were taking her voice worldwide. Her popularity was such that she was listed in the 1944 edition of *Who's Who*. A small entry initially, but it signalled her arrival as a soprano of note. The old confusion about her name was highlighted in this edition. Those looking for 'Hammond' were redirected to 'Hood Hammond'. She must have taken steps to adjust the entry because the 'Hood' was dropped from subsequent editions and appeared only as an 'H' sitting silently in the middle of her father's name. Samuel H. Hammond — hardly the 'beloved father' she had in mind when she sang her most popular aria!

Joan knew enough (at some point) about the origins of her name to use 'Hood Hammond' on legal documents — passport, driving licence and so on — so in effect the original listing in *Who's Who* was correct.

THE D-DAY LANDINGS along the Normandy coast gave the Allies a key advantage. The surprise attack caught the Germans off guard and the Allies were able to push forward. (A messenger pigeon called Gustav flew to Britain from the landings with news of the success, and was later awarded a bravery medal.) The tide was at last turning and the Allies were beginning to win the war.

Tony Hammond telephoned to say he was in England. He was with the RAAF in Bournemouth and had been given leave to visit London. Joan went to meet his train at Waterloo station next evening. He'd been a lanky, fidgety 16-year-old when she'd seen him last, and she had been a plump, gauche and rather innocent 24-year-old. Now she was nearly 31. She had a lean yet solid figure, a strong handsome face, wore lipstick but no other make-up, and had a hairstyle that was unfashionably short. She wore the standard dark suit: fashion didn't interest her and clothes rationing cut down the choices in any case. The overall effect was neither masculine nor feminine. She looked strong and somewhat serious until she smiled, and her smile often turned into a laugh. She had the same aura of protective reserve she'd always had, and the same mischievous twinkle in her eyes, though you had to be observant to spot it.

Hundreds of RAAF men disembarked from the train and there was a great sense of excitement, but as Joan peered at every young man's face in the half-light of the blackout she couldn't find her kid brother. The crowd gradually thinned but she still couldn't see him. A tall, strikingly handsome young man was walking up and down the platform with the same worried look. He wore a RAAF uniform but was nothing like her brother. The crowd dwindled to a handful and the anxious pair glanced at each other for the umpteenth time. Joan said 'Tony' without any conviction and the handsome man frowned; then he suddenly exclaimed 'Joan? Joan!' and they hugged each other and laughed and cried and looked at each other and hugged again.

They had a marvellous evening back at Eaton Mews, with Essie, the dogs and a feast of a meal, the merriment enhanced by a powerful drop of Russian vodka.

Tony had experienced a great deal in a short time. He was a fighter pilot, first with Lancaster bombers then as a Pathfinder, and he had a wife and baby daughter back in Sydney. Tony was also something of a womaniser, though the extent of his activities was probably concealed from his morally minded sister. Joan was more worldly than she used to be but this hadn't weakened her sense of right and wrong. Infidelity was 'wrong', and a touchy subject given her father's background.

Tony visited his sister quite often and one of their favourite things was to go cycling. Tony, Joan and Essie (and dogs in baskets) rode all over London. This trio was extended when an old friend arrived on Joan's doorstep: Eber, the young man in the Vienna Boys' Choir who'd escorted her to the theatre and taken her mountaineering. Very surprisingly, he'd become a major in the US Army. Eber was hesitant about being seen on a bicycle until he saw an American lieutenant-colonel riding across Chelsea Bridge—clearly it was the done thing. The foursome would go on long rides to see the sights, or take the dogs for a run on Hampstead Heath or Wimbledon Common; a picnic lunch, then the slow ride home—tired, satisfied, glad to be alive.

HITLER MADE AN impressive onslaught against Britain from mid-1944 to March 1945. Long-range ballistic missiles known as 'doodlebugs' began to shower down with horrible regularity. An average of fifty doodlebugs hit London every day in June 1944. They were vicious things, low-flying rockets that made a distinctive noise, then became silent—then they dropped. Joan saw these things fly over quite often when she was walking the dogs. They held a strange fascination and she rarely ran for cover. Some landed very close; she'd hear the screams, the shouting, the sirens. One of the side-effects of this new mayhem was that the people who'd come back to London suddenly changed their minds and left again.

Joan had the most terrifying train journey of them all as a consequence, not because of bombs but because of people en masse. She was booked to sing at Sheffield in the Midlands. When she got to the platform she was caught by an overwhelming surge of people pushing to board the train—fortunately the one she'd intended to catch. It was like a stampede. The force pushed her into a carriage, down the corridor and with nowhere else to go, into the toilet cubicle, or 'W.C.'. Six soldiers were crammed in there with her. Once in, it was impossible to get out. Her legs were pressed against the toilet bowl; her suitcase was wedged against her kneecaps; there was barely room to breathe let alone move. The cubicle was dank and redolent of a urinal. She felt a cold sweat break out over her body but couldn't even get her hand to her brow. Nausea and claustrophobia started to engulf her. A soldier broke the small window next to the toilet cistern, which brought in some fresh air. She breathed, slowly, evenly, and told herself to be calm, told herself she was somewhere else, anywhere else. The soldiers were kind but nothing could be done. They were trapped in the same position for most of the journey. She could hardly walk when she got off the train. Then she had to sing.

The night train back to London was bliss by comparison, she even got a seat, but she swore she'd never put herself through that again. She refused out-of-town engagements until she was in a position to afford a car, which wasn't so long in coming. She bought a second-hand Hillman Minx for £475. It was a large sum but she paid it outright, which shows that things were definitely looking up financially.

Petrol rationing restricted her journeys but she was at last free to travel as she wished. This meant Pippo could keep her company. Pippo was such an important part of her life that he went to rehearsals and even joined her on the concert platform on some rare occasions. He sat under the piano while she sang, perfectly behaved. Essie was sometimes the pianist, which meant that the four of them—two women, two dogs—could travel in the Hillman Minx together. It was a wonderful new freedom.

The next large financial outlay was the purchase of a house. The owner of Eaton Mews was returning to London so Joan had to find somewhere else to live. Bomb-damaged houses were selling very cheaply and there was a house 'going for a song' just around the corner: 75 Eaton Terrace. It was a typical Georgian terrace (basement and three floors) in need of structural repair and renovation, but a great buy given its Chelsea/Belgrave location. Joan took possession in April 1944 and moved in with Pippo, Jani, and the person who was increasingly the mainstay of her life: Essie. They camped on the top two floors while the builders worked all round them. Joan had almost no furniture, which was probably just as well given the conditions. Essie was able to bring a few things but Joan's contribution was limited to a portable gas ring, a desk and chair, the wind-up gramophone she'd brought from Australia, and the Minipiano, a parting gift from the Eaton Mews friend. Living conditions were basic for the first few months, not least because there were no floorboards on the ground floor, but it was the beginning of a very happy phase.

SHE TRANSFERRED TO the popular HMV label and continued to make numerous recordings of arias and songs—and Alec Robertson continued to review the results. Her recording of two duets from *La Traviata* with Dennis Noble pleased him so much that he declared his optimism for the future of English opera. Three solos from *Il Trovatore* also gave pleasure:

> It is very pleasant to be able to give almost unqualified praise to
> this recording. Joan Hammond sings with much more discipline
> and control than I remember her to have showed before. Her soft
> high notes in "Love, fly on rosy pinions" (what a translation!)
> are really lovely, she does not shirk the top D flat, and she does
> the cadenza beautifully. A little more care in the distribution of
> accents in the vocal phrases, a greater roundness of tone on top
> B flats, would add to what is already very good singing.

But he took it all back again a couple of months later. She'd recorded two of Liu's arias from *Turandot* and he could hardly believe it was the same singer. He didn't like her interpretation: 'Liu is supposed to be a child but there is little child-like poignancy in the heavily underlined emotion'; and he didn't like her 'wavering tone and overstressed explosive words'. She was one of the best singers around yet she was unpredictable—and flawed. All in all it made him pessimistic about the future of English opera all over again.

His comments would have stung, yet Joan probably accepted some of them. She would have argued the point in relation to interpretive choices, but she knew she had vocal flaws. She knew her voice still had a long way to go, and it distressed her that it wasn't progressing as she felt it should. Something was wrong with her breathing, or some aspect of her technique, but she couldn't pinpoint it. She didn't seek the help of a singing teacher, perhaps because she found none she could trust, but she worked on it constantly by herself.

H. B. Phillips (of Carl Rosa) could find little fault with Joan's voice and dismissed her anxieties as 'temperament'. In his experience all singers liked to give themselves something to worry about. This was true in a way: Joan was extremely self-critical. A perfectionist, she was doomed never to be satisfied.

Unlike Robertson, Phillips was very optimistic about the future of English opera. Carl Rosa had done well at the box office, partly thanks to Joan's growing reputation. He was at last in a position to pay for new sets and costumes. He offered her the first 'new look' *Tosca* and she was delighted to share the line-up with Frank Titterton as Cavaradossi and Otakar Kraus, the Czech-born baritone, as Scarpia. The conductor was her friend, Walter Susskind, one of the best conductors she'd ever worked with. Indeed the whole creative team was good.

Never before had she had a designer create new costumes just for her, with even the accessories made to match. Not everything was new of course. Some of the props were recycled, and the same musty old mattress was used to break Tosca's fall when she leaps from the battlements at the end of Act Three. A leap Joan liked to achieve with generous athleticism.

The production opened in Newcastle on 20 March 1945 and toured the major venues. The most memorable performance was in Glasgow on 8 May. The good old Theatre Royal was packed, its bell-shaped auditorium providing lovely acoustics. The performance had proceeded as usual till they reached the second interval. The stage manager walked on stage as soon as the curtain came down and announced that 'V. E. Day' — Victory in Europe Day — had arrived. Hitler was dead and the war would soon be over. It was an electric moment, yet everyone stayed put. There was the faint sound of people celebrating in the streets outside, but the audience wanted their last act of *Tosca*, so that's what they got. Joan could hardly contain herself as the last scenes were played out, and finally the last few phrases:

Spoletta:
Thou shalt pay full dearly for his life
Tosca:
With my own!
Oh! Scarpia we shall meet on high

Tosca, Act 3

And she threw herself as usual from the battlements as the soldiers chased and the orchestra thrilled and the curtain came down with terrific speed. There was no time to ponder. She rushed back on stage to take her place for the curtain call. The audience applause was for the opera at first and then something else began to grow. An overwhelming relief, a rushing exhilaration as the realisation took hold. Peace is coming! War is over! The applause grew louder and louder and went on and on and everyone was clapping — principals, chorus, orchestra, stagehands, usherettes — cheering, crying, hugging, kissing, dancing, laughing. War was over. It was over, it was (almost) over!

CHAPTER 5

ILLUMINATION

LIFE IN JOAN'S new home at Eaton Terrace began to settle after some shaky beginnings. The house suffered bomb damage before the end of the war, and just as they'd finished the repairs a gang broke in and stole much of the contents—shifting it straight into a furniture van. It happened on a Sunday afternoon when Joan was singing at the Albert Hall (Beethoven Mass, Sargent conducting). Essie was in the audience and luckily Joan had the poodles in her dressing-room: she felt sure the robbers would have stolen even the dogs when she saw how methodical they'd been. It was a horrible experience but they eventually made things comfortable again.

Joan established a music room and bought a Steinway grand, Essie took charge of the kitchen, and Pippo and Jani, plus a couple of stray cats, took over the whole house. It was home sweet home at last.

Ivor Newton (Joan's frequent accompanist) told a friend years later that he always assumed Joan and Essie were 'a couple'. There's no doubt Joan and Essie were close, but how close is uncertain. Essie was brilliant in some ways and strange in others. She'd been an odd and gifted child who'd grown into an odd and gifted adult. Some people explained her strangeness as acute shyness, but that probably simplified a more complex condition. She was a loner—and yet she was very happy to be with Joan. She was warm, generous and lovely—but also 'odd'. How this manifested itself is unclear, but Joan and some of her closest friends knew that Essie wasn't always the easiest of people to cope with. Perhaps there was a moodiness sometimes, a resentment when her generous nature was exploited?

Essie was never forthcoming, so it's uncertain how much Joan knew about her family background. Strangely enough, there was a strong Australian connection. Essie's mother, Elaine, had been born in Melbourne, the fourth child of Judge Molesworth, an Irish Anglican whose father was Sir Robert Molesworth of Dublin. Elaine was a recognised beauty who married the not so handsome but highly decorated Captain William Walker, VC, in 1907. William had been born in India, the son of the Deputy Surgeon General of the Indian Army. The couple lived in India till the beginning of the First World War, when Walker served in France. Essie was born in London in 1916, the second of two children. The Walkers moved to Seaford on the south coast of England when Walker retired, and Essie grew up there. Her father died in 1936 after a long illness, and the following year Essie's aunt met Joan in Vienna, and began the friendship that resulted in the request that Joan befriend her painfully shy niece.

Whatever the terms of the relationship, Joan and Essie found comfort in each other and agreed to live together long-term, Essie rent free. It was an excellent arrangement from Joan's point of view because Essie supported her on all fronts—musically, administratively (she was a high-speed typist) and domestically. Essie, meanwhile, gained a purpose, a home, and a stimulating artistic environment, one that she could take part in from the periphery if she didn't want to join in fully.

IN SEPTEMBER 1945 Joan was sent to Germany with ENSA. She was a guest artist with Sadler's Wells and the company's mission was to take opera to British occupation troops.

Madam Butterfly was the opera performed but the company also gave impromptu concerts wherever needed. One of these was at Belsen, the Nazi concentration camp. The camp had been burnt to the ground because of the typhus epidemic, yet much of the horror was still in evidence: the gallows, the mass graves neatly terraced with signs reading '2500 bodies buried here'. The survivors had been moved to a camp nearby and it was here that Joan sang.

There was no 'debrief' after such an experience, for soldiers let alone artists, so she returned to London and carried on as usual — or tried to. A niggling vocal problem took her to a throat specialist for treatment, and then she contracted bronchitis. This meant she had to cancel a much-anticipated Christmas recital with Gerald Moore, which upset her terribly. She was worried about her voice. Anxious about its weaknesses and flaws, which of course added extra tension — which made the problem feel worse. The enforced rest was frustrating rather than relaxing.

She hid her insecurities behind a protective veneer, but it was a stance that could work against her. Her inner tension, combined with her obvious desire to reach as high a standard as possible, could make her seem arrogant, or 'difficult'. Yet in truth she was her own worst critic. Consistently good reviews and ever-increasing popularity didn't wash: she knew she could do better, should do better, and pushed herself hard.

She continued to make guest appearances with Carl Rosa but she wasn't invited to sing with Sadler's Wells in London, which seems surprising given she'd broken into that company with the Germany tour. Maybe her 'arrogant' tag influenced the decision makers who were themselves jostling for power in the post-war phase. Sadler's Wells and Covent Garden were in a state of reformation and it was uncertain as to who would be 'in' or 'out', even at the highest levels. The one consistency was that opera was to be sung in the English language—a strategy designed to foster an English opera identity, something that hadn't existed before.

APPRECIATIVE LETTERS BEGAN to pour in from near and far. Servicemen wrote to describe how her voice had sustained them in prison camp or distant outpost. Housewives wrote about their lost loved ones and the comfort that her singing had brought. People who'd seen her performances wrote adoring letters reminding her of a Tosca in Burnley or a Mimi in Hammersmith, when she'd signed their programme, chatted in such a friendly unassuming manner afterwards. Loving and often moving letters, and Joan, with Essie's help, answered them all.

When Tony Hammond returned to Australia Joan missed him very much. He'd spent most of his leave at Eaton Terrace and they'd grown close. Perhaps Joan felt some homesickness, for when the ABC asked if she'd consider an extensive concert tour for the latter half of 1946 she said yes.

When she signed her agreement she understood that Gerald Moore would be her accompanist, but when it came to the final negotiations the ABC declined to pay what he asked, so he reluctantly refused the offer. What had been a perfect arrangement was scuttled from the beginning. Gerald's presence would have given her confidence. The ABC said they had an excellent accompanist in Australia so she wasn't to worry.

Yet worry she did. She'd been asked to prepare at least eight different programmes, some recital, some orchestral, and was told that one half of each programme would be broadcast (meaning it had to keep within a strict time limit). It was a massive amount to prepare, let alone memorise and rehearse, all without one's accompanist. Essie spent hours with Joan at the piano, helping her to piece the material together: variety, pace, key changes, content, timing, style, mood, language—all had to be carefully considered.

She selected a range of mainly German, Italian, French and English songs for the recitals and saved most of her big-gun arias for the orchestral concerts. The ABC had asked for a sophisticated repertoire so her selection included lesser-known classics and a smattering of contemporary works.

The most interesting and personally challenging of the contemporary works was Benjamin Britten's *Les Illuminations*, set to a prose poem by Rimbaud. Benjamin Britten (1913–76) composed the song cycle in 1939 when he was still in the USA, and although his partner, Peter Pears, made it his own later on, it was originally written for a favoured soprano. Joan first sang it in London in 1944, and Britten coached her for the performance. She had a great respect for Britten's music and was keen to find another opportunity to explore the depths of this complex, multi-layered work. The prose poem is a magnificent exploration of the industry and debauchery of 1870s London, and unlike anything she'd sung before:

J'ai seul la clef cette parade sauvage . . .
    Gracieux fils de Pan! . . . Tes crocs luisent. Ta poitrine ressemble
à une cithare, des tintements circulent dans tes bras blonds.
Ton cœur bat dans ce ventre où dort le double sexe. Promène-toi,
la nuit, en mouvant doucement cette cuisse, cette seconde cuisse et
cette jambe de gauche.

[I alone have the key to this savage parade . . .
    Graceful son of Pan! . . . Your fangs glisten. Your breast is
like a cithara, tinglings circulate in your blond arms. Your heart
beats in this belly where sleeps the dual sex. Walk, at night, gently
moving this thigh, this second thigh, and this left leg.]

Les Illuminations, from parts 1 and 3

Joan was far more worldly than she used to be, so she may or may not have been aware of the homoerotic thread that ran through the work. What she fully appreciated was *Les Illuminations'* importance as a new composition, which is why she wanted to share it—and many other interesting selections—with an Australian audience.

SHE FLEW TO SYDNEY in a Qantas Kangaroo Service flying boat and arrived on 1 July after eight days of 'hopping' from country to country. The plane landed at the flying-boat base in Rose Bay so she had a chance to see the oh-so-familiar coastline from a new perspective. The harbour, the bays, the clustered rooftops, the wetlands and estuaries, the beaches and cliffs, the fishing boats and yachts, and there, so clearly, the green-brown expanse of Royal Sydney Golf Course. It had been ten years since she'd walked that course, ten long years in which so much had happened.

Her appearance hadn't changed so very much from the girl who'd boarded the *Dagfred*. She was solid of build, but not as plump as she'd been in 1936. That had been puppy fat; now she was a woman of 34, a 'success story' coming home to show her worth. The touchdown was bumpy—and not just because of the waves.

She knew there'd be some kind of reception when she disembarked but was unprepared for the avalanche of enthusiasm that greeted her. She was swamped from the moment she stepped from the plane. There was hardly time to hug her parents and brothers before reporters, newsreel people, cameramen, dignitaries, friends and strangers pressed towards her. It was as if she were a film star. Charles Moses, the General Manager of the ABC, drew her towards a platform set up with microphones and newsreel cameramen and invited her to make a speech. Footage of this moment shows a hearty if rather startled looking woman wearing a fur coat over an ill-fitting wartime suit—and digging deep to come up with a few words. She spoke, staccato fashion, with an unmistakably Australian accent: 'I'm now looking forward to singing to you. And it will be my joy and pleasure to come back as a singer, and to meet my old friends: [big smile] the golfers'. She nods, smiles some more, then adds 'It's wonderful to be back — and I've never seen anything as beautiful as the Harbour today!'

It was a fantastic welcome. There were so many people, so enthusiastic, so happy to see her, so eager to shake her hand and say a few appreciative words. She found herself in front of a diminutive lady in fur wrap and felt hat. It was Leo Wray, the woman who'd sent the cheques to Vienna. Joan held her hand, craned forward to hear what she said — a solemn little speech full of pride and admiration. Joan wanted to say how important, how grateful, but was overrun by yet another reporter wanting an interview, then another person wanting to speak, and another. People were telling her they were looking forward to greeting her 'properly' at this function and that function, at this cocktail party and that reception. She had no idea she'd be so well remembered, so well known, so much in demand. One radio interviewer introduced her as 'the greatest English-speaking soprano of the present day' — a marvellous but nervous-making compliment.

The emotional intensity of those first few hours was overwhelming. Seeing her mother's big smile, seeing her father who looked noticeably older though no wiser — he irritated her immediately. Embracing her brothers, Len and Noel, grown men with wives and children, and Tony of course, handsome Tony. And so many friends — the Lloyds, the McCays — but so little time to talk. Just being in Sydney again, seeing familiar streets again, the blue sky so high above, the bright clarity of the sunlight. It was all so much to take in. When she eventually reached her hotel bedroom she found beautiful bouquets and the most wonderful sight: baskets of fruit. Robust, fresh, colourful fruit, the like of which she'd not seen, let alone tasted, for years.

But from then on it was the tour from hell.

Tony was her tour manager. It was an idea that must have sounded good in the planning but in practice he failed to look after her well-being. She had nine days before her first recital, which was to be given in Melbourne, so her priority was to rehearse as much as possible with her as yet unmet accompanist. The last thing she wanted was a string of formal functions where she'd have to make speeches and exchange chitchat with dignitaries. But that is exactly what happened—in Sydney, and again in Melbourne.

She had very little time to rehearse with her accompanist, and wasn't reassured when she did. Raymond Lambert was a highly regarded pianist with the ABC, so much so that he'd insisted on having his own solo spot in each performance. This disrupted the balance of her carefully constructed programmes. She found Lambert to be a good soloist but an average accompanist. He didn't 'breathe' with her musically so she didn't get that marvellous rapport: two minds, two instruments, moving as one. Lambert improved during the months of the tour but it was a rough start—for him and for her.

Joan was insecure from day one and as the weeks passed the feeling intensified. She'd prepared for the demanding itinerary—a tour that crisscrossed between Melbourne, Hobart, Launceston, Perth, Adelaide, Sydney, Canberra and New Zealand—but she hadn't prepared for the social demands or the unrelenting public scrutiny.

She felt besieged. For some people her clothes seemed more important than her singing. Her long sleeves and gloves, the design and even the cost of her gowns, her fur coat—all were subject to comment. Phone calls from all and sundry were put through to her hotel room. Mail containing invitations, questions, compliments and complaints piled up waiting to be answered. Her repertoire was a constant point of criticism: some wanted more highbrow, others more popular hits. People seemed to have no conception that she might like to save or rest her voice. Even Tony had little understanding of her customary need to eat her main meal after and not before a performance, preferably sitting down rather than standing at a formal reception nursing a plate of dry biscuits. Tony did what he could but he was a pilot, not a manager, and they argued.

The pressure resulted in displays of 'temperament'. This was caught somewhat mischievously by David McNicoll, the journalist husband of her old friend Mickey McCay. He was disgruntled when she refused to see him during the interval of her first Sydney concert, and couldn't resist printing a barb in his column:

> Conductors like Sargent, Ormandy, Goossens, and Abravanel never objected when music-lovers dropped in to see them at half-time. But there were some tense moments backstage at Joan Hammond's concert on Wednesday night. She had complained about her dressing room; and when at interval A.B.C. general manager Moses went round to discuss the matter, he found the door locked. Everything was finally ironed out. But one fact emerged—Miss Hammond wants to be alone.

Joan was very angry as well as hurt. She saw it as a mean-minded misrepresentation, and her friendship with Mickey never recovered.

The performances were greeted with cheers and even foot stamping. Reviews were mostly complimentary, comments running along these lines:

> Her singing of the Brahms group was as near perfect as one could wish . . . Of the operatic numbers, the recitative and aria "Thy Hand Belinda" from Purcell's Dido and Aeneas, was outstanding. The singing of the touching recitative with its magical fall of a third on the phrase "darkness invades me" was an unforgettable moment.

But Neville Cardus, the well-known British commentator on music and cricket, made some particularly incisive observations:

... she is essentially an opera singer, or she is at her happiest
in the setting of orchestral tone and range; her voice does not
assume many shades of colour, and for this reason it is not easy
for her, despite a keen intelligence and sense of style, to make
those impulsive and natural transitions demanded by lieder,
or by any song seriously wedded to the piano. Her interpretation
of a group by Brahms was so admirably studied that criticism
is quite reluctant to point out where the singing fell short of the
aesthetic intention ... It is Australia's misfortune that whenever
singers of Miss Hammond's style or genre return home, there is
no opera house in which they may naturally realise themselves
... When the canvas of a song extended to some dramatic or
poetic range, Miss Hammond at once created the mood and the
character ... She is a singer who, away from opera, needs
a programme that appeals to and calls for the full measure of
her very responsive understanding of truly poetic words; and if
a music critic may make a "request" it is that she will sing, at
her next recital, the Britten settings of poems by Rimbaud—"Les
Illuminations".

When Joan looked back on this tour she said that the stresses and
strains of the war years had weakened her resilience more than she'd
realised. She'd thought that the Australian tour would help her regain
strength—the sun, the food, the sea—but the pressure, let alone the
itinerary, made her feel worse.

Willpower pushed her through the first part of the tour but then
her health began to suffer. A thirteen-hour flight to Perth resulted in
an ear infection and by the time she'd flown back to Melbourne she
had an assortment of symptoms described as 'flu'. She retired to her
hotel room and refused to speak to anyone except Tony.

At this point Lolita Marriott, the friend who'd waved her off at
Port Melbourne ten years before, tried to make contact. Tony turned

her away a couple of times but at the third attempt she managed to squeeze through the door. She found a red-nosed and unhappy Joan struggling with a pile of correspondence, and immediately offered to help. Joan had little faith in Lolita's secretarial skills but was too fraught to argue. Lolita took the bundle away and returned with the job efficiently done, and asked if there was anything else she could do. There was. It was as if a heavy load was being lifted from her shoulders, piece by piece. The more Lolita took care of, the less Joan had to worry about. It was the beginning of a remarkable partnership.

Lolita had been a fun-loving but somewhat aimless friend when Joan knew her in the 1930s. She had a privileged background, a good Catholic education, and played a tough game of golf, but she was an unlikely candidate for secretarial duties. The war had revealed her talents. She'd been a volunteer with Melbourne's Red Cross Transport. An officer, she'd driven trucks and managed her own section of two hundred drivers. A friend and fellow officer, Miss Burtta Cheney, remembers her distinctive abilities:

> Everything ran to clockwork when Lolita was doing it—and she
> made sure it *did*. She turned out to be a very good organiser—she
> had a charm about her, got all these section girls under her wing
> absolutely. They'd do anything for Lolita because she'd just have
> this manner with her . . . She used to bring recordings and a
> wind-up gramophone and she used to play beautiful music . . .

When Joan resumed her tour and went to New Zealand Lolita rather than Tony went with her. She organised the travel, the wardrobe, the press interviews, the timetable, everything. In later years she tried to keep a low profile but in the early days her presence caught some of the limelight. The journalist who interviewed Joan for the *New Zealand Listener* mentioned Joan's 'secretary, Miss Marriott' more

Lolita Marriott

than once. He portrayed the pair as a kind of double act, exchanging knowing looks and finishing each other's sentences—the 'secretary' chipping in with clarifications.

Lolita's 'chipping in' probably helped the interview along, for he found, as so many interviewers found, that Joan was 'a very easy person to talk to, excepting only that she can often answer your question with a laugh or a look that leaves nothing more to be said, and the laughs and looks do not fill your pad with notes'.

Even so, she became more vocal when they talked about the touchy subject of repertoire:

> "I sing lieder quite a lot. But as for building up a programme—
> you simply can't do it with operatic arias, and I am *not* going to
> sing a lot of operatic music with piano." . . . Miss Hammond and
> Miss Marriott began to look restless, and there was talk of work
> to be done . . . A general movement began towards the lift.

The New Zealand tour was a success, but when they returned to Sydney Joan's health broke down again, this time with tonsillitis. She took to her bed in the Australia Hotel and Lolita stood guard. Hilda Hammond and Bertie Lloyd were allowed in for a visit but after a short time they were ushered out: Joan needed her rest. Bertie was deeply offended and Hilda was furious: who was this woman ordering her away from her own daughter's sickbed?—A woman with charm and authority! Joan had found her soul mate.

Joan recovered sufficiently to complete her remaining concerts, which included a broadcast performance of *Les Illuminations*.

When she next went to Melbourne she stayed with Lolita in the Marriott's palatial home. Somewhere around this time the pair made a life-changing decision. Burtta Cheney remembered the moment when Lolita told her what it was:

Lolita had a Packard Roadster, beautiful car. She and I were
driving down Exhibition Street and just before we got to Flinders
Street Lolita said to me 'I'm going back to England with Joan.
I'm going as her secretary.' [pause] Everything just stopped dead.
What?! . . . Lol was looking for something to do. She enjoyed the
job in the Red Cross . . . people standing to attention 'yes Madam,
no Madam', she had enjoyed that . . . And from the word go they
clicked. They clicked in the way that—well Lolita had been used
to having everything the way Lolita wanted it . . . But so had Joan,
in a different way. [Joan] couldn't purchase whatever she wanted
[as Lolita could] but she was so strong willed that she *would
have* what she wanted. Lolita was prepared to accept that, and to
bend over backwards to learn the job she was going to do, and to
look after Joan . . . And Lolita went as her companion-secretary.
She'd never done anything secretarial except at Red Cross!

Joan wanted Lolita; Lolita wanted Joan. Tony's services were dispensed
with and non-essential commitments cancelled. Lolita packed her
trunk—and Joan's trunk—and the pair left for London two weeks
earlier than originally planned.

What an interesting welcome it must have been when the two of
them arrived at Eaton Terrace!

THE AUSTRALIAN TOUR had exposed weaknesses that Joan was
determined to overcome. She resolved to make some changes, the most
fundamental being the decision to strip back and rebuild her vocal
technique. The problems and niggles that had persisted for so long
were to be identified and eradicated. She became her own experiment.
Exploration, self-instruction—including the study of anatomy—plus
regular consultation with her trusted ear, nose and throat specialist
were all part of the process. Singing engagements were used as 'test

drives' and the results were analysed from all angles. She wanted to be the master of her voice. Mastery meant she would know how to use it and look after it in almost any situation; mastery was total control, which ultimately meant total release. The process took three years.

She also devised some ground rules to improve her working conditions. She would always tour with her own accompanist; always complete rehearsals with the accompanist in London *before* travelling; always tour with a personal representative/secretary; always decline interviews or social functions on the day of a performance. She would also endeavour to construct programmes with greater variety; try to relax more when meeting people; and pay closer attention to her appearance.

There was another reform that had a distinct effect on her finances. Her tax bill that year was enormous, partly because she had to pay double income tax and partly because artists visiting Australia couldn't claim accommodation as a deductible expense—a restriction that stopped many artists from visiting. Joan had spent almost every night in a hotel for five months. She decided to fight the ruling, and eventually won. It was a small step for the Australian Taxation Department but a mighty leap for international artists.

The likely reason she caught flu on the tour was because she'd been so cold in her Hobart dressing-room, which had rainwater running down the wall. The audience kept their overcoats on in the fridge-like auditorium but she didn't have the nerve to do the same. It seemed impolite. She would never make that mistake again.

Joan's resolutions were supported absolutely by her 'in-house team'. Lolita the organiser and Essie the home-keeper.

Eaton Terrace was a happy household for the most part. The common purpose was Joan's voice, Joan's career, Joan's wellbeing: everyone was pulling in the same direction.

It was in character for Joan to take stock after an experience like the Australian tour, but it seems more than coincidence that her reforms were instigated, and realised, from the time that Lolita was on the scene. And what a scene for Lolita to find herself in! She'd travelled overseas with her parents in her youth, but this was entirely different. London was very grim in its post-war dishevelment but Joan's world had plenty of sparkle. Living in Eaton Terrace was an eye-opener in itself. Vivien Leigh had a house just around the corner.

Joan introduced Lolita to friends such as Otakar Kraus, Kathleen Ferrier, Walter Susskind and Lady Gowrie. The Gowries were back in England because Lord Gowrie had been appointed Deputy Constable and Lieutenant Governor of Windsor Castle. Lolita, and presumably Essie, accompanied Joan when she visited the Gowries in their new place of residence: the Norman Tower at Windsor Castle.

Joan and Lolita had much fun together, and were always laughing and teasing one another, yet both knew who was boss. Lolita's desire to assist Joan was a pure and somewhat obsessive form of devotion. Her motivation, in its purest form, was to serve Joan so that Joan could serve Art. By so doing she'd found a vocation, and a very interesting way of life. She told a friend many years later that one night during the war she was drifting off to sleep with the radio still on when she suddenly became aware of Joan's voice wafting through the airwaves. In that moment she simply knew she was destined to go to London and support her. It was as if she'd had a vision—something no Catholic could ignore. Maybe the story was enhanced over time, but the fact remains that Lolita made it happen.

Lolita's talents included financial management. She was her father's daughter in that regard. If she'd been born male she would have directed the Hecla family business and very likely made a better job of it than her non-business-minded brother. Joan's income was spasmodic, and when she had it she spent it. This meant that the lean times were very lean indeed. Lolita organised Joan's money so she could spend but also save. Joan gave her carte blanche, happy not to have to think about it, and a nest egg started to grow.

Lolita taught herself a multitude of relatively humble skills in order to do her job. She learnt to type and cook; she became an expert packer (velvet gowns must not be placed next to beaded gowns) and wardrobe organiser (cleaning, storing, transporting). She also devised a listing system to show what had been worn where, and when, so the same dress didn't appear at the same venue twice in succession. She acted as secretary, publicist, bookkeeper, chauffeur, dresser, false eyelash applier, travel agent, shopper, mediator, doorkeeper, queue regulator for autograph signing, hair and wig dresser, negotiator, receptionist—anything and everything she could think of to make Joan's life easier. And she did so with love.

Joan's colleagues also appreciated Lolita's presence for she had the knack of easing an artist's tension. There'd be a calming hand on the shoulder, or a perfectly aimed settling remark.

Lolita and Joan with Walter Susskind

EMI's PUBLICISTS HAD KEPT Joan's name and photograph to the fore while she'd been in Australia for there'd been a steady release of recordings. Alec Robertson's reviews in *The Gramophone* were critical and complimentary by turns, but on the whole she was recognised as a singer of great stature. Undoubtedly one of the top ten singers in Britain.

It was on the strength of her gramophone recordings that she secured her next big engagement. The Vienna State Opera offered an attractive contract to perform *Tosca*, *Traviata* and *Bohème* (in German) during the April/May season. It was a significant honour given that native English-speaking singers hadn't appeared there for some time.

The train journey across Europe was full of difficulties. Joan must have been relieved to have Lolita by her side for they were searched and questioned at every border. A friend advised them to travel with packs of quality cigarettes and these turned out to be very useful. All the customs guards were intimidating but the Russians were frightening.

Vienna was split into four zones: British, French, American and Russian, so movement was restricted according to one's pass. The pair were billeted at 'Sacher's British Officers' Hotel'. When Joan had last seen that hotel it was one of the most exclusive places in the city. Grace Palotta had taken her there once to have hot chocolate and a divine piece of torte. Now the building was overrun with soldiers in British uniform: a weird sight.

The happiest moment of the whole trip was seeing Alfred Komma again, the gentleman dentist. The saddest was to find no one else that she'd known. Rector Schnitt had been killed by the Nazis, Countess Kinsky had probably died a natural death but no one knew—and the palace was out of bounds because it was in the Russian zone. She looked for her old singing teacher, Frau Eibenschütz, but was told she and her son were dead, the daughter still alive, maybe. Enquiries about the Baroness drew a blank.

So she made the most of her time with Alfred Komma. Amazingly he still had those few possessions she'd left with him all those years ago, her old umbrella being a particular treasure. He even returned the money she'd left in his care. Alfred had survived the war with no apparent catastrophe. He still had his dental practice and his apartment, still had his gentlemanly charm, but she could see he was a broken man. His health was poor but it was more than that, a sickness of spirit. She couldn't help but feel that his days were numbered—and she was right, he died a few months later.

The Vienna State Opera House (Wiener Staatsoper) had been bombed so the two other main theatres were being used. Joan performed *Traviata* at the Theater an der Wien, and *Tosca* and *Bohème* at the Volksoper, where she'd sung before. Working conditions were trying, but there was a sense of vitality in both theatres. Some marvellous musicians were returning to Vienna and the State Opera was working hard to reinvent itself. Not all artists were allowed to return, however. The Allied authorities banned certain people because of their wartime activities or associations. Conductors such as Herbert von Karajan, and singers such as Elisabeth Schwarzkopf were banned by one or other of the four occupying countries—though there were ridiculous inconsistencies between zones.

Joan wasn't particularly happy with her performances as it was early days in her 'master of my own voice' regime, but she allowed that one performance was good. She especially liked the Chief Conductor, Joseph Krips. He'd been forced out of the Vienna Opera during the war and survived by working in a factory. Musicians from the opera used to visit him secretly and pay for his advice. He accompanied Joan on the piano for a concert and she thought him brilliant. She knew from his playing that he would be an excellent opera conductor— and he was. As she described it, Krips could 'make the orchestra play as a single instrument . . . a test which few [conductors] could pass'.

Joan may have come across Walter Legge while she was in Vienna because he was scouting for talent at the time. He signed up a number of artists to record with EMI—most famously Elisabeth Schwarzkopf, whom he later married.

Ironically, Schwarzkopf made her debut at Covent Garden a few months before Joan, and was a permanent member of that company from 1948 to 1951 (singing in English). Schwarzkopf had a fabulous voice and the looks to go with it, so she probably stole away some of Joan's potential work. It was a sign of the times: sopranos of greater and lesser magnitude were emerging from the war-torn world. Competition was keen, but Joan held her own.

Rejoice, rejoice, rejoice greatly!

Messiah, Handel

Lots of enjoyable work propelled her through the next few years: concerts, broadcasts, Carl Rosa productions, a highly successful tour of South Africa, four Promenade Concerts, a season in Dublin, her debut in Paris, in Amsterdam, in The Hague, and at Covent Garden as Leonora in *Il Trovatore* in 1948. There were extensive recital tours throughout Britain, two tours in the USA (her debut in New York), further performances at Covent Garden with *Aida*, *Fidelio* and *Bohème*, a memorable Verdi *Requiem* and *Messiah* in Wales, a BBC broadcast of *Eugene Onegin*, *Tosca* and *La Traviata* in Glasgow, a Beethoven's Ninth with the great conductor Wilhelm Furtwängler, another with Beecham, a Verdi Requiem under Victor de Sabata in the USA, concerts with Sargent, BBC broadcasts of *Thais* and *La Forza del Destino*—and the list goes on.

Sargent asked her more than once to sing 'Land of Hope and Glory' on the last night of the Proms. It was a delicious opportunity to lift the roof of the Albert Hall; but alas, the music was better suited to a contralto. She tried and tried to find a key that would suit, but it was no good. She regretfully had to decline—'for Elgar's sake'.

One of the most rewarding experiences during this period was a second visit to Australia in 1949. Joan called it her 'Thank you tour'.

She'd long wanted to clear her debt to 'the golfers'. She'd wanted to give something back to the community that had worked so hard to raise money for her overseas studies, and at last found a way of doing it. She sang four fundraising recitals, the proceeds to go into an international fund that would send an Australian team of women golfers overseas. She hoped to raise enough for a team to be sent to Britain to compete in the 1950 British Open Championship. There were two recitals in Sydney and two in Melbourne and they were wonderful events. Packed to the rafters and full of joy. Joan also played some fun-filled but rusty games of golf in the Victorian and New South Wales championships, which helped to raise the profile of the fundraising effort. At the end of proceedings she was able to present the Australian Ladies' Golf Union with a substantial cheque. The international fund was boosted to such a degree that the ALGU could send a seven-member team to Britain and still have money in reserve.

Joan and Lolita gave themselves a brief holiday before continuing on to America, the next part of their world tour. They saw family and friends and enjoyed lots of relaxing golf. Joan was especially happy and not at all prepared for the bad news that arrived.

Essie sent word that Pippo had died, her four-legged friend of nine years. Their last parting had been difficult, if amusing. He always knew when she was going on a long trip, and always wanted to go with her. On many occasions he did go with her, but never on an aeroplane. Joan had said goodbye to him at Eaton Terrace but he'd somehow managed to wangle his way into the car when Essie drove Joan and Lolita to the airport. So Joan said goodbye to him again at the barrier before boarding. Airports were fairly casual places in terms of boarding and security in 1949. Pippo suddenly slipped his collar, rushed across the tarmac, up the boarding steps and straight on to the plane, causing much hilarity as he sought out his mistress. So they had a third goodbye. She walked Pippo off the plane and returned him to Essie, one last kiss on his curly head.

Joan cried and cried. She loved Pippo so much she would have cancelled the trip—even New York—if she'd had an inkling he wouldn't be there when she returned.

> Oh the green hills o' Somerset
> Go rolling to the sea,
> And still today the violets
> Are blooming there for me;
> The shadows kiss the waving grass,
> Beside the kirkyard wall,
> But the song the blackbird sings to me
> Is the saddest song of all . . .

'Green Hills o'Somerset', Coates

It was just as well the news came when Joan was on holiday: tears ruin the voice. Lolita's answer to moments of sorrow was to open a bottle of champagne (her answer to any big moment was to open a bottle of champagne). Joan took a deep breath, controlled her tears, and tried to focus on what lay ahead.

Next was Honolulu and the start of the USA tour. She'd been on the American circuit just a few months before and received a mixed response, but her second visit was more successful. Her performances of Aida, Butterfly and Tosca were praised highly, her singing recognised for its 'truly exquisite texture'.

Howard Taubman, the music critic for the *New York Times*, reviewed her Carnegie Hall debut with cautious satisfaction:

Joan Hammond, the Australian soprano, was the soloist at last
night's Philadelphia Orchestra concert at Carnegie Hall, and
for this opportunity she owes thanks to Eugene Ormandy, the
orchestra's conductor. Her singing last night helped to set at rest
doubts about her capacities as an artist that other appearances
in this city had raised. She has a good voice and can use it like a
musician, provided she turns to the proper musical milieu.

At the City Center Miss Hammond sang the leads in
"Butterfly" and "Tosca," and in her recital last season she did
things not meant for her. Last night she sang the Mozart scene and
aria, beginning with "Misera, dove son" (K. 369), the big scene
from Beethoven's "Fidelio," beginning with "Abscheulicher, wo
eilst du hin?" and the Letter Scene from Tchaikovsky's "Eugen
Onegin." The grand scenes by Mozart and Beethoven were
especially right for her.

Miss Hammond sang them both with purity of style and
with ample vocal reserves. She phrased the Mozart music with a
sensitive regard for its classic line, and she captured the passion
and ecstasy of Beethoven's music. Her tones were clear and
accurate through all shades of soft, medium and loud. She colored
the voice with taste, and in the climactic passages she let it ring
out with resonance and power. To do her best work she seems to
need music of large utterance and of some discipline and classic
restraint in its design.

Mr. Ormandy and his orchestra gave Miss Hammond fine
orchestral support. At no point was she overwhelmed, and at no
point was the orchestra so subdued that the music lost its balance.

A photograph accompanied the review—a far more feminine and
sophisticated looking portrait than earlier shots. The classier image
was part of her 'pay more attention to my appearance' campaign, but

it was also a response to America's obsession with style. The publicity machine was aggressive in the USA and image was important. Joan looked like a prima donna of quality in her photograph and she endeavoured to live up to that image in person. Her gowns and dresses were specifically designed, her hair was well styled, her make-up, jewellery—everything was stylishly, thoughtfully done. She began to 'perform' the role of prima donna when she presented herself in public. This image and way of being became her trademark. It also worked as a protective shield behind which the private Joan could feel more comfortable.

Of course her other protective shield was Lolita. A companion-secretary cum personal representative made all the difference to her wellbeing, and was a luxury that most divas couldn't afford. Lolita volunteered her services, though it's uncertain who paid her travel expenses. Joan's friend, the contralto Kathleen Ferrier, was also doing the American circuit but she had no one but her accompanist to help with practical matters. Kathleen Ferrier's star had risen rapidly since the end of the war; she commanded high fees and was always in demand, but she couldn't afford a personal assistant.

Joan and Kathleen had the same English agent, and probably had similar touring contracts for the USA; they certainly had similar complaints. The fees were enormous but the deductions were huge. Joan said that the USA sold artists like a can of baked beans—Europe *asked* for you whereas America *sold* you—and it was the selling that dug into the fees. Joan didn't reveal specific figures, but a letter written by Kathleen Ferrier in 1949 shows how exploitative the system could be:

> I've been telling the Chicago manager what I think of him and the whole managerial set-up here—and what's more I didn't cry! . . .
> I've really been miserable until now with my money disappearing down a drain of advertising and manager's pockets! I said
> I wanted to know where, if the concerts were non-profit-making,

the money went. I have an average of 3,000 in the audience—
which means at least 3,000 dollars and they pay me 800, out of
which I pay an accompanist 105—20 per cent. manager's fees—
rail travel for two (which is a colossal amount here) hotel, taxis,
porters and tips—and income tax!

Lolita, rather than Joan, would have tackled such issues with
managers, and her negotiation skills were very sharp.

Joan always felt that her overall success in America might have been
greater if she hadn't declined an invitation from the most important
lady in the country, Eleanor Roosevelt. Lady Gowrie had introduced
her to Mrs Roosevelt the year before at Windsor Castle. It was a
successful piece of social engineering because Mrs Roosevelt made
a point of attending Joan's second recital in New York. The First
Lady then sent an invitation for Joan to sing at a special luncheon.
It was an event that would have enhanced her reputation and forged
good connections, but Joan had to refuse. She had an opening night
with *Tosca* that evening and a rehearsal that morning. She thought
Mrs Roosevelt would understand and offer an alternative date, but
communication went cold.

She completed her season with the City Center Opera Company,
sang a Morning Concert at the Waldorf-Astoria, and flew off to
Ireland to give recitals in Belfast and Dublin. She had good friends in
Dublin but there was little time to enjoy them for she had to be back
in London for a New Year's Eve booking with the BBC.

Home at last after six months of touring. Home sweet home, but
no Pippo.

JOAN OVERCAME THE last of her vocal insecurities during the early
months of 1950. Abdominal breathing became natural and easy—an
action so simple yet so difficult to achieve! She was finally in command

of her instrument: 'Clearing this last vocal hurdle set me up for the busiest and most rewarding years of my career. I could now sing for any unlimited period without tiring vocally. The slightest trouble could be rectified by a few scales'.

She was confident about every aspect of her technique—and it showed. Tenseness vanished and humour took its place. Her new sense of ease was most noticeable in recitals. Nothing seemed to phase her: a creaking floorboard, a clanging clock, the big foot of her accompanist standing on her train—they were dealt with calmly and turned into jokes to share with the audience.

Everything was in place: voice, image, confidence, support. She was at the peak of her powers on the crest of an almighty wave.

CHAPTER 6

LOVE AND MUSIC

BELGRAVIA WAS LOSING its charm. Post-war development had brought more traffic, more noise and less privacy. Fan mail was welcome but some of Joan's more persistent admirers (male and female) would telephone, or even bring bouquets to her door. Essie and Lolita were gracious on Joan's behalf but the attention could be intrusive. A new bus route bringing double-deckers along Eaton Terrace was the last straw.

Joan found the perfect secluded cottage at Burnham Beeches, a beautiful area of countryside nestled between Farnham Common and Beaconsfield in the county of Buckinghamshire, less than an hour's drive west of London. She knew the area well because she'd sometimes played a round of golf at Burnham Beeches golf course since the early 1940s. The club had been the easiest to travel to in times of petrol rationing because it had its own railway station.

The Old Cottage was a wonderful find. The central part of the building dated back to the sixteenth century while two substantial wings had been added at hundred-year intervals, plus modern additions—all architecturally blended. The seven-acre property was on the fringe of Burnham Beeches, a vast expanse of ancient forest.

The grounds included formal gardens close to the house with dense woodland extending out on three sides. The official location of the cottage was Egypt Lane, Egypt—so called because it was an oft-used encampment for gypsies in the 1700s. The local stream was called The Nile.

The auctioneers selling the property described The Old Cottage as a picturesque old-world residence comprising:

> Entrance hall, two reception rooms, staircase hall (with large cupboard), dining room, loggia (leading to the garden), billiards room, five bedrooms, two bathrooms, dressing room, attic, well equipped kitchen with AGA, scullery, pantry, W.C.; fireplaces; oak panelling, oak beams, oak floorboards; mains electricity and water; septic tank drainage. External larder and fuel store, double garage, workshop, cycle shed, potting shed, games room. Conveniently close to Farnham Common village for post office and shopping facilities.

Joan became the owner on 6 June 1951. Much preparation, emotionally as well as practically, must have led to that moment. The size of the cottage indicates that it was bought with three expansive residents in mind: a bedroom each for Joan, Lolita and Essie, and two to spare. Clearly the 'Triumvirate' (as friends had dubbed them) was happy to live and work together as an ongoing team.

Joan loved her new home. A narrow spiral staircase led up to her bedroom, bathroom, dressing-room (the master suite), and the attic housed her costumes, wigs and props. This part of the house was the oldest and had very low ceilings. Legend had it that Sheridan had written part of *The School for Scandal* in that very attic. The cottage had atmosphere and the surroundings were full of enchantment. An early morning walk through the woods would reveal the sight or sound of woodpeckers, woodcock, tawny owls, foxes, finches, dragonflies, hedgehogs, and the sweet scents of country air.

At The Old Cottage

The increasing number of household pets was another reason for the move. The trio had five cats and three dogs: Jani, the white standard poodle, Mr Chips, a miniature black poodle belonging to Essie, and Pippo the Second, a standard black poodle bought in honour of Pippo the First. Joan added hens and an aviary of budgerigars to her menagerie—and was always willing to accept waifs and strays. The first of these was a pheasant: it arrived one day and never left.

The pheasant may have come from nearby 'Cliveden', the Astor family's stately home. Viscountess Astor—Nancy to her friends—

had been the first woman to take a seat in the House of Commons in 1919. Nancy included Joan in some of her élite luncheons and dinner parties, and they once played an impromptu game of golf on her immaculate front lawn. Yet Joan was ambivalent about her witty, outspoken neighbour. They were both Conservatives but Nancy's politics were erratic and her stance on religion was aggressive. Nancy Astor was a Christian Scientist and anti-Catholic.

Anti-Catholicism wouldn't have bothered Joan a decade earlier but her attitude had changed. After all, she'd lived with a Catholic (Lolita), for five years. She'd enjoyed the good friendship of the Marriotts in Melbourne and also the McDonnells in Dublin: two Catholic families that had brought her much joy. Also, the majority of the operatic characters she portrayed were of the Catholic faith: Tosca, Desdemona, Mimi, for example. Joan had made a point of learning about the faith's rituals so she could convey them accurately on stage.

Her interest intensified when she began reading about the Reformation as background research for her role as Elisabeth in *Don Carlos* for Sadler's Wells in 1951. Her reading widened and her thoughts deepened. Two particularly influential works were *One Lord One Faith* by Vernon Johnson, which described an Anglican minister's conversion, and *Come Rack, Come Rope* by R. H. Benson, a novel set in Elizabethan England where chaste young lovers subjugate their passion for a nobler, purer devotion.

It was a spiritual journey that deepened and intensified. One morning she woke and simply knew she would become a Catholic. She was received into the Catholic Church at St Mary of the Angels in Dublin on 21 May 1953 by her friend, Father Senan. Her sponsors were Dr Colm McDonnell and Lolita Marriott.

The news—for it was news—circulated quickly. Nancy Astor fired off a telegram that summed up the thoughts of many: 'How could you?'

Joan declined to discuss her conversion with journalists; it was too personal. She didn't have much to say on the subject to non-Catholic friends either. She told Bertie Lloyd she'd absorbed the religion without really realising it, even from the time when she was in Vienna, and the more she'd absorbed the more it seemed to make sense. Joan denied that Lolita had been the major influence, but Bertie wasn't convinced. Joan was never quite the same, in Bertie's eyes, after Lolita came on the scene.

Lolita must have had at least some influence with regard to Joan's conversion but Stephen Marriott, Lolita's nephew, says there was a much greater force at work. Stephen came to know the McDonnell family in later years and experienced Colm McDonnell's charismatic personality firsthand. He feels that Colm 'would have been the most outstanding spiritual influence by a very long margin'.

MAY 1953 MARKED Joan's forty-first birthday. It was a landmark month in every way because she was named Officer of the British Empire in the coronation and birthday listings. Joan Hammond, OBE—it was a proud moment.

Yet there was also sadness that year. Kathleen Ferrier began to lose her battle with cancer. Joan stepped in on a couple of occasions at short notice, notably with an *Aida* at Covent Garden replacing *Orfeo* when Kathleen couldn't continue in the title role. Kathleen's illness, and the way she dealt with it, was perhaps another influential factor as Joan struggled with mighty questions about the meaning of life. Joan visited Kathleen in hospital; she looked radiant—she laughed and joked and her extraordinary spirit shone through. She rallied during the summer but died in the autumn, greatly loved and sadly missed.

YOUNG AND MAGNIFICENT sopranos began to take the stage in all the major opera houses: a plump Maria Callas, a shy Victoria de los Angeles, a glowing Renata Tebaldi—with many more waiting in the wings, not least Joan Sutherland. When Joan Hammond succumbed to the flu during a tour of *Aida* with Covent Garden in 1954 it was the inexperienced Sutherland who stepped in at short notice. Joan Sutherland had first heard of Joan Hammond when she was a child. Her mother was friends with Lute Drummond, the Sydney coach. News of Joan's progress in Europe filtered through over the years and Sutherland took note, as did so many young Australian aspirants.

Joan never forgot how tough or how lonely it could be for a budding singer in a foreign country. Her policy of 'giving back' prompted her to help with fundraising schemes that would assist young Australians to further their training in Britain. One such was for the establishment of a Joan Hammond Scholarship at the London Opera School. Joan gave a recital at Festival Hall with Walter Susskind as accompanist, and a healthy sum was raised. But her enthusiasm was dashed when she discovered that relatively large amounts of money had been deducted for administrative and promotional social activities. A cocktail party wasn't her idea of money well spent. She was furious and said so. It was another moment of reassessment and she adjusted her method of 'giving back' as a consequence. Organised projects were sidelined in favour of private gestures.

Life was good: offers of work flowed in; recordings continued to sell well; and The Old Cottage was a haven to return to after long overseas tours.

A MATURE JOAN was once asked by a journalist: 'Why did you never marry?' Her answer was immediate and succinct: 'Art is a jealous mistress.'

Joan's answer to the marriage question was a quote from a lengthy sentence written by Ralph Waldo Emerson (1803–82), the American poet and essayist: 'Art is a jealous mistress, and, if a man have a genius for painting, poetry, music, architecture, or philosophy, he makes a bad husband, and an ill provider, and should be wise in season, and not fetter himself with duties which will embitter his day'.

The use of 'mistress' in this context is tantalising, for it highlights the nuance around the question of Joan's sexuality. There are no neat answers. The private thoughts and actions of Joan, Lolita and Essie remain private. Observers of the relationship formed their conclusions over the years: some saw Joan and Lolita as a lesbian couple, others saw a close friendship. Maybe the truth, if there can be such a thing, rests somewhere in between. How close is 'close'?

Being an artist as well as a wife was an impossible equation in Joan's view, she advised young singers against it. But what of love? Joan knew all too well that marriage wasn't the only option. Puccini's famous character, Floria Tosca, the songstress of Rome, gave love and music equal billing. Jealous Tosca was Mario's lover, not wife. Her plan, before everything went wrong, was to escape to their hideaway after her evening's performance—her Catholic faith notwithstanding.

Dost thou not long for our cottage secluded?

Tosca, Puccini

One of Joan's crowning achievements was to sing in Russia in the Russian language, something that no British soprano had done before. She'd proved that her Russian was good enough when she sang with a Russian company (oddly enough) in Spain.

She sang Tatiana in *Eugene Onegin* in Leningrad, and at the famous Bolshoi Theatre in Moscow, and *Aida* in Italian. It was a marvellous experience all round. The Communist regime restricted her (and Lolita's) movements in that she wasn't free to go where she pleased, but she was treated with great generosity.

The way the theatres were run impressed her enormously. There was more than enough staff, all well trained, and ageing artists were always found some kind of job. There was respect for the work, and for the workers. For instance, the stage was mopped after every major scene by a gang of women—thus keeping the dust to a minimum for the singers; the lighting was refined, providing side and back lighting instead of the usual blinding central spots; and when Joan performed Aida, the Ethiopian slave, her dresser came into the shower with her to help remove the body make-up! She found the audiences sophisticated in terms of musicality and appreciation, and the Russians adored her. She received the loudest and longest ovations of her career in Russia.

RECORD SALES FOR 'O my beloved father' had passed the half-million mark by 1952. When she entered places like the Savoy the band would play her signature song and everyone would know who'd walked in. Then she recorded another little-known aria and that too became a great success. The new recording was 'O silver moon', also known as 'Song to the moon', from *Rusalka* by Dvorak.

It was a melody and lyric that stayed in the head:

O silver moon in the sky above, shedding thy light over all
Wandering through the great big world, seeing and knowing all mankind
Wandering through the great big world, seeing and knowing mankind
O silver moon, stay thy course
Tell me where is my beloved
O silver moon, stay thy course
Tell me where is my beloved

Her popularity was further enhanced when she was invited to appear on various television programmes. She sang favourites such as 'The Green Hills o' Somerset' and performed arias, sometimes in costume with a simple set. Her warmth of personality, her stylish gowns, her ability to create a believable emotional world within a television setting, all helped to endear her to a wide cross-section of the viewing public. Joan's success in the medium also helped to make opera more accessible.

If there was a downside then it was that Covent Garden only used her sparingly. She had a powerful physical presence, a solid, robust appearance—ideal for Aida and Tosca but visually incompatible when it came to consumptive Mimi or teenage Butterfly. Joan's extraordinary artistry on stage could seduce an audience to suspend their disbelief. But the task had become more difficult, for every prima donna, since Callas had pushed the boundaries with her dramatic powers.

Joan's fans complained to the papers when they didn't see her at Covent Garden as often as they thought they should, but it wasn't always Covent Garden's fault. Joan was busy as well as choosy and her fees were high.

LOLITA'S MANAGEMENT OF Joan's financial affairs had been a marked success. Joan's next major purchase (perhaps with the help of Lolita?) was a custom built Rolls-Royce. A magnificent black, four-door vehicle, with two enormous front lamps. The *Spirit of Ecstasy*, the Rolls-Royce emblem, spreading her wingèd arms on the forefront of the huge bonnet. Its registration number was: LXU 366.

The Roller became a trademark announcement: 'Joan Hammond is arriving'. She used it for all her British tours and some of the Continental ones (it was purchased in about 1955 and had 99 500 miles on the clock by 1960). The Rolls even saved Joan and Lolita's life when a drunk driver caused a head-on collision. A lesser car would have buckled.

Joan and Lolita travelled the length and breadth of Britain, happy with their Roller but generally unhappy with provincial hotels. The dingy and sometimes damp rooms were unappealing. A little lateral thinking and they came upon a novel solution: a caravan. A compact, top of the range, all mod cons, caravan. They hitched it to the Roller and went on the road. They camped at pre-arranged places—farmers were very obliging—and there were many country areas where they could stop in a secluded spot without needing permission. They would make their camp, unhitch the caravan, and commute to the city or town where Joan was singing. They had independence, privacy, total control over their accommodation—and much pleasure in the process.

The 'gypsy' system worked very well most of the time though there was one particular glitch that brought much unwanted attention. They were doing a recital tour of Wales organised by the Arts Council. Joan was due to sing at the village of Caldicot, east of Newport, on 1 October. Ivor Newton was the accompanist and he arrived in good time, as did the audience. The village hall was packed, but there was no sign of Joan. Forty-five minutes went by and the back row started singing 'why are we waiting?' Ninety minutes went by and the last of the faithful went home. Joan and Lolita, meanwhile, were bedding down for the night after a relaxing day by the sea. Lolita had mistaken the date. She'd somehow got it into her head that there were thirty-one days in September. They sent telegrams of apology next day, mortified at the mistake, but the *Daily Express* got hold of the story:

Singer angers fans—"It was in the hope of 'getting away from it all' for a few days that Miss Hammond and her secretary drove their caravan to a quiet hillside overlooking the sea at Fontygary Bay, 10 miles from Cardiff," said a spokesman for her agents in London . . . At her caravan yesterday Miss Hammond was "Too upset to talk of the mistake," said her secretary . . . "The error is my fault. I am completely heartbroken to think I have put Miss Hammond in this position. I thought today was October 1."

Lolita, Odette, Essie and Joan

The atmosphere must have been somewhat strained in the caravan that evening!

Essie rarely joined the pair while on tour. She had her own car, and would sometimes seek out suitable places for the caravan to be parked, but camping wasn't her style. Tour managing wasn't her style either. She never wanted the responsibility of organising so many practicalities away from home, especially overseas. She was happiest being the anchorwoman, fielding the phone calls and correspondence when the other two were on the road—which they could be for months on end when it was a world tour. 'Miss Walker' was quoted almost as often as 'Miss Marriott' when Joan wasn't available for comment. Essie would cook for special occasions but she wasn't overloaded with chores. The three shared household duties, Joan invariably doing outdoor jobs, and they had domestic help on a daily basis. Holidays were sometimes taken all together. Essie joined the other two, for instance, when they took a break between engagements in France and Italy.

'The Triumvirate' was interdependent in many ways, but the old saying comes to mind: 'two's company, three's a crowd'. The trio was really a 'two plus one' arrangement. Hotel rooms were booked as 'twin share plus single' when the three of them were travelling, and the 'plus single' was always for Essie.

Australian friends and relatives would stay at The Old Cottage from time to time and Essie would do her utmost to make them welcome; yet she never invited any of her own friends or relatives, not when Joan and Lolita were there to meet them anyway. Joan never met Essie's mother or cousins, for instance, not even after a concert, though she knew they existed.

One of Joan's most devoted fans was Betty Davison, a youngish woman who lived in Broomhill, Sheffield, and who worked in a biscuit factory. Betty's obsession with Joan was such that she confessed to depression if she didn't receive some kind of acknowledgement—a card or signed photo—after a few weeks of waiting. Essie's response to this confession gives us a glimpse into her way of dealing with things: 'You must try and snap out of it for your family's sake. One often has to try and hide one's depressions, I find; and it is the hardest thing to do!' Essie's caring nature is most obvious in the postscript to a later letter: 'Let me know always if I can do anything to help you, Betty'.

JOAN AND LOLITA were enjoying a brief respite back at The Old Cottage in early 1956 when Lolita received bad news. Her mother was seriously ill. She left for Australia next day—leaving Essie to fill the breach. It would have been interesting for all three women to see how Joan managed without Lolita but events took a different turn. Joan became ill herself and had to be rushed to Windsor hospital with acute appendicitis. She was still convalescing when Lolita returned some weeks later.

Lolita's mother, Nance, had undergone a major operation for cancer of the throat. There'd been some hope within the Marriott family that Lolita, the unmarried daughter, would stay on to look after her mother at home. Clearly Lolita didn't choose to. Nance's health deteriorated fairly quickly and a second operation became necessary. Lolita rushed back to Melbourne for a second time, and Nance died a couple of weeks later.

Lolita adored her father, Clarence, but had always been somewhat ambivalent about her mother. She'd managed to visit her family almost annually since 1946, usually because of a recital tour in Australia but sometimes purely for a holiday, no tour involved, and Joan always accompanied her. There was mutual affection between Joan and the Marriotts, though there was always some private eyebrow raising and speculation on the Marriott side as to how 'close' Joan and Lolita were. Nance had always suspected her daughter of being 'different', and this may well have been part of the mother–daughter ambivalence.

Rosemary Wilson knew the Marriotts from the early 1920s because she lived opposite 'Hawthroy' when she was growing up in Toorak. Rosemary and Lolita were in and out of each other's houses every day from the age of about eight. The two families were forever connected when Rosemary's younger sister, Peg, married Lolita's brother, Ron. Rosemary recalls that:

> Lolita always envied Ron, and wanted to have and do everything he had and did! . . . I can't claim to have been close to Joan in any way, but I was to Lolita of course—but not after Joan came along . . . It would not be an exaggeration to say that Lolita worshipped Joan . . . Joan was everything. Lolita was a very courageous person . . . when she was a little girl she was knocked down outside—she used to run across the road to our place, with or without the little dog, and she was knocked down by a car—but it was nothing serious. But I remember Mrs. Marriott saying, when Lolita said she was alright and so on, she said 'She's cracking hardy!'—It's a good description of Lolita . . . She never had a boyfriend really. She had a little bit of a fling with a naval officer during the war. But that didn't last, it was very short . . . Lolita was given to pashes on people. There was somebody up here [in Sydney]—Brownie Ross I think was her name—I mean they were very passionate friends. And then the woman got married and that finished. And when Lolita was driving for the Red Cross, a Mrs Fairly I think was in charge of it, and she [Lolita] had a crush on this woman—I mean they weren't terribly great friends, but she used to be very devoted, you know?—and it was just in her nature to be like that . . . Joan certainly cared for Lolita and relied on her for everything, whereas Lolita *doted* on Joan and regarded it a privilege to look after her.

Stephen Marriott's memories of Aunty Loly and Aunty Joan—simply known as 'JoLo' over time—go back to the mid-1950s when he was a boy. Whenever Joan and Lolita visited Melbourne they always stayed at his grandparents' house, 'Hawthroy', which was close to where he lived:

> They shared a double bed there because when I was a kid we
> would play kids games—'anaconda' under the bedclothes. I was
> about nine. They'd call each other darling, they shared the same
> bed. My grandmother, [laughs] was not impressed—would say
> with an annoyed expression about her daughter 'She's got a kink!'
> . . . They were nevertheless welcome at 'Hawthroy', even though
> grandmother had her reservations. Grandfather simply overlooked
> it all, basically because clearly Joan Hammond was a first-class
> person. 'Hawthroy' was gigantic, they could easily have had
> separate bedrooms if they'd wanted.

The speculation within the Marriott family about Joan and Lolita's relationship was never brought to a conclusion. There were indicators such as the double bed and the loving quality of their familiarity, but there were other factors such as their faith and their conservative sense of morality. If it was a sexual relationship then it seemed extraordinarily unfettered by guilt or secrecy.

Stephen Marriott discovered the pleasures of golf when he grew older and played with Joan on numerous occasions. He marvelled at the number of strong, independent, single women who strode across the golf course. Some he saw as masculine, but not Joan:

> There was nothing butchy about Joan. She was quite self-effacing,
> had a humility about her. Most courteous person, right in her
> soul. Always take the time to write a letter of thanks after a lunch
> etc. Great woman. Spent five hours a day in study, polishing up
> her Russian etc. Meticulous, thorough. But as to sexuality—isn't
> it anybody's guess whether a kiss is a kiss or a stroke is a stroke?
> No doubt it was satisfying, tactile, who knows for the rest.

In the late 1950s Nancy Spain, journalist, novelist, celebrity panellist and most 'out' lesbian of the era, visited The Old Cottage to write a feature on Joan. The 1950s were still very much a time when gay men could be jailed as criminals and gay women, though never legislated against, were stigmatised and ostracised.

Suppression, guilt, angst, ignorance and secrecy surrounded the not so happy gay experience. Nancy Spain, by contrast, was wonderfully and wittily subversive. Good looking and close to 40, she wore slacks or tailored trousers, well-cut tweed jackets, crisp shirts with elegant cufflinks, and neckerchiefs or cravats—and she never compromised when she appeared on television. Even children noticed that the slim woman with short dark hair looked extraordinarily different from any other female on TV.

Nancy's appearance and manner gave the clue, but she made a point of flirting outrageously with fellow panellist and wit, the very masculine Gilbert Harding, himself gay and firmly in the closet. Nancy Spain lived relatively openly with her female partner, but it would have been professional suicide if she'd acknowledged her sexuality publicly. Her 'outness' was in the subtext, the in-jokes. She had a two-tier audience for her writing and broadcasting: an uninformed heterosexual one that simply enjoyed her high spirits, and a far more knowing and sophisticated one that was in tune with her gay double-speak.

It's interesting, therefore, that Nancy Spain chose Joan as the first interviewee in a new feature column for the *Daily Express*. The column was designed to discover what famous recording artists were like at home: 'Millions know their voices—but few see the side of their lives not on record'. Nancy was greeted by Lolita and Essie in the first instance, and a certain amount of whisky was consumed before Joan even made her entrance. The resulting article captured a unique if somewhat inebriated and not entirely accurate view of life in The Old Cottage. The piece is reproduced in full apart from one edit as shown. All ellipses and occasional print errors are Nancy's.

Eamonn Andrews, Gilbert Harding, Godfrey Winn, when they are doing "Housewives' Choice," quite often put on something "classical."

When they do depend upon it, they are usually asked to choose something sung by Joan Hammond.

Quite often this turns out to be "One Fine Day," but housewives have also been known to ask for her recording of "The Green Hills of Somerset," or "O, My Beloved Father."

Joan Hammond is a splendid 45-year-old deep-chested, good-looking Australian who lives in Buckinghamshire surrounded by beech trees, good food, good fellowship and budgerigars.

She has three poodles and 23 budgerigars, though this was a bad year for eggs.

"Not one fertile egg out of the litter."

Joan is attended by two charming ladies, rather like herself: good-looking, forthright and calling a spade a spade.

"When we are downhearted we three," they told me, "we open a bottle of champagne or play it off with ping-pong up in the games hut in the woods."

As far as the eye can see through the beeches, the land is Joan's. She has acquired this in spite of the fact that she won't talk about money because it looks so vulgar in print and also has said that classical music doesn't pay.

"I think I went into the red to buy my Rolls and I daresay I did it again when I installed the new oil central heating."

It is quite difficult to know which of the three ladies of Old Cottage is speaking as they all speak such a lot and so well and so excitingly.

Joan's personal representative, Lolita Marriot [sic], greeted me, explaining that she had known Joan ever since they were at school together in Australia where Joan was known as "ham and eggs."

The third lady, Estrees Walker, said she did the French and fancy cooking.

"I am for the plain," said Lolita, excusing herself by handing me an enormous plate of small ham sandwiches and a whisky and soda.

Lolita plays the violin, Estrees the piano and all three have a musical evening from time to time (these have not yet been recorded).

Joan now appeared, fresh from the golf course, wearing a salmon pink cardigan and a straight skirt.

She has extremely good legs. She was golf champion of Australia. She has gold and silver medals for life-saving.

There is no one I wouldn't [sic] rather have on my side in a scrap.

She plays golf off a handicap of four (this is very good) saying modestly that it will soon be seven if she doesn't pull her socks up.

She played off a handicap of two when she was a champion.

Joan thinks Bing Crosby is rather good and she says the most important thing about any singer is rhythm.

She hardly drinks at all. "It makes my voice chords feel furry, so drinking can't be good for them. I am a maniac about brushing my teeth, too, always brush them before I sing.

"I am a terribly early riser. I am usually up at seven, taking the dogs through the woods. I breathe deeply then. Yes. Then I come in and go straight to my work. Work at the moment means Madame Butterfly. I am singing Madame Butterfly on television on Tuesday night."

Joan has an unashamed Australian accent, to which she clings, just as she unrepentantly sings opera in English whenever she can.

I saw her music room with the grand-piano and a bookcase

Marguerite in *Faust*

Leonora in *Fidelio*

Title role in *Aida*

It's Joan Hammond sing
the Suez Opera–in Mos

Bolshoi, Moscow, February 21. Joan Hammond as Aida (at left, between sphinxes

IRONY OF HISTORY NOTE

Eighty-odd years ago that same Khedive of Egypt who sold Disraeli our stake in Suez commissioned Verdi's "Aida" to celebrate the Canal's opening, and it was first sung in Cairo. Last year "Aida" was being banned in white-hot East-West anger over Suez. But—last month, in the artistic shrine of Nasser's allies, two British singers triumphed...in "Aida." PHOTONEWS gets the picture. Write your own moral.

nstance Shacklock as Amneris (on throne). Centre: Dmitri Uzunov as Rhadames.

Title role
in *Salome*

Elizabeth in
Don Carlos

Title role in *Tosca*

crammed with operatic scores. Each one (even the Russian) was translated by Joan herself.

She can sing in Russian, Italian, and German as well as English. "The phrasing is exact," explained her secretary, "The English stops exactly at the end of a phrase just as the music does. That is the big difference between Joan's English singing and other people's . . ."

[Joan shows Nancy the scars on her left arm and tells her about the early years of her career. Then says:]

"But the greatest bit of luck I ever had I now think was when I got appendicitis in 1956."

I was amazed.

"Oh, yes," said Joan, "I was really grateful to appendicitis. I had time to lie in bed and take stock of myself. Until that time I had never really learned how to relax. I was just doing, and singing, and going from one recital to another without thinking or considering what I wanted out of life.

"It was when I was recovering from my operation and discovered I wasn't made entirely of old iron, I decided to concentrate on my acting. So when I went to Moscow in 1957, I made a success of it."

Joan paused and tugged at the short, ever so slightly silvering hair in the nape of her neck and turned to her two friends.

"Where's Mrs Thorn?" she asked. "Mrs Thorn always comes in to cut my hair before I wear a wig like I shall do on Tuesday.

"Why aren't you eating, Nancy? You've got a journey back to London and you need to eat . . ."

I gathered Mrs Thorn was the hairdresser. I also gathered that one of Joan's real hardships lay in the fact that she can't eat a thing, not even lunch, when she is singing in the evening.

Then slightly dazed, I found myself gripping a greaseproof

paper parcel with the ham sandwiches inside. I also realised that I was wonderfully relaxed.

I had been having a very good time, indeed. This quality of relaxation is so rare that when we find it we should never take it for granted.

I had lolled in Joan Hammond's house completely at ease. Just as I had so often lolled back listening to her gramophone records, knowing that she would not let me down . . .

You listen to her latest recording, Dvorak's "O, Silver Moon" released this week. You will see exactly what I mean.

There cannot really be much wrong with the wicked old world if a story like Joan Hammond's can come out of it . . . to produce a God-given voice like hers.

The article showed a photograph of Joan cooing at a budgerigar perched on her shoulder.

THE 1950S AND EARLY 1960S SAW Joan at the peak of her powers. She sang all over the world: Europe, Russia, South and East Africa, North and South America, Asia, Australasia, and a multitude of places in between. Round the world she went, thrilling the glitterati in magnificent opera houses and charming the curious in remote and makeshift venues—all with Lolita by her side. There were the inevitable frustrations and excitements: hours of tedium spent in a transit lounge, emergency landings, gun-toting audience members, extremes of temperature and conditions. But the positives outweighed the negatives: the fascinating cultures, the breathtaking scenery, the kindness of strangers, the genuine appreciation and applause.

Joan had some marvellous operatic highlights during this era. Return seasons of *Butterfly* with the Welsh National Opera proved phenomenally successful, so much so that the *Daily Mail* was prompted to comment on an oft raised issue: 'While the Australian soprano's fans—few singers have more—will be pleased at her Welsh success, they will be confirmed in their contention that the London opera stage should use this star much more'.

Covent Garden seemed to take note for in 1959 she was engaged to sing *Aida* after a five-year gap. Sadler's Wells was more responsive—and adventurous. Her recording of 'O silver moon' was such a hit that the Wells invited her to play the title role in *Rusalka* (1959). It was a particular honour because *Rusalka* had never been produced professionally in Britain before.

Australia, meanwhile, was at last able to see the famous soprano on its own opera stage. The country's embryonic opera company, the Elizabethan Trust Opera Company (ETOC) programmed its 1957 season around two of its home-grown stars: Joan Hammond and Elsie Morison. Ballarat born and twelve years younger than Joan, Elsie Morison was a well-loved soprano singing with the major companies in Britain. The ETOC idea was to present five popular operas—*La Bohème, Tales of Hoffmann* and *The Bartered Bride* for Morison, and *Tosca* and *Otello* (Desdemona) for Joan. The line-up was further enhanced with rising stars Ronald Dowd (tenor) and John Shaw (baritone), drawn back to Australia with the ETOC clincher: 'We've got Hammond'.

It was an all-Australian cast and a rare opportunity for developing opera singers to gain experience and employment. Joan performed with ETOC again in 1960 when she sang *Salome* and *Butterfly*, with Donald Smith, another rising star, joining the line-up.

JOAN HAD BEEN preparing for the extraordinarily taxing role of Richard Strauss's *Salome* since the mid-1950s when the idea was originally raised. She said she had first heard the opera in Vienna and the music gripped her: 'But the story seemed horrific. Both musically and histrionically this opera is electrifying from end to end'. The particular challenge of this role, apart from the excruciatingly difficult score and the fact that Salome is a teenager, is that near the end of the opera she performs the 'Dance of the seven veils'. Salome dances for her salacious stepfather after much coercion, but only so that she can demand the head of Jokanaan (John the Baptist) in return. The opera has no interval, Salome has about eighty minutes of straight singing, then an eight-minute dance, then thirty seconds to gain her breath while still on stage, then the extremely dramatic final section (about twenty minutes). The vocal range is G flat below C to high B, and the orchestra is very large.

It was not uncommon for a stand-in to do the dance but Joan wanted to perform the whole role or not at all. She knew it was a huge and perhaps unrealistic challenge, so she asked Robert Helpmann for advice. He took her through some movement sessions and concluded that she could do it and that the choreographer, Pauline Grant, was the perfect person to help her. So Joan rehearsed with the excellent Pauline Grant. They worked with the music and concept of the dance, whereby a girl discards seven veils till she stands semi-naked, until they found a style, integrity and motivation that suited both Joan and the role.

Joan's style of performing was of the old school, one that was steadily going out of fashion. She had her own specially designed costumes and she had her own set way of doing signature roles—Tosca always made her first entrance wearing a poke bonnet and carrying a stick. She had particular moves, gestures, props and costumes that worked well for her and the music, and there would have to be a very good reason for her to consider a change. This said, she'd been keen to learn new movement and relaxation techniques, and she'd integrated this new knowledge into her work. She was aware of where the energy was in her body and knew how to make a good body-line. She moved well within her chosen framework, but the framework was of the old style; either you accepted this or you didn't.

STEPHEN HALL WAS a young Australian journalist in 1957, with a passion for opera. He remembers the Sunday evening when the famous diva arrived in Newcastle. He was standing outside the theatre, a converted cinema known as the Old Vic, on the lookout for her arrival when a Rolls-Royce with a caravan hitched behind came to a halt at the kerb. Out stepped Joan and Lolita—who asked if he knew of anywhere they could get a meal. He said there was only one place open on Sunday, a Greek milk bar that did 'wonderful steaks and the works'. 'That'll do us,' they said, so he took them there and it sowed the seeds of a friendship. Stephen Hall became a key member of the Australian Opera team in later years, and he never forgot the effect of that ETOC season:

> What the recordings don't prepare you for is the size of the voice in the theatre. It was humungous, really big voice. We don't make voices like that any more . . . Joan Hammond gave people what they wanted. They weren't a sophisticated audience. They weren't used to seeing great performers. A good opera singer who could pull out all the stops and sing all the notes and look vaguely glamorous was very appealing . . . Joan was a great shot in the arm to all the performers that worked with her. I doubt if any of the singers from that company would have a bad word to say about her. She became a member of the company, she played with them, ate with them, she mucked up with them—was into the spirit of the thing wonderfully.

John Rohde was a business manager with ETOC during the 1957 season; he distributed the wages every Thursday evening. John's memories of the opening season of *Tosca* in Adelaide are especially vivid because his mother had just died and he was emotionally vulnerable:

Joan and Lolita were very kind. Invited me to lunch at the Pier
Hotel in Glenelg one day and were absolutely marvellous to
me [and they became friends] . . . She had a beautiful voice that
used to go right to my heart really. Up in Brisbane when she was
singing Tosca, I used to go in every night—my office was up in
the dress circle at the old His Majesty's Theatre. In the dress circle
foyer there was not a wall above the stalls but a heavy curtain
(it was to do with the climate I think) and I stood there and
every night I never missed her singing 'Vissi d'arte'. Never missed
it. It was the most beautiful voice, glorious. It was a pure rich
soprano voice . . . If you think of what we think of as an Italian
tenor—she had that kind of full bodied voice—which came from
that quite large frame she had.

Greg Dempsey sang minor tenor roles with ETOC in the early years
of the company. He was the second youngest member of the cast and
went on to establish an international career:

Rehearsals were in Sydney for *Tosca*. We rehearsed at the
Elizabethan Theatre in Newtown. Her reputation came before her;
we were all in awe of her . . . Elsie Morison was equal to Joan—
though she never had quite the voice. Two great performers here
at the same time, it was marvellous, marvellous . . . The best thing
I ever heard in my life was Joan Hammond and Donald Smith
singing the love duet in *Butterfly* . . .

[In the rehearsals] Joan had her own ideas as to how it should
have gone. Stefan Haag, the producer, I think he just tailored
things around her, because she'd done it umpteen times. It would
be hard, when you get people like that, to say I'm going to do it
differently. If he was to say 'you lie down here' she'd say 'I don't
lie down here I stand up' [gentle laugh]. She was very positive.
Eric Clapham was the conductor. I remember her saying: 'Mr

Clapham, the brass cannot be that loud there' [laughs]—but she
was right! That was the thing about her. It's a bit like working
with Placido Domingo or Fischer-Dieskau—they knew more
about the orchestra than the conductor—and Hammond was
like that . . .

We treated her like royalty, even Stefan Haag, it was Miss
Hammond this and Miss Hammond that; no one else got that
treatment . . . She brought her own costumes [but] the costumes
for Tosca didn't suit the set colours too well; they clashed! No one
would challenge that, because that was how it was arranged—she
would bring her costumes. Sutherland used to do that too.

She was a very consistent singer. Most singers sing one night
very good, then ordinary the next, but she was consistent every
night . . . I suppose we all felt she was severe, but there was
also a lot of warmth there. Indeed in *Otello* I had to go on at
short notice to do Cassio (because the man singing Cassio, Ray
MacDonald, was the cover for Otello and Ron Dowd got sick)
so I had to go on at short notice—and I forgot the handkerchief!
And of course I've got to give her the handkerchief in the scene.
And I'm trying to tell her on stage [whispers] 'I forgot the
handkerchief.' She says under her breath 'Don't worry. Just cup
your hands and give me the handkerchief like that and no one will
notice'—she did it all terribly in character. I was distraught after,
went round to the dressing-room in great perturbation, and she
just said, 'Oh everybody forgets. You did go on at short notice and
you sang marvellously.' Very gracious.

Lolita was a lovely person, very matter of fact, very warm . . .
always there, assisting Joan at the theatre during performances
. . . She gave a big party for the whole company at her house
in Melbourne ['Hawthroy'], a magnificent place it was.
Whole company invited, she didn't mess around with just the cast.
She was a generous person.

The company decided to throw a surprise party for Joan after the final performance of *Tosca* in Adelaide. They cooked up an idea that would get her out of the theatre while they were setting up the food and decorations. Greg Dempsey and two companions dressed up as 'hoods' with dark glasses, spivvy hats and bandit masks. They burst into her dressing room (Lolita had been alerted to the plan) and said she was being kidnapped. Joan played her part with good humour and allowed herself to be blindfolded and bundled into a waiting car which drove round the streets of Adelaide for the next twenty minutes. Joan knew there was to be some sort of party (she provided eight cases of champagne) but she was astonished to find herself back in the theatre when the blindfold was removed: Surprise!

Members of the Elizabethan Trust Opera Company, 1957

The cast ceremoniously presented her with 'The Trophy', a big ugly china jug worth 7s 6d which they'd all written on, and an elegant coffee set. Joan and Lolita were among the last to leave the party and when this small group reached the big iron gates at the back of the theatre they found them locked. Greg was there:

> We'd all drunk a lot of grog so we decided to climb up the gates
> and get over . . . And of course Lolita got her underwear or slip
> or something caught on the top. We were all trying to undo her
> to get her down the other side. Joan had hauled her up ok, but
> then she got stuck up the top . . . I can remember the police on the
> other side of the road were looking, you know, at all this—which
> made us laugh even more. True story.

When Joan arrived at Sydney airport in 1960 to perform *Butterfly* and *Salome* she gave an impromptu radio interview that revealed something of her approach to the Salome role and the tour in general. The young man who interviewed her had a difficult job because Joan, as usual, spoke haltingly, or simply laughed and smiled instead of speaking. He began by asking her to say a few words:

> JOAN: So very pleased to be here—was here last year for a
> holiday. A golfing holiday.
> INTERVIEWER: This time it's work?
> JOAN: Yes, I'm looking forward to it. [long pause]
> INTERVIEWER: Can you tell us the details?
> JOAN: . . . Er . . . Well [laughs] Two operas, *Madam Butterfly* and
> the . . . er . . . controversial *Salome*. Both are very great roles and
> . . . both strenuous. I shall be here I think about five months, and
> a month rehearsing before the opening night, the Adelaide Festival
> on March the 17th, and then on tour after that: Melbourne,
> Sydney, and a short visit to Brisbane.

INTERVIEWER: I believe that you're dancing.

JOAN: Yes! [laughs] Umm—I used to dance a lot, of course as a child, I've been very keen on it and . . . I . . . have . . . started taking lessons again about three years ago and doing quite er strenuous exercises, and steps because I'd made up my mind that I wanted to tackle this very, very er exciting role of Salome. And I believe that one cannot divorce the dance from the opera. If you're going to sing the opera you must certainly perform the dance. Having a ballerina come in and do it was not Strauss's intention *ever* and I think he would have been horrified if, if that had been done. Simply because she wasn't a ballerina, she was a Princess of Judea and *loved* dancing and obviously had this fascination and Herod was mad, always, at the thought of her doing this dance, which is the taking off of the veils. As you know the Eastern women wear many, many, veils, and it is part of their custom. And . . . I don't think anyone's very interested in the six veils, they want to know what's happening to the *seventh*! [chuckles]

[Interviewer asks about a family connection with the other opera]

JOAN: Er, yes, *Madam Butterfly*. My parents went to Japan many years ago and brought back a very lovely wig for me—er—then it was for a fancy dress I think. Parasols, and kimonos, all of which I've been using throughout my career. And I've brought back again the wig, which, in its old form is still a very wonderful wig, and er my wig maker in London re-dresses it and keeps it looking absolutely right for me. It is the original hair, but of course it's been added to over the years to keep it modern. The Parasol is—just beginning to get a little mothy here and there—but one doesn't notice that and I'm very attached to it. [laughing under the following] And I hope it'll go on being useful for me for a long time to come.

INTERVIEWER: Do you still play golf?

JOAN: Oh my word—when I get a chance. I haven't lately of

course—and the weather is not very—I'm not a winter player. I must say I can't stand the cold over in England, and I don't like the damp very much so—I play as often as possible in the spring and autumn when I'm there—and summer, when it's possible. I get out because—I love the game, first of all—and I also find it very beneficial to my health.

INTERVIEWER: Welcome back.

JOAN: Thank you!

Greg Dempsey was in the *Butterfly* and *Salome* productions. He remembers Joan arriving with Salome's dance and costume fully prepared—and understood why:

She wasn't going to make herself look silly. A real sensitive thing it would be, taking off all the veils. It was done very well, done with a lot of shadow, lot of wispy curtains floating around, she took off the final thing and—I thought it was done with great taste. I don't know what the press was, but I would have thought they'd be pretty positive about it. But she sang! Ah! Salome is such a difficult thing to sing. She was such a fantastic singer.

Joan was a 'tall poppy', an easy target to be cut down to size. Some reviewers hacked away at her old style of performance. Her Tosca in particular upset one critic because of her solidly traditional presentation of '*Vissi d'arte*'. It was sung to God in the direction of 'the gods' and he wanted more Callas-like drama. But there was a general respect for her performance of Salome. An extraordinary achievement considering she turned 48 during the tour. Audiences voted with their wallets. All Joan's performances were sell-outs but *Salome* proved especially popular. Melburnians were so keen that an extra performance was put on—the huge Palais Theatre in St Kilda was filled to capacity yet again.

Children as well as adults were introduced to opera during those history-making ETOC seasons. A young Stephen Marriott remembers being allowed to stand in the wings during a performance of *Tosca* with strict instructions not to move. He was fascinated by the amount of make-up people wore, and how much sweat poured off the principals when they came off stage. A boy called Moffatt Oxenbould, destined to become Artistic Director of Australian Opera, managed to see almost all the productions—his first experience of grand opera on stage. He remembers the brilliance, brightness and 'blaze' of Joan's voice: 'It had a big sort of sheen, an opulence to it'. And he was particularly struck by Tosca's costumes: 'I thought they were the most glamorous things I'd ever seen. Today I don't but when I was a kid—black velvet and a bit of diamond, ermine and stuff like that—she looked fantastic'. Her Butterfly was a visual disappointment to Master Oxenbould, but her Salome impressed; he wasn't allowed to see her Desdemona because he hadn't finished his homework.

The other really important aspect of Joan's presence during those early ETOC tours was that she never shied away from speaking up for Australian music, opera and singers. In newspaper, radio and television interviews she asked Australians to value their art and artists in the same way that they valued their sport. She also said that talented young singers needed to be supported at a grassroots level while they were developing, and that a permanent national opera company that toured extensively was essential to that process: 'Australia will never get professionalism in opera while it allows young singers to treat their art as a hobby. Opera must be full-time'. She believed in the potential of ETOC and was distressed that the company was disbanded at the end of each tour, her colleagues left stranded without work. She expressed her thoughts very forcefully to Dr H. C. Coombs, chairman of the Australian Elizabethan Trust, and he agreed with her.

Joan supported the *idea* of the Sydney Opera House, and helped raise funds for it, but was sceptical about the interior design when she saw the plans. She thought it was too small for a true opera house and was concerned that the seating arrangement was lengthwise, as opposed to the European U-shape. She said that it wasn't really an opera house at all but a multi-purpose concert hall.

Joan also made a point of supporting Australian singers overseas. John Shaw made his debut at Covent Garden as Rigoletto in 1958, sight unseen, because Joan and also Elsie Morison recommended him. Joan sang with Shaw in England the following year (*Tosca* in Cardiff), and with Ronald Dowd (*Butterfly* in Manchester); she was also an advocate for Donald Smith (recipient of a Joan Hammond Scholarship). Numerous Australian colleagues were helped along with an influential 'nod' in the right quarter.

JOAN AND LOLITA managed their Australian tours with aplomb. They drove between cities and stopped by the roadside to make 'billy tea' and a midday meal—according to the press anyway. They stayed in the best hotels when in the larger cities, or at 'Hawthroy' when in Melbourne. Lolita was 'Aunty Loly' to Joan's nieces and nephews, and Joan was godmother to Ron and Peg Marriott's second child, Miranda.

Joan's parents had moved to a basement flat in Double Bay by this time. Joan visited but never stayed. Somewhat estranged from Noel and Tony, she was closest to her middle brother Len. Joan and Lolita stayed with Len and his wife Monti at least part of the time when in Sydney. An especial joy was to join them when they went sailing. It was during these trips that Monti Hammond came to know the pair quite well. One thing was obvious—Joan was 'boating mad':

The show would end, she and Lol would get in the car and come racing down to Newport. We'd be waiting, the boat all primed ready to take off—and usually with a lamb stew or something on

Joan with her parents

the stove because she didn't eat before a performance. She was always starving when she finished so the first thing she did when she came on the boat was eat . . . It was a 36-foot cruiser so there was plenty of room. We used to go up to Broken Bay, the Basin, and one of my memories of Joan is early in the morning, waking up, and Joan walking up and down the beach singing.

The foursome enjoyed each other's company so well that Joan and Lolita invited Len and Monti to return with them to England for a holiday after the *Salome/Butterfly* tour in 1960. They travelled via Hong Kong, Rome and Paris, Joan and Lolita acting as tour guides all the way:

They were a pair of madcaps, they used to do the funniest things
. . . in Paris, in the middle of the night, they came in and said
'Come on, wake up, you've got to come and have a look at this' —
something was going on [in the street] . . . They were a good
combination, full of fun.

Fun and relaxation were becoming key words in Joan and Lolita's
conversation. Work and endless travel were beginning to wear them
down, especially Joan. Congestion on the roads, the smog, and another
unsettling car accident made driving less of a pleasure.

Then there came a terrible moment that had never happened
before: Joan forgot her words during a concert. She prided herself
on her phenomenal memory and it disturbed her terribly. She went
through a phase of feeling lacklustre about singing—a feeling that
was entirely new and disquieting. Perhaps the menopause, as much
as the car accident and treacherous road conditions, was to blame.
She began to mull over plans for retirement: she and Lolita would
move back to Australia for the sun and the sea. She was candid with
journalists, saying that retirement was between one and five years
away. She had engagements for the next twelve months or so, but
after that, she wasn't sure.

In the meantime the pair felt they needed 'something else', something
invigorating. The something they decided upon was special: a boat of
their own.

It wasn't to be just any boat. It needed to be designed with their
particular requirements and sailing abilities in mind. Lolita's maritime
skills were limited or non-existent, but their aspirations were high.
They wanted an ocean-going vessel, one that could comfortably cross
the English Channel—and keep going. Joan approached a childhood
friend, the naval architect Walter Rayner, and he designed the boat of
their dreams: a yacht with a substantial motor.

It took a year or two from planning to completion but the end result was very classy. Officially known as a twin screw motor launch, the vessel was a 38-footer (plus four inches), had a streamlined mahogany superstructure, single mast, white hull, blue water line, two 56-horsepower engines, a fore cabin with two berths, a settee and a full length berth in the saloon, a galley complete with gas refrigerator, a toilet with separate shower, two berths in the after cabin, with wardrobe, dressing table and washbasin, and the mod cons included a radio telephone. The standard price for this 'Tasman Class' model was £7500 plus extras (and there were a lot of extras). They called her *Pankina*, an Aboriginal word meaning 'to be happy'. She was launched with much hilarity and fanfare in 1963 at Poole Harbour in Dorset, where she had been built and moored.

Joan and Lolita loved their boat, and went sailing as often as they could. Essie also, though she didn't step into the 'sailor mode' as much as the other two, who revelled in wearing old clothes and calling out impressive nautical terms. Joan took the role of Captain and Lolita called herself 'The Hand'.

Once they'd found their sea legs they were eager to show off their purchase—even to the press:

"Come aboard!" the grey-haired woman called as our tender drew alongside a brand spanking new yacht. "Careful you don't slip. I had a dip yesterday and nearly froze."

And with little more ado, singer Joan Hammond started up the twin diesel motors of her recently acquired 15-ton yacht, Pankina, gave her for'ard hand Lolita Marriott the order to "up anchor," and headed out of Poole Harbour into the English Channel.

Steering clear of the treacherous rocks and sandbanks at the harbour mouth, where an expert yachtsman had been wrecked just a few days before, Joan told me of the new enthusiasm which has entered her life.

"A lot of people thought two women couldn't manage a boat

this size," she said. "But we've shown them . . . I've been taking Pankina out into the Channel just to get the feel of her. We've also practised coming up to our mooring and going alongside the wharf for fuel and water, and I think we're getting pretty good.

"Later on I'll be taking Pankina across the Channel to France, then perhaps to the Mediterranean.

"I plan to ship Pankina to Australia when I retire, but I don't know when that will be—I find that since living on the boat I'm singing better than ever.

"I don't know what it is . . . probably the effect of the sea air or the relaxation or something."

Lolita's presence was often mentioned in interviews like these. Casually as in the article above or more specifically as in Joan's 'companion, business manager, and co-owner of the yacht'. Lolita was personable and charming, always there to help an interview along if need be, and journalists tended to weave her into their story. Her presence in Joan's life was public knowledge.

Joan and Lolita met a young naval officer, John Crisp, through their mutual friend, Ivor Newton. John Crisp had long admired Joan's voice but she soon got him talking about sailing and navigation and meteorology. She wanted to sail across to Cherbourg to give *Pankina* her first big test but was tentative about her navigation skills. Rough seas never worried her but she was nervous about losing sight of the coast. John offered to act as navigator for the adventure and the offer was happily accepted. *Pankina* could sleep five and Joan, Lolita, Essie, John and Ivor sailed to Cherbourg one long weekend without a hitch. It was the first of many such trips.

John, and (later) his partner Ian Kirk, became lifelong friends of Joan, Lolita and Essie—or 'JoLoEs' as they collectively called themselves. They shared birthday parties and dinner parties and sailing excursions. Sometimes they'd all meet up at Ivor's house in

Portsmouth and enjoy a meal prepared by Andrew, Ivor's live-in valet and companion. Ivor, who seemed to know something about everyone, had previously told John about Joan and Essie's history and the sudden arrival of Lolita. What (if anything) Ivor told the trio about John's affairs he never knew. When John introduced the threesome to Ian Kirk they took to him immediately. Joan gave him his first 'Horse's Neck', a potent cocktail that was a favourite tipple on the *Pankina*. John says that they shared many good times together over the years, yet they never said anything intimate about their respective relationships, never discussed their sexuality. Assumptions were made, rightly or wrongly, but nothing was said. That's simply how it was.

JOAN WAS HAPPY. She was loved, she was sustained by her faith, she had a devoted following, and she was enjoying herself. To cap it all, she had the satisfaction of 'giving back' through charitable work in the form of recitals in Her Majesty's prisons. This was an initiative started by Ivor Newton, and Joan, though fearful at first, found the experience extraordinarily rewarding. Wandsworth Prison, Wormwood Scrubs, Parkhurst Prison, and Holloway the women's prison, became important engagements in her working calendar. Her Majesty rewarded her for this and all her achievements with a CBE, Commander of the Order of the British Empire, in 1963.

Love and music, these have I lived for

Tosca, Puccini

ROYAL ALBERT HALL

Wednesday, December 10th at 7.30 p.m.

Lynford Joel announce

JOAN HAMMOND

LONDON SYMPHONY ORCHESTRA
STANFORD ROBINSON

A programme of popular operatic arias including excerpts from :

Madam Butterfly	*Puccini*
A Masked Ball	*Verdi*
Manon	*Massenet*
Tannhauser	*Wagner*
Adriana Lecouvreur	*Cilea*
Mefistofele	*Boito*
Fiery Cross	*Max Bruch*

Tickets from 2/6 (KEN 8212) and Agents

CHAPTER 7

'WHEN I HAVE SUNG MY SONGS'

JOAN SCORED A hole in one at Yarra Yarra golf course on 19 December 1963—which inadvertently brought attention to her presence in Victoria. She'd been quietly holidaying for five weeks, successfully avoiding the press, but the hole in one blew her cover: it was drinks all round at the bar. Joan and Lolita were staying at 'Hawthroy', taking the opportunity to catch up with Clarence and the rest of the Marriott family. She told journalists that she'd come back to Australia to spend Christmas with her mother, something she hadn't done for twenty-seven years. What she didn't tell them was that her father had died some months earlier. Samuel had died without Hilda by his side for she'd been staying with Joan at The Old Cottage at the time.

Joan and Lolita's future plan for retirement was to settle in Victoria, so they spent some of their holiday time looking for land on which to build a house. They wanted to live near the sea. Burtta Cheney and her companion Alison Searle invited the pair to stay with them at Anglesea, a couple of hours west of Melbourne along the Great Ocean Road. The foursome had known each other for many years. Alison, like Burtta, had worked with Lolita in the Red Cross, and Burtta was one of Victoria's best golfers. Joan and Lolita were particularly attracted to Aireys Inlet, a lovely bush-meets-ocean area close to Anglesea. There was no land for sale that suited their needs at the time, so they asked Alison to keep a lookout for them. Months passed and then Alison rang them in England to say there was a 63-acre block at Aireys Inlet that fronted the Great Ocean Road. Lolita bought it sight unseen.

MATTERS OF HEALTH began to take prominence in Joan's life—or rather more prominence than usual, for anything that threatened her health threatened her voice. She had a troublesome right knee and occasional pain in her arms, but these things were nothing compared to the onset of a middle-ear infection. She heard noises inside the ear and there was increasing deafness. Joan was frightened by the prospect of not being able to sing again but her specialist said that three months' rest would cure the problem; and he was right.

All began to look rosy again but then Lolita's world suddenly deteriorated. Her father had a relapse and she rushed back to Melbourne to be with him, and stayed away for many weeks.

Joan was in good voice again by September 1964, when she was scheduled to record a collection of songs with Ivor Newton. It was a special recording for both of them—a long-playing record that celebrated a working relationship that spanned more than two decades. Ivor was 72 and still in good form. Well-known favourites were gathered under the title of the first track: *On Wings of Song*. Tracks included 'Bird song at eventide', 'Love's philosophy', 'At the well', 'Home sweet home' and, somewhat prophetically, 'When I have sung my songs'. The final track was 'Green hills o' Somerset'. It was recorded at Abbey Road and was one of the happiest recording sessions she'd ever experienced.

The aches and pains that had come and gone in previous months began to occur more frequently. A pain in the arms and shoulders, a constriction in the chest after deep breathing, but nothing that lasted very long. She only knew in retrospect that they were the warning signals known as angina. Then in November, when she was gearing up for the busy Christmas season, she had a coronary thrombosis (a blocked artery radically reducing the supply of oxygen to the heart). Lolita flew back to London to be with her.

When Joan came out of hospital she was weak in body but determined in spirit, although she was appalled at how long it would be before she could sing again. A letter to Bertie Lloyd shows how she was feeling.

The Old Cottage
18th January 1965.

At last I am allowed to write, or type, two or three letters a day. I think the doctors are glad to find any reason for keeping me stationary! To be inactive for over 2½ months is making me rather impatient and now I know that I shall not be working until September—it seems like a lifetime. They assure me, however, that if I do as I'm told and carry out the prescribed routine, by about September I shall be as good as new! And able to do just everything as before. At the moment I have my on and off days when I feel I am progressing then I feel that I have got nowhere! I am still having to have the blood tested, but more infrequently, but I have to continue taking the anti-coagulant pills. Enough of health . . . I am thinking of selling The Old Cottage as there has been a family very keen to buy it from me for some time, and it is too large for us now and I do want to begin making plans to return home to Australia. The three of us are making plans for our future. Essie is going to buy some land up at the Barrier Reef where she will build a small easy to run home where we can go during the cold weather!! I shall buy a flat in Melbourne and Lolita will build a home down at Airey's Inlet so we shall have a variety of nests! Essie, of course, will not be able to come out until her mother passes on so we shall buy a smaller house, on one level if possible, here. I am permitted to come downstairs once a day only so we shall seek a bungalow!

Determined though she was, Joan's progress was unsatisfactory. Her doctors recommended a long sea voyage, and Joan and Lolita boarded a liner bound for Australia, Joan having to bear the indignity of being carried aboard in a wheelchair. She was unable to go ashore at any of the ports due to the steps; but in any case she was still very weak. They stayed with Clarence at 'Hawthroy' initially, and by Easter Joan was strong enough to travel to Sydney. The extended rest and the warmth of the sun achieved the desired effect. They flew back to England in May.

Joan went to see her fairy godmother, Lady Gowrie, and found her much changed: she too had been seriously ill. They talked of many things. Lady Gowrie's extraordinary spirit was as buoyant as ever. Then she became more serious. She took Joan's hand and asked when she'd be able to sing again. It was pointless trying to hedge, so Joan told the truth: she didn't know. Lady Gowrie reminded her of the first time she'd heard Joan sing—the peerless voice awakening her on that humid afternoon in Sydney long ago. Then she talked about the most recent occasion: a function at Australia House in aid of the Australian Musical Association with the Queen Mother and various dignitaries present. Joan had sung particularly well and a fine speech was made about her achievements, much to Joan's embarrassment. Lady Gowrie looked deep into Joan's eyes and smiled.

Lady Gowrie died ten days later. The young Earl of Gowrie consulted Joan about the memorial service, for it had been his grandmother's wish that Joan sing the Bach–Gounod 'Ave Maria'. There were two major obstacles to this, Joan's health, and the fact that the service was to be held in St George's Chapel, Windsor. No woman had ever sung in the Chapel and special permission had to be granted by the Queen. Permission was granted and Joan was determined to sing, whatever the consequences.

On 30 July 1965, two months after her fifty-third birthday, Joan sang in public for the last time. To her great relief she sang from the organ loft—out of sight of the congregation and unable to see the coffin. Her disembodied voice floated to the heavens. She'd begun her career in like manner, heard but not seen when she sang the solo in Vaughan Williams's *Pastoral* in Sydney in 1931.

Joan's heart stood up to the strain of the memorial service without mishap and this gave her hope. She wanted to fulfil at least one last commitment—to make a recording at York Minster with organ and choir. It was a wonderful opportunity and the people at EMI were prepared to delay the recording date as long as necessary. It was a lifeline that she clung to. Public performances might be too much pressure but perhaps she still had a future as a recording artist. She began to rehearse, and slowly but surely she built up her strength.

Her voice was as lovely as ever but the physical and emotional stress that came with the act of singing was too much. A series of telltale pains in the chest and arms caused her to postpone the date—once, twice, three times—and then a mild coronary forced her to face the inevitable. As soon as she made her decision she made it public. She informed the newspapers on 10 September 1965 that ill health had forced her to retire. There would be no comebacks. It was finished.

Joan always believed that things happened for the best—it was Fate or God's will—but it was hard to see the positives. The thing that she lived for had been taken away.

THE RETIREMENT PLAN was put into action. Preparations for this, and the answering of solicitous fan mail, kept her occupied; but her spirits were very low. The Old Cottage was sold and a smaller house called 'Lilliput' at Farnham Common was bought. Leaving The Old Cottage was a wrench in itself. There had been much happiness there, not least with dearly loved pets. There was a place in the garden where deceased pets had been buried and a gravestone was made to mark the spot. The stone indirectly marked Joan's term at the cottage also: 'Here Lies The Hammondry, Four-Footed and Feathered Friends, 1951–1966'.

Early in 1966 Essie's belongings with some of Joan's and Lolita's were moved down the road to 'Lilliput', the rest was packed up ready for shipment to Australia. They had three Rolls-Royces by this time. Joan's, Lolita's, plus a third bought for Essie. Essie used to get around in a red Mini but Joan and Lolita felt she needed something more substantial, a Rolls-Bentley to be exact. Joan's Roller was shipped to Australia, along with *Pankina*.

In the meantime Lolita's dream home was being built. She went back and forth to Australia to oversee things and Joan went with her at least once to observe how the building process was going. It was Lolita's house, Lolita's design ideas, Lolita's name on all the cheques, but when the press got wind of it—for the house was newsworthy in terms of extravagance—it was constantly referred to as Joan's house, despite her protestations to the contrary. One reporter eventually listened to what Joan was saying and wrote:

That house of Joan Hammond's—is it hers or not? Just after she snuck into Melbourne the other day—almost as secretly as the house is being built down at Airey's Inlet—she says she is sharing it. "But no one will believe me. I've just given up saying it." She's sharing it with her friend of 35 years standing, her secretary, her business manager—Miss Lolita Marriott . . . All the negotiations, the signing for the land title and all the rest, are signed 'Marriott'.

Yet the assumption that it was Joan's house remained.

There was much curiosity about the mansion that was taking shape. The district, indeed the state, had never seen anything quite like it. Rumours circulated about the cost. One newspaper suggested $200000 and sent a reporter to investigate. Joan and Lolita had wished to keep the project private but a 'helpful' councillor revealed that it was to be a single-storey double-brick white painted house laid out in a form resembling an X. There was to be a very large central reception area (60 feet x 25) with five 'wings' leading off it at different angles. There was a wing with an indoor heated swimming pool (30 feet x 14), a wing with four bedrooms and two bathrooms, a wing with large lounge (30 feet x 18), a wing with den, dining, kitchen and laundry—and a carport extension wing made for four vehicles (50 feet x 21). There was to be a wine cellar and two cocktail bars; the swimming pool was to have underwater lighting, the bathroom taps to be gold plated, the cupboard handles to be crystal, and the roof to be green slate. A sophisticated system of underground tanks would provide the water supply. A more conventional dwelling, 'The cottage' had already been built for domestic staff (measuring 12 squares compared to 80 squares for the main house). They'd named the property 'Jumbunna', an Aboriginal word meaning 'here we sit and talk together'.

Lolita chose a master builder, H. J. Fudge of Toorak, to draw up the plans, and used an Anglesea contractor, B. J. Butterworth, to carry out the work. Butterworth said it was the biggest job he'd ever undertaken. Rumour had it that the costs blew out to an exorbitant degree. Rumour also had it that money was no object.

Lolita's income had risen considerably since 1957 when her father passed on his inheritance, a decision influenced by forward thinking and

Lolita at 'Jumbunna'

a keenness to avoid certain taxes. Hecla Pty Ltd was doing extremely well and Lolita's share of the profits was considerable. Joan's income, meanwhile, dropped dramatically when she was forced to retire. Lolita acknowledged that she was paying for 'Jumbunna' when asked, but she and/or her builder made an interesting choice when ordering materials. Consignments of timber arrived on site with the delivery name 'Hammond' rather than 'Marriott' scrawled upon them, a factor that added fuel to the various rumours about ownership.

The duo's finances were kept separate; they never shared a bank account, for instance, and they had different accountants, but Lolita did 'reassign' monies in quite intricate ways to minimise tax. She kept a close account of domestic expenses (phone and fuel etc.) and these balanced out as a two- or three-way split, depending on what they were.

Joan, Lolita and Essie settled into 'Lilliput' during the English summer, and then Lolita went back to Victoria to oversee the final touches to 'Jumbunna'. Joan gave Essie the gift of a return ticket to Australia as a fiftieth birthday present, so they flew to Australia together in early November—Essie's first trip to the land of her mother's birth. Lolita had everything ready, or as ready as it could be by the time they arrived. Joan had seen the land, seen the plans, seen the caretaker's cottage finished and the main house take shape; but even she was taken aback by the sight of the dream home. She hadn't envisaged anything quite so large, quite so extravagant. Her grand piano looked strangely small in its new, light and airy setting. Everything looked extremely impressive, not least the swimming pool. And the setting was marvellous: the sight and sounds of the bush, the view and distant roar of the ocean, the night-time blink of the lighthouse—lovely.

Everything had gone to plan and Lolita in particular was to be congratulated. The trio raised their glasses to Christmas and then the New Year of 1967 with a sense of hope and revitalisation.

Essie's holiday was almost over, her suitcase open ready to be packed, when she developed a blinding headache. She lay down on her bed and when Lolita found her she was very ill indeed. She was rushed to hospital in an ambulance, Joan by her side, and it was discovered that she'd suffered a brain haemorrhage. It was touch and go whether she'd survive. Joan and Lolita visited her in hospital for weeks on end and slowly, very slowly, she began to show signs of recovery. She said afterwards that she'd heard them talking to her but couldn't respond, and that it was Joan's voice that kept her going.

The prognosis wasn't good. Her life expectancy was radically reduced—a matter of months to a few years. She was told not to drive and advised not to travel by air or sea for at least twelve months. Essie was stranded in Australia.

'Life certainly does some cruel things at times', wrote Lolita to a friend. She was writing from 'Lilliput', catching up with correspondence after the flurry of selling that house, organising Essie's affairs and packing up belongings ready for shipment. Essie's mother was in a nursing home, so that part of the equation was already dealt with. 'It has been a terribly sad time for us all', wrote Lolita.

Yet the sad times were far from over. Lolita had been back in Australia but a couple of weeks when her father died. She was fortunate to have been close by, considering the amount of travelling she'd been doing. It was a painful loss; she loved Clarence dearly.

'Hawthroy' was sold and another round of sorting and packing had to be done. Lolita bought a fourth-floor flat in a new apartment block at 46 Lansell Road, Toorak: two bedrooms, living room, and a balcony with a northerly view across the city.

THE NEXT MEDICAL PROBLEM concentrated itself around Joan's lower lip. For years she'd had a sensitive patch on her lower lip, a soreness, especially when using stage make-up. A check-up revealed that it was a melanoma. The lip had to be removed: two operations, very painful, but the outcome was good. It was non-malignant and the plastic surgeon did an excellent job. As Joan put it: 'I now have a new lower lip. It is smaller, and if there are a few lumps and bumps they are only seen and felt by me'.

Then they had problems with their choice of domestic staff. They'd brought a married couple out from England who'd worked for them before. All was well until Lolita's builder alerted them to an 'issue'. Rather than take all the rubbish to the tip, the couple would fossick through the wastepaper bins and select items of curiosity or interest and share them with the locals at the pub. The couple were sent packing; but suitable replacements were hard to find—and keep. Joan and Lolita were difficult to please; they knew this, but it didn't seem to help. Joan's fastidiousness regarding cleanliness was obsessive but inconsistent. She couldn't stand to see dust but she was tempted to put food down if there was a mouse in the house. Lolita may have been more consistent (mice were to be killed) but her 'to do' list would have been comprehensive.

Their problems with domestic staff were never fully resolved, which is why Essie's presence, when she eventually returned to 'Jumbunna', became as significant as it had ever been. Her recovery was very slow but eventually she was able to function almost as well as she'd done before. So the kitchen, once again, became her domain. It was her sense of freedom and independence that was forever impaired.

Essie, an English rose of the first order, applied herself as best she could to her new country. Joan and Lolita, meanwhile, had to adjust to the altered plan. Projected trips to Europe to see friends and soak up the culture had to be postponed, and postponed again. Essie couldn't be left, couldn't travel. All three had hoped that Essie would be able to return to Britain in due course, but it wasn't to be.

The one thing that Joan and Lolita refused to do was dwell on the negatives. If the projected trip to Europe had to be put off then it meant that Joan had more time to spend on her two pet projects: creating a garden and writing her autobiography.

She'd sworn that she'd never take on a big garden again after the demands of The Old Cottage. The 'garden' round 'Jumbunna' was to remain native bush. But then visitors started bringing presents in the form of potted plants. A small garden was inevitable, and once she began it just kept growing. Roses were a particular delight, also her vegetable plot. Her competitive nature, always to the fore, drove her to grow the best possible specimens. Her artichokes were a marvel.

Writing her autobiography was a new kind of challenge, though she didn't lack confidence as far as writing was concerned. She liked to write. It was one of the things she did when illness forced repose. She'd written the occasional article (on Verdi, on the Moscow theatre experience) and dabbled in anecdotes (on playing golf in the British

Open). A handful of these items had been published over the years. There was also the experience of being a reporter in her youth. A whole book was a big undertaking but she had a ready-made structure to draw upon: her five-year diaries, scrupulously maintained since 1936. There was also Lolita's extensive archive of reviews and promotional items, all neatly dated and filed.

Joan began her task at the end of 1967. She wrote some of the chapters aboard *Pankina*, now moored at Church Point, Pittwater; the rest was written at 'Jumbunna'. The influence of sea and bush is evident in her opening paragraph:

> The roar of the surf, of heavy seas pounding the shore, the calm
> undulating swell after a storm, the feel of hot sand on bare feet,
> the prow of a yacht surging through the waves, maybe dancing
> as through a curtain of foam, a horse's mane flying in the wind—
> these things are woven into the fabric of my childhood. And more:
> the smell of the bush and the leaves of gum trees twinkling silver
> after the rain, the boronia and the wattle; sunrise and sunset,
> trees, birds, animals—the whole of nature's riotous pageant.
> Then the glory of a great symphony or opera, the simplicity of
> a lovely song, the sometime beauty of prose and poetry, of art.
> Children's playtime laughter, the trust and companionship of good
> friends—all these I love.

There were moments of lyricism but on the whole the autobiography was a practical, vigorous yet restrained re-telling of the highs and lows of her career. It was Joan wearing her 'proper' public face. The reader was left in no doubt that times had been tough monetarily, and that income was always hard won. She was keen to stress the hardships and loneliness of the early years, but was less forthcoming about the better times and the private times. There was no mention of a Rolls-Royce, for instance, nor her conversion to Catholicism—and she never mentioned her parents' first names let alone any reference to 'Hood'.

She was diplomatic when it came to referring to her colleagues. She praised when praise was due, or made no comment, or simply left names out that might ordinarily have been in. Conductors in particular received this treatment—Karl Rankle's name was nowhere to be seen when she discussed the *Salome* production, for instance. Yet she wasn't afraid to speak her mind when it mattered. She'd worked with Eugene Goossens in Australia in 1946 and more recently when she sang the title role in *Yerma* for the BBC in 1960. It's uncertain how much she knew about the infamous events that led to Goossens' sudden exit from Sydney but her feelings were clear:

Australia lost a conductor of the highest calibre and musical integrity when Gene was forced to leave. He had that very special gift of being able to build and create an orchestra. Knowledge and patience were the necessary adjuncts when he took over the Sydney Symphony Orchestra for the A.B.C. The unfortunate circumstances that brought about his dismissal were, without doubt, a cause of hastening his death. *Yerma* was the last opera this impeccable musician conducted. We lost a master musician, a builder of players and a conductor Australia could ill afford to be without.

She concentrated on the difficulties rather than the triumphs in relation to her own career. Key engagements marked the footsteps of her progress through the years and, though there was no hint of gossip, she dropped some impressive names—from conductors such as Wilhelm Furtwängler to celebrity artists such as Rudolf Nureyev and Julie Andrews.

Lolita was mentioned rarely but her presence was clearly invaluable. The lack of dressing-room facilities when Joan and Ivor performed at Parkhurst prison, for instance, proved a memorable challenge:

Lolita, who was as usual trying to ease our backstage discomforts by acting as table, chair and hallstand, even tested the floor in certain dubious places to see if it was safe to place anything on! Our cases became chairs, and Lolita had to hold my mirror as there was nowhere to put it.

But even Lolita couldn't improve the toilet situation: a bucket in the corner.

The final paragraphs of her action-filled story suggested that she'd come to terms with her enforced retirement:

> How true it is that when one door shuts another opens! The hinge of my next door creaked and grated for a time but it is now well oiled and has opened fully, on to a new world. I am back among old friends and new interests . . . I look at life with new vision. Thinking of the thousands of miles I have travelled and the interesting places I have visited, I realise that I have in fact lived in a cocoon, cramped by the exigencies of my profession. I saw the world through the restricted area of a small window in a jet airliner. Life has swished past me because every thought, nerve and muscle was used to sing, sing, sing . . .
>
> The very thing you love isolates you from all else. Nothing kills that love, but when the pressure is eased it becomes more temperate. It permits other facets of life to show themselves, and this brings about a change of values . . . I am learning the names of flowers, plants and shrubs, and pottering generally in the garden which surrounds our house . . . I can now give myself the luxury of listening for hours on end to my extensive collection of records . . . I can listen and go about my weeding at the same time . . .
>
> I am fit and life is full to the brim. Reading, writing and having endless discussions on all manner of subjects leave no time for idleness. I can swim, and play the odd game of golf. The strain

of a pressure existence has gone, and I can learn about anything and everything . . .

I have no regrets. I had a wonderful innings, and now I am having a second innings, more tranquil than the first, but equally full of the joy of discovery.

But there was a darker side. She said years later that she tried to block out her sorrow. 'I wanted to forget about it. I wanted to feel that it hadn't happened . . . For a year I think I can honestly say that I thought I would never, never, get well again.' Photographs taken around the time of her illness show a diminished woman. Gone was the handsome physique, the radiant energy. She looked middle aged, overweight and dowdy, a woman you wouldn't notice in the street. But slowly she'd regained full strength, and locked away her sorrows.

On 27 August 1969 at EMI House in London she was awarded a Golden Disc, a unique achievement for a classical singer. The disc celebrated her career—86 records under the EMI banner and sales of 'O my beloved father' passing the one million mark. It was a wonderful and deeply moving occasion. Photographs of the event show Joan to be fit and vibrant. She even had the confidence to wear a sleeveless dress, the scar on her left arm revealed for all to see. And why not? She was a new woman, enjoying a new life.

Her autobiography was published by Victor Gollancz, a high profile publisher whose list had included such authors as George Orwell, Daphne du Maurier and Kingsley Amis. Joan had her own ideas for the title but Gollancz called it *A Voice, A Life*. It was launched in London on 2 July 1970, and Joan promoted it with much vigour. There were radio and television interviews and 'meet the author' talks in major cities. Fans lapped it up. The book was immediately reprinted and entered the top ten best-seller list.

She was feted and praised in all manner of ways and returned to Australia with a great sense of achievement. There was another flurry of author talks and book signings in Sydney and Melbourne, and then there was time to relax.

> My days of sorrow, no more remembered,
> My health returning, shall dawn anew.

La Traviata, Verdi

The main entrance of 'Jumbunna'

When public duties were done, Joan and Lolita would race back to their idyll, their 'dream house secluded'. Essie *in situ* with the air conditioning running, a meal waiting and the swimming pool ready for two large ladies to leap in.

Joan and Lolita, and maybe Essie too, dispensed with bathers when at their most private in the pool. They splashed and swam and cavorted in their 'birthday suits', playing with their floating toys or swimming sedately up and down, classical music piped through from the stereo, drinks and nibbles ready on the side table.

'Jumbunna' was a house with a view of bushland stretching southward to the ocean. As the sun set, the blink of Aireys Inlet lighthouse would become apparent to the right, and the pinpoint glow of fishing boats and freighters would crisscross through the night. Kangaroos would travel their private paths, sometimes venturing on to the front lawn to graze until dawn, while wombats, rarely seen, would leave their calling cards. Cockatoos, parrots, rosellas and galahs would screech their calls as Joan went on her early morning walk with her two dogs: a black Labrador called Kim and a bitsa terrier with attitude called Sandy, both refugees from the lost dogs home. There was also a Siamese cat, passed on by a niece with a cat allergy.

Joan, Lolita and Essie weren't overly sociable but when they entertained they did so in style. It was at these kinds of occasions that friends and relatives saw the other side of Joan—or at least *some* friends and relatives. Burtta Cheney and Alison Searle were part of Joan's inner circle. One of the things that struck Burtta was that Joan could hold her alcohol: 'She could drink anyone under the table!'—except Lolita:

It was a magnificent home. And Lolita made it a home, believe me, it could have been a museum, because it had all these wonderful things. Books to begin with. When you came in there was this big area, the bar was there, beautiful woodwork . . . Joan's bar. She'd get behind the bar and heaven help you what you got to drink! She used to love to have people a little bit more than they should have I think. She had trouble with me because I didn't drink.

. . . We'd be asked to lunch [for] 12.30. So at half past twelve we'd drive around the bedroom wing and the swimming

pool wing, round to the front and park over there, and come
in. Now we'd see Joan in her room (usually) as we came past,
blinds all open, and about quarter past one Joan would emerge.
She never came to greet you or anything like that. You know,
when she was ready she would come to meet us. But she was
good then, she saw to your drinks and saw you had everything.
Essie would come out and say 'Lunch is ready when you are
Joan'—'Yes, alright Essie. Would you like another drink?' Half an
hour later she'd say to Essie 'Oh we'll come to lunch now'.

. . . Joan could act the giddy-ox like nobody's business—but
only in certain company . . . She'd collect hats and scarves and
things and come out and play Carmen Miranda or something—
she was a great actress—but that was all in private company.
You never saw her put a foot out of step in any direction, either
she or Lolita—but get them behind closed doors!

On very rare occasions there'd be mixed naked bathing—though not
the orgiastic kind, not by any stretch of the imagination. There was
an unabashed quality about Joan and Lolita's approach to nakedness;
it was natural, uncomplicated.

Lolita's nephew, Stephen Marriott, was in his mid-twenties by the
time 'Jumbunna' was built. His memories confirm that Joan and his
aunt were very different when in private:

Joan was no prude. They liked their drink, quality drink and lots
of it, and could hold it . . . Down at Jumbunna, when we'd go
down, after lunch there'd be—you jumped in the pool—and you'd
have naked water-polo. Joan, starkers there,—and Joan would
always take me to the deep end . . . and she'd have no hesitation—
while Lolita walked around, Aunt with her big breasts (and me
thinking: I'm not sure I like this!) approaching me at the side of
the pool saying 'Have another champagne dear!'—and this is just

David McLeish, Stephen Marriott and Joan

before Joan would—since the volley ball would be coming our side—push me under the water Ahh!—then throw it back to my sister and her husband to get . . . They needed to be seen publicly as sober citizens, but when it came to their own world—it was a very lively one.

Miranda McLeish, Stephen's sister, remembers drinking champagne out of Waterford glasses while bobbing around in the pool, a glass sometimes falling to the bottom. She doesn't recall swimming naked, but then it was difficult to recall anything at all: 'The good fun thing about being with them was that you'd be drunk!' Conversation with JoLo was always interesting and lively but memories of what was discussed invariably dissipated into a haze: 'JoLo pulled up very well the morning after, unlike everyone else.' Miranda and her husband saw JoLo quite frequently initially, but when they had children things changed: 'They were quite happy to see me and David but not the children. Which was fair enough, they just had a blanket rule, no kids around . . . I took new baby there once thinking that a non-moving baby would be acceptable but really it wasn't.'

Lolita said that children upset the dogs. Joan and Lolita weren't keen on children, that's clear, but the blanket rule may have had something to do with safety. Sandy, the bitsa terrier with attitude, was known to bite.

Joan, Lolita and sometimes Essie went up to Melbourne to see a show or lunch with friends and it was through this activity that they met a young man called Peter Burch. Peter worked at the Comedy Theatre as the assistant manager and one evening he noticed three distinctive ladies enter the foyer. He'd been an opera buff since a boy in Bendigo and immediately recognised Joan Hammond. He told the box office to give them complimentary tickets and when the trio sought him out to thank him he invited them to interval drinks. It was a hot summer and the theatre didn't have air conditioning and by the time interval came around Essie wasn't feeling too well. They said they'd better not stay—but Peter suggested that Essie sit by the big fan in his office while Joan and Lolita saw the rest of the play (Googie Withers in *Plaza Suite*). Peter says they were very appreciative afterwards:

Joan said they were going up to Sydney shortly for a couple of weeks to be on their boat *Pankina*—'When we get back we'll catch up, we'll be in touch.' Well I thought that's sweet but I'm sure they won't. Sure enough, about ten days later I get a postcard from 'the girls' saying we're out here and thanks for looking after Essie— the three of them signed it: JoLoEss. They used to sign everything JoLoEss. Sure enough we had lunch together at Florentino. All the staff there knew them and adored them. We sat at 'Joan's table'—when you walk into the inside room there's a window over

'JoLoEs'

Bourke Street and the table in the middle of that window is where Joan, Lolita and Essie were put. And in those days, over the road from Florentino, on the corner of Bourke and Exhibition Street, there was the Mickey Powell Dancing School and (being on the same level) you could look over and see silent Tango lessons and Waltzes—it was so funny, like your own floor show!

Retirement in its most tranquil sense was short lived. Formal requests and invitations arrived almost daily asking Joan to make a speech, give an interview, become a member, give advice, become a patron, adjudicate, support a cause, attend a performance, join a committee, give a prize. Many requests were declined, but then Peter Burch arrived with a proposal that interested her greatly. The Victorian Opera Company (mainly amateur) and Ballet Victoria (mainly professional), had received funding from the newly formed Australian Council for the Arts for a joint administrator, and Peter had been approached to take the job. It was an enormous undertaking and he felt reluctant to accept without some kind of backup. He went to see Joan:

> She indicated that she had been approached by the Victorian Opera Company a couple of years before to be its patron and she very strongly felt that it was time for there to be a properly established, Melbourne based, opera company—a small company—that would do work that essentially complemented the Elizabethan Trust Opera Company . . . she said 'Don't worry, you have my absolute support' . . . Socially, politically, newsworthy, at every level, she was just a fantastic icon to have attached to the company. So I took that on; and we then went on through the delicate and tedious process, over about eighteen months, to persuade the committee that ran the company at that stage . . . that they needed an independent board that was not their friends and relations . . .

An Advisory Board was assembled with Joan as a member and Alfred Ruskin as chair. Progress was slow but positive as the foundations for a professional opera company were laid:

> We set out to find a Music Director. I'd seen Richard Divall up in Sydney, and Joan had encountered him in Queensland . . . We both very strongly felt that he would be a good person for a couple of years. Joan at this stage was in hospital, making one of her frequent visits to hospital for surgery and, as I recall, at the Mercy Hospital at the same time Bob Menzies was there for something and Dick Casey [Governor-General of Australia 1965–69]. And the three of them were on the one floor, so they all had whatever they had to have first thing in the morning, then

they would all zoom in to one or other of their rooms and spend
the day yarning about old times . . . You'd never know who'd
be in the room with her or whose room she'd be in. It was just
fantastic. She wrote this letter to the Board that essentially said:
'This is what you should do, this is where you should go, you
need this sort of person'—and all that stuff. Of course we adopted
all that . . .

Joan had met the young conductor, Richard Divall, when she went
to Brisbane to give a series of master classes for the newly formed
Queensland Opera Company in 1971. Richard was the Music Director
in training. He recalls:

When Joan came up [to Brisbane] there was one tenor but he was
a bit slow and so she had to—she wanted things to be done with
the tenor, and as I had done a lot of singing in Sydney, I'd sung
about 30 solo roles in opera, and a lot of chorus work—she said
'Well Richard, you'll sing for us.' So there was I, in the end, singing
Cavaradossi, the most under-voiced Cavaradossi—and young, I was
only 25 I think—to Joan's Tosca! Well, it was sort of a bit of overkill
on her part and extreme under-kill on mine! 'Underwhelming
experience' I think Peter Burch would have described it as, my
singing. But we got on really well. And she was just such a magnetic
operatic presence that she carried you along with her.

Joan was a good, sensitive and highly entertaining teacher and her
master classes were a success. She was impressed with the potential
of some of the singers but appalled by their lack of future prospects,
their lack of adequate training, their lack of opportunity to see top
artists at work—and she said so publicly. She told one reporter that
Queensland was a cultural desert, and accused the state government
of being apathetic with regard to funding and organisation. Indeed

none of the states impressed her as far as support for the arts and artists was concerned. She saw it as her responsibility to agitate for improvements—and agitate she did.

IN THE EARLY 1970S Joan was in and out of the spotlight, part reclusive and part celebrity. There'd sometimes be a master class, and sporadic feature articles on 'the diva at Jumbunna' with photographs showing Joan and sometimes Lolita at home in 'Joan's house' (the assumption of Joan's ownership now firmly established). Essie's presence wasn't acknowledged in such articles. She was, however, loved by members of Joan's inner circle. Alison Searle, who lived at nearby Anglesea, became a close friend and would stay with Essie at 'Jumbunna' when Joan and Lolita made their almost annual trips to Europe—for holidays but also for Joan to give master classes.

Honours continued to come. The newly named and reconstituted Australian Opera Company (formerly ETOC) made Joan an Honorary Life Member, along with Dr Coombs and Gertrude Johnson—each for their contribution to the development of opera in Australia. Joan was delighted but it didn't stop her from openly criticising the unsuitability of the company's new home: Sydney Opera House was still under construction and still controversial.

She celebrated her sixtieth birthday in London by having a party at her club, The Belfry. Halfway through the evening she popped across to the Strand for the opening of the new New South Wales House, a function that was attended by the Queen, who shook her hand and wished her a happy birthday, then she popped back to her party again.

Royalty had not been blind to her achievements for she received the Companion of the Order of St Michael and St George the same year, 1972. It was extremely rare for a female to receive the CMG so it was a distinct honour. The Order's motto is *Auspicium melioris ævi*—'Token of a better age'. So perhaps it was with this in mind that a brand new Rolls-Royce took up residence next to Joan's 1956 model in 'Jumbunna's' garage. Its numberplate JOL 010.

Yet 1972 had its sad aspects. It was the year Joan's mother died. The Hammond siblings had bought Hilda a flat in Double Bay after Samuel's death but her final months were spent in a nursing home. Essie's mother also died that year. It was the end of an era.

THE TIMES WERE A-CHANGING. Innovative reforms began to influence all areas, including the arts. A new wave of thinking and doing began to flush out the old and bring in the 'alternative', or at least try to. Joan was asked to serve on three boards to this end: the newly formed Victorian Council of the Arts, which advised the Victorian Government's Minister for the Arts; the new Victorian College of the Arts, brainchild of sculptor Lenton Parr and in the process of establishing its School of Music; and the new Opera Panel set up by the Australian Council for the Arts as a think-tank for the future of opera in Australia.

The vigorous and sometimes overheated chairman of the Opera Panel was Joan's old friend, Ronald Dowd, the tenor. Another friend, Stephen Hall, and a new acquaintance, Moffatt Oxenbould, were often at meetings as they were both on the directorial/managerial team running Australian Opera. The purpose of the panel was to discuss strategies that would address the problems faced by regional opera companies: how to create steady employment for artists and technicians, how to bring opera to more people. These, and other pressing issues relating to budget, casting, standard and repertoire were the major concerns of Joan's other commitment, the Victorian Opera Company (VOC).

Joan had strong opinions and a wealth of experience to draw upon, but her knowledge came from a singer's point of view, and an old-style way of doing things. In Joan's day it was usually an entrepreneur who called the shots. The younger generation of practitioners, the managers and music directors employed to run government funded companies, saw the problems and solutions from a different point of view. There was respect on both sides within the boardroom, but both sides tended to believe that they knew better.

Old-style or no, Joan was invited to become the Artistic Director of the Victorian Opera Company in 1971. It was an advisory rather than leadership role so she had influence rather than power. She helped to raise standards and she supported Richard Divall in every way she could. Richard remembers that:

> [She] was very happy to see both older [e.g. Baroque] works done—works that we could afford to perform, and also contemporary works . . . She was right behind the schools' company, and doing alternative repertoire and country touring. She was a good thinking person, she tried to create employment for people . . . She just gave as best she could. So her influence, whilst it may not have seemed great, just on an historic level, was actually quite strong . . . not on an administrative level though.

She had a narrow-minded approach to economic management. The key word was frugality: work within an overly tight budget and spend as little as possible. This was realistic in one sense—the VOC's financial situation was always precarious—but it was restrictive artistically. Times and tastes had changed and the cheaper option wasn't necessarily the best. Her advice was respected but it didn't mean that things were done her way; nor did she expect them to be.

A good team effort produced positive progress. The VOC began to build a loyal audience by presenting an alternative repertoire that complemented the Australian Opera's Melbourne seasons; it also brought opera to schools and country areas and produced new works by Australian composers. Some federal and state funding was procured, the latter through the particular support of Rupert Hamer (state premier from 1972 to 1981).

There was a great deal to do, so the idea of 'tranquil retirement' became less and less of a reality.

PETER BURCH AND RICHARD DIVALL were 'adopted' by Joan, Lolita and Essie to the extent that they shared Christmases together at 'Jumbunna'. These were highly festive occasions where the food, drink and music flowed freely. Richard would play the piano and they'd have a somewhat raucous singalong. Sometimes Joan would offer a full-blown aria, just for the pure love of singing, and there'd be no doubt that her voice was as beautiful as ever.

A strong bond was formed between Joan, Richard and Peter—so Peter was shocked when Joan suddenly cut the friendship. He'd decided to leave the VOC to work full-time with Ballet Victoria:

> She was furious and for about three years she would not speak to me. Just wouldn't talk. And of course we would see each other constantly at performances and there would be this half frozen smile—if you got to that . . . Lol would come up and talk to me and Joan would [stay back].

Then one evening during the interval of an opera performance Peter felt a presence behind him and turned to see her standing there, looking uncomfortable but wanting to speak. She apologised for her 'inaccessibility' and hoped that they could resume their friendship. It was, in effect, an apology; she'd got it wrong.

> And for Joan that would have been an absolutely cataclysmic admission, because she was not someone who was used to putting

herself in that situation. So I walked around from the seat
I was in and we hugged each other. And then off she went and
things—[snap] just like that—resumed. As though it had never
happened.

Joan tried to do everything for the 'greater good' but her approach
could be misguided. Her shortcoming was that she saw things as either
'right' or 'wrong', black or white. Her very high standards in terms of
dedication, self-discipline—the striving for perfection—could obscure
her understanding of someone else's needs or motives. Lolita could see
the grey areas, the broader picture, so she often acted as intermediary
or rescue agent, mopping up in Joan's wake. It was a role she'd always
played, and would continue to play as Joan's second career as mentor
and teacher took shape.

IT HAD BEEN ten years since Joan had sung in public or made a
recording, but EMI still felt she was a sellable artist for they brought
out a new LP under the HMV Treasury series. It was called *Joan
Hammond—An Anthology of Unpublished Recordings* and featured
ten works, arias and songs that she'd recorded between 1946 and
1964 but rejected for reasons of quality. EMI's engineers had managed
to fix some of the technical faults and though Joan's appraisal of her
performance was still harsh she was amenable to publication.

It was a fortuitous (or canny) piece of timing in terms of publicity,
for Joan received yet another honour from the Queen the same year
(1974). She would have liked to have travelled to London to receive
it—and promote the LP—but for the first time in a long while she was
feeling the pinch financially. Inflation was very high and the economic
situation troublesome, so much so that even Lolita's income was on
the slide. Yet life was good:

Private Bag 101,
Geelong P.O.,
Victoria, 3220
17th August, 1974.

Dear John and Ian,

Your delightful congratulatory letter gave me immense pleasure.
I send you both my warmest and most appreciative thanks. I shall
never become accustomed to my new title! And you can imagine
how my pals tease me!

The teasing came in many forms but the most frequent was the singing
of a well-known song from *South Pacific*:

There is nothin' like a dame,
Nothin' in the world,
There is nothin' you can name
That is anythin' like a dame!

Joan was the first Australian singer to be made a Dame of the British
Empire since Nellie Melba. She told people to 'call me Joan' but
there's no doubt she wore the title with much pride. Everyone made
the adjustment very quickly. It was Dame Joan who gave an interview,
Dame Joan who attended a function and Dame Joan who parked
her Roller outside the Geelong post office. 'There goes Dame Joan',
they'd say, 'the famous soprano', and girls and boys and men and
women would watch her pass as if she were royalty.

CHAPTER 8

MASTER TEACHER

THE GENERAL PUBLIC had the chance to enjoy some of Joan's expertise when a series of master classes was televised by the ABC. It was obvious from these classes that a master, albeit of the old-style, was at work. She could think on her feet, entertain, put a singer at ease—and squeeze an extra 'something' out of each performer in terms of voice and interpretation. She had the ability to reveal what was going on within a scene, song or aria on many levels, both for the singers and the audience, and the general public found it fascinating.

Teaching began to take up more of her time. The School of Music at the Victorian College of the Arts (VCA) began life in the old Police Depot on St Kilda Road. The three-level building had 'character', sometimes enhanced by the whiff of horse manure drifting across from the police stables nearby. Police cadets had trained there since 1926 and the well-worn feel of the place, with the quadrangle behind, was a reminder of activities past. Boys in blue with polished boots and straight backs were replaced by music students with unruly hair, tatty jeans, and 'make music not war' attitudes.

John Hopkins, Dean of Music, invited Joan to coach a small number of singing students in the mid-1970s, and the 'small number' steadily increased. An Englishman, he treated her with old-style gentlemanly charm, and there was mutual respect. She joined the full-time staff as 'Master Teacher in Voice' in 1978, the title later adjusted to Head of Vocal Studies. She'd found her new niche, her second career.

Discipline and dedication was paramount. Those who worked hard were rewarded with more hard work. She could seem intimidating at first, but those who truly wanted to succeed soon learnt to appreciate her manner and methods. They recognised that she was a teacher of great calibre and drive, and that she was on their side. There were detractors of course: she could be very prickly if rubbed up the wrong way, and she was especially tough on colleagues if she thought they were lacking in ability. Brian Hansford, the only other full-time voice teacher, had to suffer her dismissive attitude, though in hindsight he grudgingly saw that her constant pushing did him some good. She was tough but kind, strict but sensitive, and extraordinarily keen to do the best for her students.

She was critical about the structure of the music course because she felt it had been designed to suit instrumentalists rather than singers. She fought long and hard to reshape the vocal studies course so that essential elements took precedence over non-essential or overly academic elements. She wanted languages and movement to replace the study of advanced music theory, for instance. As she said to her friend Lenton Parr, in his capacity as Director of the VCA: 'An opera house isn't interested in whether a singer can recognise a dominant 7th or augmented 4th; and an agent will say "good voice, but can they *move?*"'

Her approach was ultra practical: vocal technique was the core but the creation of an all-round performer with high standards was the goal. She eventually managed to introduce movement, fencing and dancing to the course; and she made it her business to find the best teachers available—practitioners with professional experience.

Joan described her work at the VCA in an interview with Pamela

Ruskin. It is quoted at length for it sums up the philosophy she pursued over the next fifteen years. Pamela began her article by describing the master class she'd attended:

It doesn't take much imagination to understand that these master classes are an ordeal for a young singer who must stand up before an audience and sing, knowing that he or she is doing so under a critical and expert eye and ear.

Dame Joan will stop a student several times, perhaps, while he is in full vocal flight and make him repeat a part of the aria until a fault is rectified.

She does this with consummate tact. She praises before she blames. She may laugh at some gaucherie or wrong technique— but always with the singer, never at the singer. She is careful never to destroy confidence . . .

In addition to the lessons she gives to her own pupils, Dame Joan holds Tuesday and Thursday afternoon classes in which all singing students come to her, "bringing me whatever music they like. We go through it, and then they perform this at the regular Tuesday night master class which is, of course, only for students and not open to the public . . . I teach them a certain amount of acting, which is necessary for singing arias. They need to know the old myths which no longer seem to be taught in the schools. Many operas have a background in mythology.

I teach them posture; how to take applause; how to acknowledge their accompanist and general stage behaviour. I also teach them all about agents and contracts; what to eat and what not to eat when travelling; how to find their way about a strange city; correct behaviour towards concert managements and theatre management; something about lighting.

In fact I teach them everything that is involved in their lives as singers appearing before the public—all the things that were not, alas, taught to students when I was young. This, of course, in addition to the actual voice training.

Those who have a weakness of intonation must learn to sing unaccompanied; so, in order that no student feels singled out, I make them all do it. There are all kinds of minor details. I teach them, for instance, how to use fans as part of their general stage deportment. . . . [A few students have definite potential but this raises a particular concern] These students need to try their voices in a theatre . . . The Grant Street [studio] Theatre is too small and is unsuitable in many ways. There won't be a proper one built for the college for many years. I find this very disappointing."

. . . At her suggestion, pupils are now getting German and Italian lessons from teachers whose native languages these are . . . She also corrects pronunciation in the actual singing.

The basics of singing teaching are very important. "Scales are essential, and also correct breathing," says Dame Joan very firmly indeed—looking quite fierce. "I teach them to speak forward, not in the back of the throat. Good diction is vital and it is not always very good in Australia. After all, there is a lot of dialogue in opera, and it must be heard."

Master classes in other States and lectures to the opera school of the National Theatre, which has now been taken over by the vocal studies department of the Victorian College of the Arts, are also part of Dame Joan's very busy life, allowing her only to spend two or three days including weekends at her lovely property at Airey's Inlet. She doesn't mind.

Another of Dame Joan's concerns as far as her students are concerned is the difficulty of them gaining actual stage or concert experience . . . It is very difficult to find places in The Australian Opera and other work is very limited . . . [She would like] "to see a chain of concerts organised in country areas so that students either graduating or in the last year of their course can get concert experience and learn what it is to face an audience. This will help them to get work when they have graduated. At the moment there is a hiatus.

They wonder now, 'What are we going to do when we graduate? How will we get started on a singing career?' A few have taken part in lunch-time concerts at the National Gallery, and lunch-time concerts are certainly part of the answer to the problem."

[Another of her concerns:] "The art of interpretation. Too many singers today study other singers' work from tapes and records and that's not a good thing. You can't substitute records for a live performance, and copying isn't art. You must allow your individuality to emerge. You must also eat well and live well. A big dramatic soprano must have a big frame. This business of producers telling singers to diet is all wrong. Callas is an example. Her voice went years ago. As a young singer she was a big barrel of a girl, but her voice was beautiful. Then she was told she must diet and now she can't put on weight. Her voice should be at its peak now, and it's gone."

Joan's advice to promising graduates was to test themselves overseas. 'There just isn't enough scope here or enough competition; and competition is still the best carrot to draw any artist to the top of the tree. An artist will never get to the top unless he or she can learn from every performance and every lesson.'

One of Joan's first students was Peter Coleman-Wright, baritone and pianist. He was prepared to put up with her less appealing ideas—the study of myths and the plays of Shakespeare, the reading of poetry out loud, the formal debates on current musical topics—because the overall benefit of her training was invaluable. Peter became one of her favourites but this didn't mean she gave him an easy time; far from it. She used to call him into her room and give him 'a good talking to' if he'd been playing up. And she'd suggest ways in which he could improve himself: his clothes, his posture, his drinking habits, his gentlemanly behaviour.

They became very close eventually, but in the beginning he found her intimidating:

> I was petrified. Petrified. She wasn't scary in the lesson but she really commanded respect. That perception people have of someone being a star when they walk into a room—she would have that, the way she held herself. That's daunting for a young innocent because you think you're just this little pleby thing, but she never made you feel bad or anything. She'd expect you to do your work, expect you to know your music.
>
> She would ask you what you wanted to work on . . . She usually used to let you get to the end, and then we'd go back and dissect it . . . The more I was in the room the more she would talk about other people's interpretation . . . You could always steer her away, if you didn't feel very prepared or—you could always ask her questions about when she did it with so-and-so and then she'd tell you a story. I used to love getting her on to those things. You could steer her pretty easily. She was susceptible to that . . .

He used to play piano for her when she taught other students: 'She knew that I was struggling for money, because all students always are, and she used to pay me out of her own purse. I didn't know that initially but I saw her do it once'. It was through accompanying that he began to tune into her sense of humour:

> If someone was boring us with an endless Bach cantata or something, she used to get out the lipstick. She'd turn, so only I could see, and she'd be putting on the lipstick and giving me this 'look'. She'd catch me out of the corner of her eye . . .

She was very naughty but I adored that quality in her.

We did a concert in Gippsland. She would go and talk to the audience and then we would sing a number, like a master class type situation but we would perform. And we were doing something and I had this terrible wind and I remember going into this room and letting out the most enormous fart—which echoed—and she heard it, everyone heard it. And she said—we were going to do something from *Butterfly*—she said, 'Well there you are, that must have been the cannon shot coming from *Madam Butterfly*!' Of course the entire audience went up. She was very quick like that, very intelligent. She enjoyed that—thought it was hilarious—I didn't get told off for that!

. . . I remember once saying to her something like how fantastic Joan Sutherland was. Sutherland was around that time and really coming on and much more famous than Joan of course: 'Well she was my understudy in *Aida*'—if she said that once I must have heard that story a thousand times! So obviously that sort of thing did get to her.

If you sang something that you weren't really ready for, or the repertoire was not right, she seldom said you shouldn't be singing this . . . She would often let people do very hard things, and often you would work out for yourself whether you weren't right for it . . . I think if you're an intelligent enough person you can learn how to get round most awkward corners and most technical problems. That's what she gave us. She made us use our head . . . It's funny because people comment about Cheryl [Barker, Peter's wife] and my technique, that we must have been given this incredible grounding by her, but I think that what she gave us was this real. . . *belief*—she taught us how to believe in ourselves—because if you don't believe in yourself you've got no chance . . . Over all the years Cheryl and I have been singing, we've never had to take time out, we've never had to go and fix our voices—touch wood.

Joan also had a number of private pupils. Most, like Cheryl Barker, sought her out specifically, but a few were talent spotted—or accosted because she felt their voices were in urgent need of help. One such was Heather Ross, a young woman with a big voice who happened to sing during a master class held at the Melba Conservatorium:

> I prepared something and went to this master class and this older lady walked in. She was strong—forthright with her directions . . . I thought I did really brilliantly—and afterwards Joan came and said: 'My dear, if you keep singing that way you will have no voice left—I'd like to teach you.' I looked at her nonplussed because in my ignorance I thought my voice was fabulous. She said, 'Come to me and if I've not changed the voice within six weeks then you go on the path that you're on.' And that was it. There was something about this woman that was so direct and clean in her approach that somewhere I knew that she was right.

Joan gave Heather nothing but vocal exercises for six weeks, and the quality of the voice improved. Her former teacher had encouraged Heather to push her voice to exploit its bigness, but Joan taught the opposite: 'She pulled it back and made it more like a road map—I could go anywhere with it. She used to say: "There must always be something left to give vocally. You must never sing to the point where there is nowhere for it still to travel." And that's true.'

Heather took lessons with Joan over the next five years. She was a young mother living on a small property near Geelong—a convenient stopping point for Joan and Lolita when they went back to Aireys Inlet for the weekend. Heather was short of money so Joan accepted payment 'in kind': bags of horse manure and lemons were loaded into the back of the Roller.

I remember once it had been raining and I'd collected the manure that day, forgetting that it was going straight into their boot. So they had this wet manure in a chaff bag all the way home— seeping into the carpet of the Rolls-Royce! They laughingly said later it took ages to get the smell out! Joan didn't mind, she was real.

Heather's professional career began well. She sang soubrette roles with the South Australian opera company but the dual demands of professional singing and motherhood eventually forced her into an either/or decision. She wrote a long letter to Joan to explain that her family must come first and the reply came that explanations weren't necessary. She understood and wished her well. Her attitude toward motherhood was that it was a full-time occupation, one that should not be combined with singing: Art is a jealous mistress.

Joan was as obsessive about her teaching as she'd been about her singing. She worked for altruistic reasons but her competitive nature wasn't far below the surface: she liked to see a protégé shine. Professional experience was the only way forward and she pushed to find a suitable opening for all her students. A letter of information, a timely phone call, an informal conversation where a name or names were brought to the attention of the right person. Not every student was a winner, of course, but Joan's success rate in terms of initial employment with future prospects was noticeably high.

Ex-students kept in touch and often sought her advice. When Peter Coleman-Wright left Australia to try his fortune in London Joan gave him many letters of introduction—which opened at least some doors:

When I was over there and things were going bad, and I wasn't ready, and I was getting many many rejection letters, it was her teaching of that inner strength that kept me going. And that's the

243

first thing I would thank her for. To be a performer you have to have an ego that can deal with the knocks and the heartache.

Joan had no need of academic qualifications but it was gratifying when the University of Western Australia awarded her an Honorary Doctorate of Music in 1979. The renowned Australian concert pianist, Eileen Joyce, received the same honour at the same ceremony. Men in colourful gowns and large caps proceeded through the stages of admission with dignity, celebrating two exceptional Australian musicians with speeches and music. When Joan's turn came she stood before the congregation while the Vice-Chancellor, Professor Robert Street, read a long and detailed oration which included a splendid quotation:

In advocating music and physical prowess for the training of the young, Plato was obviously thinking two thousand years ahead of his time to this occasion when he wrote: 'The person who best blends sports with music and applies them most suitably to the soul is the one whom we should most rightly pronounce to be the most perfect and harmonious musician . . .'

And when the ceremony was completed the learned gentlemen doffed their caps.

HER ENERGY FOR WORK was insatiable, though she did step down from her role as artistic director of the VOC (soon to become the Victorian State Opera). She retained her place on the board, however, and assisted Richard Divall in every way possible—even with conducting:

She taught me *Eugene Onegin* over a couple of days. We just sat down, and she would sing and I would sit and beat and she'd say no you've got to do this, this and this. She gave me a considerable input into *La Bohème*, the first Puccini that I did. But the best thing she ever taught me to do was how to conduct the opening bar to *Aida* — every conductor finds impossible. And she said, 'I've seen the greatest and the worst do it.' She said, 'Just look as though you're doing nothing' — which is a most extraordinary thing to do but if you just glide into it it just starts out . . . many other conductors have said to me, 'You started without a bump,' and I said, 'Joan Hammond taught me that.'

Lolita and Joan with Richard Divall

Len Hammond invited Joan and Lolita to his seventieth birthday party and of course they accepted. They flew into Sydney airport on the morning of the party and entered the arrivals lounge, Lolita three steps behind Joan as was her custom. Lolita's face betrayed nothing, though she knew what was to happen next. Rather than Len stepping forward to greet them it was a young man with a microphone and TV crew. He said: 'Dame Joan, it's my pleasure to say to you: Joan Hammond, *This is Your Life!*'

Shock translated to annoyance within a second. She darted a killing look at Lolita who responded with 'innocent' surprise. Annoyance gave way to a deep sigh then a gracious smile. What else could she do? A few hours later she was in a television studio dressed in an evening gown walking on to the *This is Your Life* set with her host, Roger Climpson. The studio audience, friends and relations who'd been in on the secret for many weeks, greeted her with warm applause as she stood on her mark ready to receive—she knew not who—in the process of the telling of the story of her life. Lolita must have believed that Joan, shy Joan with a heart condition, would be able to cope. Fortunately Lolita was right.

Joan listened intently to the voice-over that gave the clue as to who was standing behind the sliding white doors, and warmly embraced each person as they arrived. Tongue-tied, she hardly said a word, yet maintained her smile, her composure and her sense of humour throughout. Ironically, the most challenging moments came when she had to listen to her own voice—something she rarely did—and, worse still, watch herself singing on various TV clips of shows past. It was at these points that her face became concentrated and critical, almost to the point where she forgot where she was; otherwise things sailed along pleasantly. Full figured and dignified in her blue satin dress, she entered into the swing of things. It was just her eyebrows, twitching involuntarily, that betrayed some inner thought, some question or annoyance, never expressed. Overall she camouflaged her feelings supremely well.

The passing parade began with a pre-recorded segment from Dame Joan Sutherland: 'Your life story and career has been an inspiration to many of us.' Then came one of Joan's students, Patricia Wright, who was about to try her luck in London. Next came Noel and Len

Hammond, Noel showing his colours by revealing that he hadn't known that his sister could sing till he was press-ganged into attending a concert. Then came Joan's old friend, Odette Lefebvre, with her anecdote about them arriving for a golf tournament in a horse and cart. The pianist Frank Hutchens, elderly and lanky, folded his arms and smiled at the audience and said absolutely nothing which compelled Joan to fill the gap by saying how much she'd learnt from him and Lindley Evans when she toured with them in the early 1930s. Sir Charles Moses spoke eloquently and finished with a flourish: 'you're a very great Australian artist, and more importantly, a great Australian, and I think you're one of the nicest people I've ever known.' The golfer Norman Von Nida, the accompanist Gerald Moore, the TV producer Paddy Foyle all added their compliments, the latter two via pre-recorded message. Stefan Haag, the opera producer, caught Joan by surprise by kissing her hands, Viennese style, rather than on the cheek like everyone else, and he made her laugh when he said with obvious candour that 'she never did leave one in any doubt as to what her opinion was!'—especially when she didn't like the set. But then he listed many praises and finished by saying, 'I will always remember her as the most intelligent artist I have ever worked with.' Then came Neil Warren-Smith, Greg Dempsey, John Shaw and Ronald Dowd— larrikins all with a joke or two to tell. One of the biggest surprises was the arrival of Pauline Grant, the British choreographer. Petite and elegant, she spoke about the artistry and integrity that Joan had brought to the preparation of Salome's dance. Richard Divall spoke with great enthusiasm about her generosity, 'Joan and the girls put together and bought me a suit to go to London with,' so that he'd look presentable when he visited all the people she'd given him letters of introduction for. 'I adore you and I am as close to you as I am to my own mum.' Claire Primrose, a voice student who'd just won the ABC Vocal and Instrumental Competition, held Joan's hand and said with much tenderness, 'You're wonderful and it's a great privilege to

After the show

be learning from you.' Donald Smith took the floor with gusto and after heartfelt compliments told a story about the throat pellets Joan had given him that rescued his voice one evening. 'Lolly brought them round to my dressing room,' they looked like rat droppings but they did the trick. Then he rounded off proceedings by inviting everyone to join him 'in that well-known song from that great opera: "For She's a Jolly Good Fellow"'—and that is how the show concluded.

The emphasis was on Joan's achievements as a golfer, singer and teacher, which is perhaps why certain lifelong friends such as Bertie Lloyd didn't appear. But where was Lolita Marriott? And Essie Walker? Only those in the know would have made sense of the 'Lolly' reference made by Donald Smith, or 'the girls' referred to by Richard Divall. Lolita had been the key informant for the preparation of the programme: her suggestions and contacts provided the leads. She had every reason, as Joan's personal representative of many years, to make an appearance; but she chose not to. Perhaps Essie made the same decision—or wasn't asked.

The *This is Your Life* programme was broadcast in 1980. The response was full of praise, which must have pleased Lolita very much. But Joan didn't watch it.

THE SCHOOL OF MUSIC moved into a brand new building along-side the old one in 1981. Joan picked the room she wanted, as opposed to the one she was assigned, and made herself at home. The school was custom built but she was never entirely happy with the music studio (Room 109) where she gave her master classes. The size and shape was adequate but the beige brick walls had no windows. She wanted fresh air and natural light, elements conducive to wellbeing. She pushed to have a large window put in, but backed down when 'Admin' told her how expensive it would be. Extravagance within a lean budget was never Joan's way.

She celebrated her seventieth birthday in 1982. Various health issues presented a challenge, not least the onset of diabetes, but this was carefully managed with the help of Lolita and Essie. There was no reason to slow her pace or reduce her workload; quite the opposite. Everything had worked out for the best; but then Fate dealt a very cruel blow.

February 16, 1983 was a terribly hot day—and prophetically it happened to be Ash Wednesday. Bush fires were spreading across South Australia and Victoria. Even city people could smell the wood smoke and see flecks of ash floating through the air. Joan had heard the news reports.

I'd been up in Melbourne. I had lunch in Melbourne. It was a
terrible day; and Melbourne, it was black, the sky was black and
getting blacker. I was lunching with the director of the college,
we were talking about the future. Then we left and got back to
'Jumbunna'—the name of our home there, at Aireys Inlet—and
the wind was already pretty fierce. But we'd heard that the fire
was along at Lorne, it had gone over through the mountains
there above. And how fierce and dreadful it was. But it was not
mentioned that it was coming along the coast at all because the
wind hadn't changed. So—we just didn't give it a thought. And
then the phone went and it was our local doctor. He said you'll
have to go. I said go where? And he said you must leave the house.
And I said, 'John, what are you talking about?' He said, 'the fire,
the bush fire, it's coming along, it's coming very fast and you must
leave the house.' And it was in that moment that I went out into
the courtyard that I heard this terrible roar. It was frightening.
In fact I what I call 'froze'. It had only happened to me a couple
of times before . . . You think it's minutes but it's seconds.
And I then—of course I was galvanised into action. I called out,
shouted out: 'look we've got to leave, we've got to leave!'

They took the two cars, Joan and Essie in one and Lolita and the old
Labrador in the other (the bitsa terrier had died). Lolita grabbed a tin
of dog food as she went; otherwise they left with nothing. There was a
gathering point at Urquhart Bluff for just such an emergency, but the
police told everyone to keep moving up the coast as fast as possible.
The heat, wind and noise was terrifying. Fireballs bounced across the
road and dead birds fell from the sky. It was awful, unbelievable.
They spent the night in Geelong, having eventually found a motel
that would accept a dog. They knew things were bad but Joan in
particular could not believe that their house had gone—even when a
policeman told her so at a roadblock next day.

The weird thing about 'Jumbunna' was that the underground telephone line still gave a ringing tone when people phoned. People ringing
from overseas in particular heard the tone and assumed all was well.
Stranger still, the caretaker's cottage, just a few metres away, survived
the fire with barely a scorch mark. The windows had cracked and let
in a film of ash, but that was the extent of the damage.

Joan and Lolita returned three days later to see what they could
salvage, and asked Peter Burch to drive down and meet them there.
Peter never forgot the experience.

One of the really bizarre things, as you drove down and hit the
fire-stricken area, was that the little round reflector things on posts
by the road, they'd all been melted by the heat; they all looked like
Salvador Dali had done a job on them!

It was very difficult to find the house because there were none
of the usual identifiers . . .

I'd never seen the aftermath of a great fire before. It was
something revelatory. The lawn—the house had a lawn descending
down the hill and then picking up the bush. The lawn was all
still there. All the blades of grass were there, but they were burnt.
Completely burnt. But they maintained their form. So it was
like the green grass had become powder grey, and when you
stepped on it, it just floated away. It was like something mystical.
The house had been burnt to the ground. Excepting the roof
had—a sort of low pitched roof—the roof had burnt along each
spine, and then the weight of the tiles on the roof had flipped the
roof over. So there were lines of tiles that had all fallen off and
the thing turned over on itself, and then there was the charred
remains of the house lying on the ground. And inside the house,
which was raised slightly from the ground, there were concrete
pillars, lines and lines of them, holding up the floor bearings, and
there was nothing left except these pillars with a big bolt in them.

Floorboards totally gone, bearings totally gone. In the library, the whole library had just tumbled in on itself, and like the grass, you could see books, you could read the name on the spine of the book. If you put your hand in, to pick up the book, you'd pick up like half a cup of powder. It was so bizarre.

. . . Joan was beside herself, she spent the whole day crying. [She wasn't a cryer] so when she cried she was seriously crying! The day was spent doing things like—There was a fountain, you drove in and around this little fountain to the front door. The fountain had this mad tortoise in it. The fountain was full of shit and burnt stuff so we drained it by sucking the foul water out with hose pipes and so on, and there was the tortoise flapping around, alive and well! So we picked it up and took it down to the dam and it jumped into the water. Amazing.

The *Age* came down to take a photo. This had been pre-arranged; they'd contacted Lolita and she'd said yes of course—! Joan had been crying all day and when the photographer came I thought—she looks so distressed she can't have a photo of her taken like that. Just as the photographer arrived I told her a really funny joke and she laughed. It was a kind of circuit breaker and she sort of held on to herself then until he'd gone. So this picture taken of her with these rubber boots on and gardening gloves, because you couldn't touch anything really with your hands, there was broken and melted glass everywhere and all that. There's this picture of her sitting on the rim of the fountain with this half smile . . .

Lol was so practical. She was terribly distressed, she loved the house—they both, everyone loved the house. But she knew that it'd happened and that it had to be dealt with and it would be dealt with—and it would be dealt with *well*.

. . . I've no idea what the [ownership] arrangement was but I know that it wasn't fully insured. They had a sort of odd payout,

Lou

they had an insurance payout and a kind of government payout, some kind of grant, a modest grant I should say. They certainly got all the insurance they could get but it wasn't 100 per cent covered; nobody's house is usually.

Burtta Cheney and Alison Searle were also on hand to help with the aftermath. They lent the trio some clothes in the first instance, and helped to pick through the devastating mess—not that there was anything to salvage. Burtta remembers that 'the piano fell in one piece—and all that was left were the keys and the metal band that went right round the inside of it'. The filing cabinets might have saved some of the documentation except that they weren't locked—when the floor dropped the cabinets fell to the side and the drawers slid open. 'It was a magnificent library, not a very big room but lined with books . . . She had original works by various people . . . One of the most tragic things you'll ever see in all your life—because there was so much history there.'

Losses included many of her annotated music scores (including different coloured markings for the requirements of conductors like Sargent); her five-year diaries; two draft manuscripts (part two of her autobiography and a book about singing); her prized stamp collection; the parchment scroll that a prisoner at Parkhurst had made for her as a thank you for her concerts (exquisite calligraphy done by a forger). Butterfly's fan, Tosca's stick; two Aubrey Beardsley paintings; rare gramophone and tape recordings; jewellery; china; silver; antiques including a 1770 grandfather clock and a seventeenth-century optical painting on glass; an extensive wine collection; letters, photographs, film reels; there was even an original letter written by Robert Burns—a gift from an admirer. The list was endless and much of it was invaluable, irreplaceable. The trio had lived at 'Jumbunna' for fifteen years. Joan and Lolita had some possessions in the Toorak flat, but other than that every bit and piece had perished.

Possessions with meaning behind them had always been important to Joan, which is why she tended to travel with too much luggage. She needed her things around her; it helped to create a sense of security. Losing everything made her feel as if she'd lost her identity.

When interviewers asked her about the items she missed most she surprised them by saying her address book. This was true to an extent. She was appalled when she realised she didn't have any contact details for friends, especially those overseas. But the answer was also her way of dealing with the question. She couldn't bear to think of the things she'd lost.

Of course Lolita lost a great deal also. Her world was inextricably linked with Joan's but there were also Marriott heirlooms. Her grandfather had been a wood carver and art metal designer before the Hecla days and samples of his beautifully crafted work had been in the house.

And as for Essie—Essie lost everything she possessed. From recipe books and saucepans to her father's citations for bravery. The only significant item that didn't perish was her father's Victoria Cross. It was still in England on extended loan to a war museum. A solicitous relative who was aware of the financial losses suggested she sell the medal, and give a copy of it to the museum. Essie took up the suggestion and sold the VC through Christie's. It brought her $18 000.

Money, or rather cash flow, was a problem for the trio. A tightening of belts had begun in the mid-1970s, when *Pankina* was sold, and the situation hadn't improved. The financial failure of Hecla had cut Lolita's spending considerably and high inflation had affected them all. Joan had investments and a fairly modest salary, and Essie had independent but not lavish means. Lolita had various trusts connected to the family but much of her money was tied up in 'Jumbunna', and the value of that property was greatly reduced. The landscape in terms of regrowth wouldn't recover for years, but in any case they had no desire to rebuild. Lolita had hoped to recuperate some of her funds by subdividing and selling, but permission to subdivide was refused, so she held on. The insurance payout and bushfire relief fund cheques were certainly helpful, but the cost of replacing the practical necessities was high.

All three contributed financially to the establishment of their new home, though not necessarily equally. It was a complicated juggling system of lending, repaying and 'reassigning' amounts between them—worked out and managed by Lolita.

Lolita valiantly insisted on accentuating the positive. She mourned the losses but immediately thought about how to move on. Her handwritten letter to John Crisp in London, less than three months after Ash Wednesday, shows how quickly she achieved that goal:

8th May 1983 Please forgive scribble!
(03) 241 4535
46 Lansell Rd.,
Toorak 3142

Dearest John,

So sorry to have taken so long to write to you, but we've had the most traumatic experience which I'll tell you about when I've got more time—suffice to say we are lucky not to have been incinerated. We 3 got away in the RR & Volvo, plus dear Kim, the old Labrador, at 7.15 p.m. when the outside temp. was 110° at that hour! We heard Jumbunna blew up about 10–15 minutes later. It proved to be the saddest & most horrific day in Australia's history where disasters were concerned. It came like a bat out of hell!

Anyway, we are safe here at the above address where we came to, which is a small flat that I bought after my father died in 1967 which Joan has used during the week when doing her teaching

at the college, & as good luck would have it, she has been able
to buy a larger flat next door to mine (it has been vacant for
18 months) & we've had permission to cut a doorway in between
& so have quite a good area for us all. As well we have just
this week managed to find, & buy, a small house at Flinders on
Westernport Bay, which is about 1½ [hours] car's drive from the
flat (shorter than Jumbunna) & when we can get in there in early
June, Essie will settle in with poor Kim, & we'll get there for our
weekends, & get our relaxation this way. It's very small but who
cares! We lost absolutely everything, it was terribly devastating
but there was absolutely nothing we could do about it. It was
all hell let loose. Anyway, we'll expand on it some day to you &
give more detail. I think the photo of Joan is terribly brave taken
3 days later—she was thrilled to bits to get your C.G. [Covent
Garden square of] curtain! That was amazingly thoughtful of you,
& I know she'll be writing soon (there's between 600 & 1000
letters to acknowledge!) to you.—Our dearest love to you & Ian.
We knew you'd be shocked, but thank God Joan didn't have a
heart attack, & Essie didn't get another brain haemorrhage!

　　Much love—Lolita

The Flinders house required alterations and the purchase of every
conceivable household item—tables, lamps, bedding, corkscrew,
wheelbarrow, typewriter, towels, everything—and Lolita took on
the task. Essie and the elderly Labrador settled into 2 Bluff Avenue,
Flinders, by the end of 1983. It wasn't a particularly attractive house
but it had a garden and a fantastic view of the sea.

　　The trio treated themselves to a holiday in the new year and flew
to a resort in Fiji, having first organised their replacement passports.
They wore ridiculous T-shirts, drank ostentatious cocktails and lazed
beneath palm trees.

CHAPTER 9

FATE

THE CAMERA ZOOMED IN for a close-up. It was the first anniversary of Ash Wednesday and the ABC's TV news programme asked Joan to give an interview. She was forced to remember scenes she'd blocked from her memory and it threw her off balance. Her face tightened, her eyebrows twitched, and for a long time she didn't speak. Tears formed and dropped one by one. She couldn't control them—in fact she said to herself out loud, 'control . . . control,' but the tears kept forming and falling. The moment seemed to last for minutes. It was a deeply moving piece of television.

Letters of complaint appeared in the papers next day. Dame Joan, they said, had been cruelly exposed and exploited. Joan responded with a letter of her own. She said she wasn't ashamed of the distress she'd displayed but was disappointed that her message of thanks to charitable organisations hadn't got through: 'like a lot of interviews, so much was deleted which was of far greater importance than my somewhat over-exposed tears'.

THERE WAS A GREAT DEAL of thanking still to do: Ricordi publications sent a new set of operatic scores; EMI organised a replacement gold disc and produced a new double album: *The Art of Dame Joan Hammond*; the University of Western Australia sent a replacement doctorate and robes; an inmate of Parkhurst prison crafted a parchment scroll with the same wording as the original; and a great many people from all over the world sent memorabilia in the form of programmes, press cuttings and fond reminiscences.

It was heart-warming; but it wasn't the same.

Work was Joan's salvation. She hardly missed a lesson after the fire and performed all her duties with a steely determination. Lolita protected her from unwanted conversations about 'the fire' and continued to look after her needs in general. The careful management of diabetes was one of those needs. The correct amount of insulin was made ready for Joan to inject into her stomach each morning, and a balanced diet was packed into her lunchbox each day—complete with linen napkin and a tiny silver salt and pepper shaker. She also carried a gold toothpick.

When the college three-year contract came up for renewal she insisted on a salary increase. She said she'd been undervalued monetarily for a long time and wouldn't consider any offer under $35 000—a significant rise but not an exorbitant sum comparatively. She must have been confident or she'd never have placed herself in such an either/or position; she was, after all, several years past retirement age. The revised offer came in at $35 099.

She continued to be an enthusiastic supporter of the Victorian State Opera but reluctantly resigned from the board at the end of 1984. In her letter she cited the demands of work, but there was another reason. A rumour was circulating that her 'insider' influence gave her students an unfair advantage when auditioning for the company. She rejected the accusation absolutely, but felt duty-bound to step down. Her contribution to the company had been enormous so the

VSO's support group, the Victorian State Opera Foundation, decided to create a special award in her honour. The Dame Joan Hammond Award was given annually in recognition of outstanding long-term achievement in opera in Australia. There was an independent panel of judges, and a prestigious fundraising dinner where Joan 'opened the envelope' and named the winner. Moffatt Oxenbould was the inaugural recipient, a choice that pleased her enormously.

The Australian Opera invited her to join its advisory group and she accepted with enthusiasm. As ever, her passionate belief in the development and quality of opera in Australia drove her to send letters of opinion or suggestion to the AO, and the VSO, whenever she saw cause. Her intentions were noble but her input wasn't always welcomed. Her attitude toward financial matters and government funding could be simplistic, and her appreciation of director-driven productions was limited: they didn't honour the music. Yet she still had a great deal to offer, especially as an advocate for singers. Forthright yet courteous, her comments could be unwieldy, pontifical, productive or even prophetic. For instance, in a paper entitled 'My Utopian Vision' she hoped that the AO and The Australian Ballet would unite and be served by one dedicated orchestra. She believed that such an orchestra, with the 'right man put in charge', would prove an excellent asset (the Australian Opera and Ballet Orchestra came into being a decade later). She also suggested that a lottery would be a good system of fundraising, though she doubted that the Government would accept such a proposal given that it depended on gambling.

On a practical and less Utopian level she offered comments and questions regarding casting and programming. She might question, for instance, whether management had thought carefully enough about the blending of particular voices and the demands that an ambitious season might make on those voices. She believed there was financial wastage and excess within the AO and VSO and made helpful suggestions or pithy observations whenever she saw the need. Managements received her comments with varying degrees of interest, thanks, patience or downright irritation. Her saving grace was that she encouraged people's efforts, praised their successes, and acknowledged their achievements.

Her ideas about opera might have been dated, but she knew how to mould a singer. Moffatt Oxenbould made it his business to see Cheryl Barker perform with the South Australian opera company because Joan said she was one to watch. He added Cheryl's name to his list of 'possibles' as a consequence. By the mid-1980s there were several Hammond protégés working their way up the ranks. They included Christine Douglas, Christopher Bogg, Simon O'Loughlin, Dianne Pitt, Andrea Aitken, Claire Primrose, Patricia Wright, Christine Ferraro, Bill Bamford, Timothy Ahearn, Helen Adams—and Peter Coleman-Wright was gaining momentum in Britain. Students just beginning their training included Nicole Youl and Steve Davislim, both already showing signs of their potential.

Joan especially enjoyed working with young people—they kept her on her toes—and was pleased when they felt able to confide in her. Pleased and somewhat surprised, for they'd want to discuss questions that would have been unutterable in her youth. Love, sex, alcohol and drugs—they were matters that affected the emotions *and* the vocal chords. She'd never shied away from intimate issues where the voice was concerned; she'd been unabashed about discussing the effects of menstruation and the menopause in her autobiography, for instance. The questions students asked were so diverse that she used them for the basis of a 'question and answer' book for singers.

Here's an example of how the book was to work, using three of the most 'up front' questions; her answers are abridged.

Q: Is it unwise to have sex on the day of a performance?
A: Sexual pleasure affects people differently, experience will show

if you are energised for the evening or left lethargic; if in doubt go without—regret is useless when in the middle of a big aria!

Q: Could the contraceptive pill cause vocal problems?

A: Yes; any form of drug/medication can affect the muscles of the throat; if you notice changes in your voice then consult your doctor and discuss alternative methods of contraception.

Q: Does childbirth alter the voice?

A: Childbirth is unlikely to alter vocal production; the more pressing concern is the effect that marriage and children will have on one's career.

She diligently researched the questions she could not answer from personal experience. Whatever her answer, the theme remained the same: the dedicated singer puts his or her voice first, whether singing classical, musical, jazz or pop. The well-cared-for voice will endure.

THINGS BEGAN TO SETTLE down on the domestic front. The view and easy access to the sea made weekends at Flinders a true relaxation—and Joan established a vegetable garden.

Kim, the portly Labrador, succumbed to her great age and was put to rest. But another dog came into their lives almost immediately. They'd been concerned about an emaciated German Shepherd they'd seen tied up day after day with no shade and sometimes no water and clearly little food. They made the owner an offer he couldn't refuse and took the dog home. They called her Cindy, short for Cinderella, and Cindy brought enormous joy into their lives—and vice versa—she put on weight and the beach was her playground.

A trip to Europe was long overdue and they at last felt in a position to do something about it. They made their bookings well in advance but then the whole adventure seemed uncertain. Lolita's health was the problem: she had cancer.

It had all started a few years earlier with a mole, a tiny melanoma on her ankle. It was a small operation, but then there was another and another, each episode a little worse than before. She underwent a major procedure plus radiation treatment about five months before the holiday. It was a worrying time—and a reverse-role time. Joan found herself in the interesting position of supporting 'darling Lol' while looking after things on the domestic front at the flat.

Lolita made a good recovery and the holiday proceeded as planned: London, Vienna, Paris, Dublin. Joan kept account of the holiday in a 'Trip Book' and wrote her first entry as they waited to board the plane: '29/12/85: We are starting off, my travelling friend through life, Lolita, and me for London. Never before have I seen such a crowded airport here at Tullamarine . . . What a change!'

She found that travelling wasn't what it was—standards of service had slipped since the glory days—but the holiday was a success. They saw the sights, soaked up the culture and enjoyed some long lunches with friends. Joan had knee trouble, and it was more difficult to manage her diabetes, but otherwise all was well. They flew back to Melbourne without incident, thankful that they'd opted to fly first-class. The cost was enormous but they just couldn't bring themselves to forsake the extra comfort: they were too used to it.

Joan concluded her Trip Book with a brief description of the sale of 'Jumbunna', auctioned just a few days after their return. They drove down to Aireys Inlet with mixed emotions, and were pleased to find that friends such as Burtta and Alison were there to lend support. Joan hadn't been near the area for a long time; it was too depressing.

Black sooty tree trunks dominated the landscape but tufts of greenery showed signs of recovery. The auctioneer began his spiel, the bidders made their signals, the third and final call was made—and 'Jumbunna' was sold:

8/2/86: It is now off our hands—not perhaps the price we should
have liked but—I am relieved for darling Lol. It has been an
increasing worry . . . It was L's dream home for us & if the fire
[hadn't happened] . . . then it would have fetched a great sum
for the sale of that splendid home. As it is there was nothing but
the cottage & an acreage that can't be subdivided for 10 years.
L cannot wait that long—she would be 80 and I—83!

Her journal dwelt on the misfortunes that had befallen the trio at
'Jumbunna' and omitted to recall the good times. She even wondered
if God had meant them to stay in England, for so much seemed to
have gone wrong after their move to Australia. But then she reminded
herself that she was a fatalist: 'I know I must accept whatever the
future brings'. And she rounded off her feelings with a flourish: 'We
await the next move by FATE'.

JOAN AND LOLITA received an invitation from the Australian Opera
Auditions [fundraising] Committee to attend a function at the Royal
Sydney Golf Club. It was to be a grand dinner with the committee's
patron, the Hon. Justice Michael Kirby, presenting the speech. The
event was to be: 'A Tribute to Dame Joan Hammond'.

It was a fabulous evening. Friends, relatives and colleagues from
the opera and golfing worlds gathered together with congenial intent.
Michael Kirby had been a fan of Joan's since he was a boy so it was
with genuine and personal pleasure that he paid tribute: 'For me, she
was nothing less than the inspiration that kindled my love of music,
and especially song . . . I pressed my ear to the old gramophone in
my parents' home at Concord. I was then so proud that this world
artist was an Australian'. It was an eloquent, affectionate speech. He
outlined the highlights of Joan's career and he briefly acknowledged
the presence of Lolita, a courtesy not generally extended to a secretary/

companion. The event was interspersed with some of Joan's greatest hits, and recorded for radio broadcast. Joan was deeply touched.

Tributes and awards in one form or another continued to come her way over the next few years. Her fame had been eclipsed by the 'other Joan', Dame Joan Sutherland, but she was still recognised in her own right. She was the grande dame of opera; a 'living treasure' with a great deal still to offer.

MOST OF HER ENERGIES remained focused on the School of Music, though the 'winds of change' brought occasional discord. There was a new dean, then a new director, and various educational reforms altered the way the college was structured. Each change brought a new emphasis or direction and there were times when she felt that her position was under attack. She was generally highly respected, but there were pockets within the college that were dissatisfied with her idiosyncratic approach. She fought like a demon to hang on to her patch, her methods, her sense of what was best for the study of voice. She was no friend of the Course Advisory Committee, for instance — especially when it recommended that singing lessons be conducted in groups rather than one-on-one sessions. She resented what she saw as interference from 'above'. When things came to a head there was a stormy meeting and she walked out, the word 'resignation' on her lips. After some face-saving mediation she walked back in again, but not entirely on her own terms. She lost her three-year tenure and went onto a yearly contract.

She continued to give master classes every Thursday evening as part of her course, and made a point of offering her services to institutions further afield. She especially liked to give master classes when holidaying in Britain and engaged an agent in the UK to help manage the arrangements. Style was still the key in terms of public appearances: Dame Joan Hammond always arrived in a prestige car, her clothes impeccable, her jewellery sparkling, her smile warmly radiant. The master classes generated publicity, useful for record sales, and the fees helped to offset the great expense of the overseas trips.

The most prestigious of her overseas projects came in 1988 when she was contracted to present a series of master classes for the Royal Northern College of Music in Manchester. The classes were open to the public and filmed for a television series produced by Granada. The format proposed by the TV producers encouraged action rather than static singing. Two or three students would present a scene from an opera in costume with simple set (*Carmen*, *Tosca*, *Butterfly*, for example). Joan's job was to advise on all aspects. White haired, handsome, vigorous and straight backed, she fulfilled her role with gusto.

She would watch the whole scene through from the side of the stage then go into action. She advised, demonstrated, gestured, explained, dissected, cajoled, praised, encouraged and joked— switching her focus from singers to audience with consummate ease. Most extraordinary of all: she sang. Her voice achieved some lovely and unlovely tones but either way she didn't seem to care. She sang to demonstrate diction, phrasing, accentuation, tempo, use of breath, intensity, nuance—and she did so for both male and female roles. It was an impressive performance. Students and audience gained much from the experience, and Joan had a wonderful time.

It was a busy working holiday as she gave master classes in London as well; and of course Lolita supported from the wings all the while. Essie could have been in the wings too if she'd wanted. She had her tickets booked, but then changed her mind at the last minute. It was this somewhat frustrating aspect of Essie's personality that Joan and Lolita knew well. To outsiders Essie seemed a warm and docile woman, somewhat fey and always kind, but from Joan and Lolita's point of view she could be 'difficult'.

Perhaps it was this difficult aspect that prompted the building of a self-contained extension for Essie to live in at the Flinders house. Close living after spacious 'Jumbunna' may have highlighted what Lolita used to call 'Essie's drinking problem'.

Essie had been drinking heavily for years, but after the move to Flinders her reliance on whisky became more pronounced. Signs of forgetfulness or sloppiness were attributed to her drinking but the symptoms gradually grew worse. There was inertia, vagueness, falling, and the real danger that she'd start a fire in the kitchen (something she'd done once at 'Jumbunna'). A urinary infection took her to hospital when Joan and Lolita were still in Europe. They returned early and found her in a sorry state. She was diagnosed as having progressive cerebral atrophy, and assessed as needing full-time care.

Joan and Lolita discovered how difficult it was to find a room in a nursing home, even with the help of influential friends, but a place was eventually found in Melbourne. It was a sad, distressing time all round. At 72, Essie was the youngest of the three.

Adjustments were made. Lolita sold her Toorak flat, leaving them with Joan's flat, and a housekeeper was employed to look after things down at Flinders. Criticism came from some quarters that Essie had been bundled into a home with undue haste. Burtta and Alison wrote a stinging letter to this effect, citing Lolita as having 'wicked' intent. The accusation was fiercely refuted and a bitter exchange followed. It soured the friendship ever after. There seems to have been some truth in the feeling that Lolita wanted Essie and her problems out of the way. Even Stephen Marriott suspected that his aunt had undue influence over Essie's affairs—an influence not necessarily in Essie's best interests. But the fact remains that Essie was independently assessed and a nursing home recommended.

MATTERS OF HEALTH began to take more precedence as the decade drew to a close. Joan had chronic knee and back pain, the latter requiring at least two operations, and recovery was slow. Her diabetes was well monitored and the insulin dose raised to two injections per day.

Joan's health always seemed to take prominence: friends became used to the fact that Joan was regularly in hospital 'having something done'. Lolita, meanwhile, was continuing her fight with cancer. There was an operation to remove a lymph gland in her groin; then a couple of years later she was diagnosed with cancer of the colon. The treatment was successful though it left her with a colostomy bag. She had some tough times but her spirit was indomitable. She refused to be afraid of her cancer and took perverse pleasure in reassuring friends and relatives that there was nothing to be scared of or squeamish about. Stephen Marriott remembers visiting his aunt in hospital and being shown much more than he wished of the scar in the vicinity of her groin.

Bertie Lloyd, Joan's friend in Sydney, had a similar experience: 'Lolita said "I've got a colostomy bag, you must have a look at it, it's the most wonderful thing, never be worried about it" — and off come the drawers and she shows me the bag!'

HEALTH ISSUES WERE never far away but the duo's quality of life was generally good. They continued to drive, garden, walk the dog, travel—and enjoy a few holes of golf—the electric buggy a godsend. Activities that were cut back tended to be social, especially if they were in the evening. Joan refused an invitation to a special party from Peter Burch, for instance, but in a very charming way:

> I must confess to feeling too old to be participating and care
> and pity will be shown, in the nicest manner, of course, but
> nevertheless, I could prove to be a hindrance and put a damper
> on proceedings. Since that last fall my back has been giving

considerable trouble . . . a sad refusal . . . I do not include Lolita.
She would truly love to be with you all. Besides she is my junior
and her arms, legs and hands are working perfectly so she would,
or could be, the life of the party! I saw the look on her face
when I said that [I] would be refusing. Incredulity and a disbelief
showed clearly in her give-away eyes!

I leave it to you to make sure that she attends, in evening gown
and all. Mind you, she does not like dressing up, but for such an
occasion I am sure she will comply with pleasure.

Joan taught full-time until 1991 when she had another serious disagreement with the college. She resigned in a blaze of indignation; but
when the dust settled she returned to teach part-time. She also coached
privately and taught some students at the University of Melbourne's
Conservatorium. She was 79 and teaching at least thirty students each
week. Retirement was out of the question: work was life.

When she recorded a television interview for *Australian Biography*
she dug deep to recall the old stories. She showed herself to be
imperious yet warm, spirited yet sensitive. As the interview came to a
close she was asked to name the most important lesson she'd learnt in
life. Her reply came immediately: 'I *hope* it's humility.'

THERE WAS A big celebration when 'the two Dame Joans' appeared
on the same platform—not singing but definitely smiling. Joan presented the Dame Joan Hammond Award to Dame Joan Sutherland
at a gala dinner in Sydney. It was a night for the glitterati. One of the
highlights of the evening was Nick Enright's spirited rendition of his
own composition: 'A Ballad For Two Dames'. Here's a snippet:

Each had to leave her country to bring glory to her nation,
And it was from this city that the journeying commenced,

Each left at home the promise of an earlier vocation,
But the loss to golf and shorthand has been soundly recompensed.

Good Weekend magazine ran an article on Joan H and Joan S a couple of days before the gala. They sat together in row D of the stalls of the Sydney Opera House concert hall and chatted merrily as the cameraman clicked and the journalist listened. Lolita must have been in row C because her role in Joan's life was observed and duly recorded in the resulting article:

> Joan H grew up with three brothers but she never married.
> She spent her life instead with Lolita Marriott, 75, a protective,
> warm woman who resembles her. They met on the golf course in
> 1932 . . . [and] now live during the week in a Toorak apartment
> and, at the weekends, at their home in Flinders.

The subtext, for those who cared to think about it, was that Joan H had a gay relationship.

There was to be a special luncheon organised by the *Sunday Age* to celebrate Joan's eightieth birthday and for some reason she decided to use the occasion to thank Lolita for all she'd done over the years, something she'd never said in public before. Lolita tried to dissuade her, perhaps because she didn't want to encourage people's assumptions, but Joan was adamant.

She prepared her speech carefully as always, using prompt cards that provided the gist of what she wished to convey. She began with some jokes about her great age: her teeth, she was proud to say, were all her own, but she lamented her wrinkled neck, her lipstick running into rivulets, her varicose veins—and other discomforts that gave truth to the adage 'you're as old as your arteries'. Her anecdotes included the time when she had trouble camouflaging her laughter after singing 'Love and music', normally a very moving moment in

Tosca. A voice had called down from the gods: 'Now sing the other side of the record!' Her acknowledgement of Lolita came towards the end of her speech; and to finish she wanted to sing to an audience just one more time and had chosen a line from *The Birthday* (a poem by Christina Rossetti set to music by Hubert Parry): 'My heart is like a singing bird'.

The celebration luncheon was held in the ANZ Pavilion at the Victorian Arts Centre on the day of her birthday, Sunday 24 May 1992. One of the invited guests was Stephen Hall who'd first met the duo in the 1950s and who'd subsequently become administrator/ director with Australian Opera. He was happy to find that he'd been placed on the main table, sitting next to Lolita:

> I remember these three brief phrases when I arrived. Lolita said: 'hoped you'd come, thought you might, glad you did'—in that short staccato way of hers. For the first time, at the luncheon, Joan made reference to their relationship. Lolita grabbed my hand at one point and said 'I'm dreading this.' She said 'she's going to talk about us, it's the last thing I want her to do and I couldn't persuade her not to.' But in fact it was a very modest disclosure that said what a wonderful lifelong friend she had been, and how she would have been lost without her advice and friendship, and how she treasured their relationship. It was nothing more than that. But to them that was a mammoth disclosure.

And for friends and relatives listening it was a mammoth disclosure— and a statement that was interpreted in different ways. Some people heard it as a timely acknowledgement of a faithful friend, others heard it as a 'coming out' declaration. Either way it registered as a deeply moving moment. Everyone stood and applauded and many were moved to tears. It was an ovation for the *two of them*—an expression of love in recognition of their love. The ovation went on for so long that it became impossible for Joan to complete her speech. So she never did sing her one-line swan song.

Joan and Lolita's relationship resists definition to the last. Their gay friends saw them as a gay couple, as did some of their straight friends, but they themselves would have been appalled by a lesbian label. They'd been born into an era where people believed that sexuality (had the word been in common usage) was about sex. There was 'normal' sex and 'abnormal' sex and Joan and Lolita seemed to have shown little interest in either. In modern times it's been seen that the subtleties of inclination, and emotion, are more complex. Sexuality is full of subtleties. Joan and Lolita preferred the term 'friends' or 'companions' for their relationship. Whatever the term, suffice to say that it was meaningful, loving and lasting.

My heart is like a singing bird

The Birthday, Rossetti

There were marvellous celebrations throughout Joan's eightieth year. Special concerts and presentations were laid on in Australia and in Britain, where Joan and Lolita holidayed for several weeks. There were also two commemorative CDs: *The Art of Joan Hammond* produced by EMI Australia, and *Joan Hammond: A Celebration* by Testament, UK. Joan could hardly have wished for more.

Yet Joan did wish for more. She wrote to a friend: 'I feel I have a lot to do before my arteries get the better of me and time for Lolita is rushing by—the days are not long enough!' So they filled their days with what they loved best. Joan taught mid-week and then they'd go to Flinders for long weekends. They'd rise early and retire early. That was the pattern until one Saturday evening in June 1993 when the world forever changed.

Joan and Lolita had their bedrooms at either end of the Flinders house. Joan had retired for the evening when she heard a tap, tap, tapping somewhere, so she got up to investigate. The noise led to Lolita's room: she found her in bed, tapping an ornament against the side-table having been in too much pain to call for help. A few hours later she was in St Vincent's Private Hospital and two days later she underwent a massive operation. A perforated bowel and peritonitis were the cause of the problem: a toxic mix that had invaded her body. It seems likely that she'd had warning signs earlier in the day but ignored them, putting Joan's needs as ever before her own. Peter Burch responded to the alarm bells and took Joan to and from the hospital over the next couple of days. When he saw Lolita and listened to the medical staff he realised the prognosis was dire. Machines were keeping her alive. Yet Joan, constantly tearful, held on to hope. She wrote in her work diary the day after the operation: 'L. seemed a little better—still not gained consciousness'.

One of Joan and Lolita's closest friends was a nun called Sister Fabian. A retired matron, she'd been a key figure in the building and running of St Vincent's Private Hospital and still had a powerful influence there. She kept in touch and knew exactly what was happening to Lolita. She lived near the hospital and sent word to Joan and Peter to come for lunch after their morning visit. The two left St Vincent's and arrived at the house in a matter of minutes:

> We got there, and Joan got out of the car and Fabian was waiting at the gate. Fabian was older than Joan, quite a bit older I think. She had a ramrod back . . . Joan walked up to her in tears and Fabian put her arms around her. She said 'Joan'—and she had this wonderfully firm voice—'Joan, Lolita is with the Lord' . . . and Joan nearly dropped on her knees . . . it was an absolutely operatic level of distraction . . . I've never seen anyone so distressed.

Peter knew that Lolita's whole existence revolved around Joan, but from the way Joan spoke at that time it was as if it had been the other way round: 'I remember her saying to me that there was really no purpose in her life any more because everything she had ever done, every performance she had given, everything in her whole life was for Lolita. And now Lol wasn't there so what was the point of it.' She was inconsolable.

She couldn't even cope with sitting among the congregation at the funeral. While Peter gave the eulogy Joan sat in a side room with the door open.

A steady stream of letters and cards brought gentle words of condolence. Her printed letter of reply focused on the positive—all that was good and wonderful about her friend—but her handwritten additions revealed her state of mind: 'life is just devastation'.

Friends such as Peter, and Richard Divall, helped with food shopping and meals initially, and Len Hammond came to stay in the flat for a few days. All three noticed that she had no idea where things were kept in the kitchen; fortunately they knew how to cook.

Work was her consolation and she prepared for the new term starting in July. Her work diary began to show entries that had never been there before: payments to housekeepers, a gas bill, a leak to be fixed. She also drafted a letter to her solicitor: 'I shall not make excuses but suffice to say that I have been inundated with many things I know little about since the death of my friend . . . I have to make a new will and find out how I stand financially'.

But she must have known she was secure financially. Lolita's will directed most of her assets to Joan in the first instance, with relatives to inherit thereafter. Joan's will, made at the same time, mirrored that arrangement.

She was emotionally drained, but still said yes when the ABC's *7.30 Report* asked if she'd comment on the Victorian State Opera's financial problems. It was only days after Lolita's funeral but she felt it her duty

46 Lansell Road

TOORAK 3142

Victoria

Australia

31st July, 1993

John dear,

This is a very hard letter for me to write because my dearest friend, Lolita Marriott, died on 23 June 1993. I know that you will understand the depth of my feelings and how sad a task this is for me. *I am devastated.*

She was a wonderful, courageous person. She spread happiness and joy and created love and trust wherever she went.

Please do not acknowledge.

With every good wish

Love

Joan.

to speak. She gave praise and criticism in her usual forthright manner but unfortunately the praise was edited out when the interview was broadcast. Her good friend Sir Rupert (Dick) Hamer, chair of the VSO board, sent her an aggressively critical letter as a consequence. He drew her attention to the company's excellent artistic record, admonished her act of disloyalty, and ended with these words:

> After the temporary setback last year, the V.S.O. is bouncing back, and will continue to occupy an important niche in our cultural life. I would have expected you to feel proud of that, and glad of the opportunity afforded to some magnificent young Australian talent. Instead you have chosen to denigrate the Company publicly and ignore its achievement, and we all find that inexplicable.

His words were so harsh that she couldn't believe he'd written them, though his signature was clearly there. It was a tough thing to deal with, given her grief-stricken state.

Hamer's letter was dated 1 July but it was mid-August before she drafted her reply, a process assisted by Sheila Scotter, friend and socialite. Joan defended herself by explaining the bias of the TV editing and reiterated what she believed: the VSO must work within its means, and those responsible should be accountable—and step down. But she ended by drawing his attention to other matters:

> I am afraid that your letter was also very ill-timed for me. Lolita Marriott had died suddenly on 23rd June, 1993. Incredibly the VSO, the Company to which I remain most devoted and with which I am most closely associated in the public eye, was the only company not to send a letter of condolence or some token of regret. Forget your anger with me, Lolita was one of your oldest and most loyal supporters, and this dismissal of her memory is both unwelcome and unworthy.

She gathered herself together and carried on as best she could—
the same procedure as before: teaching, and then weekends down
at Flinders. Each day was a challenge because Lolita had done so
much. She'd soothed, bolstered, advised and of course managed every
practicality. Even her sharper memory was missed—Lol used to drop
the correct name into Joan's ear just as that person came forward to
greet her.

Joan and Len at the Golf Club luncheon

She reluctantly agreed to fulfil a long-held commitment to speak at
a special luncheon at the Royal Sydney Golf Club, but only after Len
and Monti persuaded her. She gave her speech with brave aplomb,
having asked beforehand that no one mention Lolita's name.

Ironically, the RSGC was the site of her last public appearance. In
early September she was at Flinders for the weekend having driven

down in the Roller. On the Saturday afternoon she walked the dog as usual, ate her meal and injected herself with her second dose of insulin. She retired early but did not rise next morning as usual. When the housekeeper went to see if Joan was all right she found her deeply unconscious. She was taken to hospital and revived, but it was clear that there'd been some brain damage. There was short-term memory loss and confusion. A mild stroke was suspected, but the cause was eventually tracked down to an insulin overdose (hypoglycaemia). She must have forgotten she'd already administered the second injection—or maybe misjudged the dose. A premeditated overdose seems extremely unlikely: Joan's religious faith and sheer determination wouldn't have allowed it.

Independence was no longer possible so she was transferred to a nursing home in Melbourne. She was hazy about the present moment but knew with absolute clarity that she wanted her life back. She wanted to go home, so much so that she became aggressive and even managed to escape a couple of times.

Few people settle into a nursing home easily, but Joan's distress seemed to be aggravated by the conditions. She would ring Len or Peter almost every day, crying and begging to be taken out of 'this terrible place'.

The 'terrible place' was a well-regarded nursing home managed by a woman who liked to be known as 'Sister' (or matron). Sister was obviously delighted to have such a high-profile resident in her establishment; but her delight didn't seem to be reflected in the quality of Joan's care. Joan had a single room, but there was barely space between bed and small wardrobe. She shared a bathroom with a man who kept locking the door against her; staff consistently called her 'love'; the food was repulsive; there was a persistent bad odour, and everything seemed grimy.

Monti Hammond and her daughter Aurora were so dissatisfied that they started looking for an alternative nursing home in Sydney. The task proved difficult because of long waiting lists but they eventually came across Kenilworth Gardens at Bowral in the Southern Highlands of New South Wales. It was lovely and there was a place available. They came back to Melbourne and prepared for the intended move, and that was when the proverbial hit the fan. Joan was suddenly in the middle of a custody battle. Monti picks up the story:

> Len rang up [from Sydney] and said 'I've just been told that the matron has applied to the Guardianship Board that Joan shouldn't be taken away!' They were having a hearing in the nursing home on the Sunday morning—and this was Saturday night. The only one of Joan's friends that I actually knew in Melbourne was Sheila Scotter—and Peter. I got Joan's address book and I rang everyone—could they come? Well it was amazing how many of them came.

The Guardianship Board assessed the best interests of someone in care and had the power to overrule a family's wishes. The hearing was held in the nursing home's dining room—bad odours and all. Joan wasn't in the room but Peter, Richard Divall and many of her friends were. It was a tense situation. The Sister/manager accused Len and Monti of having no regard for Joan whatsoever. She said the only reason they wanted her moved to New South Wales was to get their hands on her money. Monti couldn't believe her ears and burst into tears: 'Sheila Scotter was patting me on the shoulder, and everyone was carrying on. It was all very dramatic'.

Then it was decided to bring Joan into the hearing to see what she wanted. She looked vulnerable and confused when she was brought in, a confusion intensified by seeing a room full of friends—all seated as if they were some kind of audience. The man in charge of proceedings asked if she wished to remain where she was, and Joan, feeling that she needed to be polite, smiled graciously and said yes. Everyone on the Hammond side groaned inwardly. Fortunately the examiners decided to talk with her in a separate room and it was during this exchange that her fog of confusion lifted enough for her to say that she entrusted herself to her family's wishes absolutely—whatever they suggested she'd do. The Guardianship Board granted permission for Joan to be moved.

The transition was done with speed and style. Aurora told Joan they'd found a perfect place where she could finish writing her book about singing, and this immediately gave her a sense of purpose. They transported some of her own furniture and her typewriter so that familiar things would be there when she arrived. On the day of leaving they dressed her in her best and Peter drove them to the airport in her own Roller. They flew first-class, she was treated like royalty, and when they got to Sydney airport Len was waiting with a stretch limo ready to drive them to Bowral. The staff at Kenilworth Gardens had read Joan's autobiography, knew to call her Dame Joan, and even had her CD playing when she came through the main entrance. Joan was happier already.

And there's a coda to the story. Monti and Aurora were so dissatisfied with the Melbourne nursing home that they wrote to various government authorities to complain. Some time later there was an interesting development: 'Sheila Scotter rang me up one morning and said "Monti, you've done it!"—I said, "what have I done?" She said, "the matron's been arrested, she's been embezzling money, she owes the Health Department $450,000!"'

THERE WAS NO GOING BACK: Len sold the remainder of Joan's assets, even smaller possessions such as her jewellery. He thought it best to capitalise as he didn't want the nieces and nephews arguing over items when they eventually inherited. Unfortunately he proceeded with undue haste: some of those possessions were Lolita's, and the

Marriotts and Hammonds had to go through some legal wrangling before things were sorted out.

Joan settled into Kenilworth Gardens reasonably well. Her room was large and airy, she had familiar things around her, and there was a pleasant view of the garden. She became calmer and less confused. She had her own music, television, and the singing book manuscript waiting for her attention on her desk. She didn't progress with it but she did make copious notes about things that came into her head.

Work was Joan's central reason for being, so it must have been consoling to read a letter from Cheryl Barker who was working with the English National Opera in London. The letter was written before Cheryl heard about Joan's hospitalisation:

> In my dressing room at ENO during Boheme—since I get so much time off as Musetta!!! . . . Peter is also at ENO doing Tarquinius in the Rape of Lucretia, we have the same dressing room so leave little surprises for each other i.e. a packet of wine gums to chew on during the performance . . . I've been offered Madame Butterfly in Auckland next year. In Italian, so have accepted as a way of trying out the role. I was hoping that I could study the role with you when I come out to Melbourne in March next year—would that be O.K.? I've started working on it already—it's so daunting!! Peter and I think of you often & wonder how you are going. You mean so much to us and we love you very much.

Bowral was not the most convenient of places to get to, especially from Melbourne, so friends kept in touch as best they could. Joan could hold a conversation about things set in the past—though she might slip off to another time frame or place, then slip back again. Len came to see her once a week until he became too ill, and Bertie Lloyd visited quite regularly. Joan was pleased to see people and greeted them graciously, needing just a little prompting if they were people she didn't know so well. Her characteristics were unchanged and a certain mischievousness was still present. There was a memorable moment when her brother Tony arrived out of the blue. She'd not seen him for years and they'd never settled their differences. When he was brought to her room he found her snoozing in a chair. He sat with her, held her hand, spoke a little, but she snoozed on. Then he left. When a member of staff came in to see if everything was all right she opened her eyes and said: 'Has he gone?'

She went into a steady decline over the next couple of years. When Len died it fell to Monti to look after her wellbeing, a difficult task by mid-1996:

> Everybody came to me to make decisions. I went up [to Bowral]
> and they said to me 'The doctor has said that Joan has to have her
> leg amputated.' And I was horrified, but they showed it to me and
> it was black from thigh down, it was black. The doctor said to me
> 'If we take her leg off, she might die; if we don't take her leg off,
> she will definitely die. It will have to come off.' So I had to give
> them permission to do it.

So Joan had her right leg amputated at the local hospital. She recovered sufficiently to return to the nursing home but the decline was substantial over the next three months. She gave up.

In the final few weeks she was unable or unwilling to speak. Her face expressed little, though she would smile very occasionally. Heather, the student who'd paid for her lessons with lemons and manure, had a strong spiritual connection with her mentor. She sat with Joan over a few days and on the last day she played one of Joan's recordings. It seemed the right thing to do: to fill the room with that magnificent voice.

Bertie Lloyd spent the afternoon of 25 November with her old friend—they were the same age, 84. She comforted as best she could and as she stood to leave Joan smiled. It was the last farewell. She died in the early hours of the following morning.

> Remember me, remember me,
> but ah!—forget my fate.

Dido and Aeneas, Purcell

The funeral was held at St Thomas Aquinas church in Bowral. An adequate if not large gathering filled the pews: family, friends, artists, arts administrators, a couple of dignitaries and staff from the nursing home. Sunlight streamed in through the stained-glass windows and there was an aura of calm and beauty. The hymn singing was thin until Joan Carden put her emotions aside and floated a lovely descant to the heavens. When the coffin left for the cemetery the police provided an escort for the journey and stopped the traffic the whole way. People stood quietly as the procession passed by.

Media coverage was extensive. There were TV segments, and obituaries appeared around the world.

Had Lolita been alive she would probably have angled for a state funeral and a more prominent burial place. But Lolita was at rest in the family plot in Boroondara Cemetery in Kew, and as far as one can tell Joan never stipulated her plans for where she wished to be buried. Essie had died the year before, her ashes scattered on the river at Anglesea—Alison, Burtta and Stephen Marriott doing the honours.

On 17 December a 'Tribute to Dame Joan Hammond' was held at the Melbourne Concert Hall. An open invitation was issued and the auditorium was packed. Speakers included Moffatt Oxenbould, Jenifer Eddy, Lenton Parr, Nance Grant, Sheila Scotter, Leo Schofield, Frank van Straten, Peter Burch, Richard Divall and Aurora Hammond. The artists were Cheryl Barker, John Bolton-Wood, Joan Carden and David McSkimming. Images of Joan as golfer, singer, teacher and friend were portrayed on a large screen. It was an affectionate celebration of a life well lived. The ABC broadcast its recording of the event nationwide. And in Sydney, PLC Pymble held a memorial service to commemorate one of its own.

It was a good send-off.

The final task was to place the headstone: a block of black marble with gold lettering. Peter Burch had volunteered to manage the funeral arrangements months before, so it was due to his influence that the wording on the headstone appeared as it did—with the Hammond family's approval:

DAME JOAN HOOD HAMMOND
DBE CMG
24-5-1912—26-11-1996
LOVING COMPANION OF
LOLITA MARRIOTT

SINGER, SPORTSWOMAN, VOCAL TEACHER
A GREAT AUSTRALIAN

Controversial to some, a simple statement of fact to others, it stands in line with the other headstones: an unmistakable sign that an exceptional woman had lived, loved and achieved.

CODA: THAT WHICH REMAINS

Life is all about opposites: ups and downs—and I've had many of those throughout my career—laughter and tears. One needs the balance. We must expect to cry, occasionally, and we do that in private, with friends. But we can share the joy with everyone, each of us through our own special talents.

IN THE COUNTY of Buckinghamshire in England there is a forest of beech trees and on the edge of that forest there stands an oak tree. The oak tree was planted by Joan with due pomp and ceremony in 1977, a commemorative plaque at its base to honour her name. Its branches are alive with birds, its acorns provide food for squirrels, its canopy is gracious in all seasons. This is Joan's tree.

In the Visiting Artist Room in the School of Music at the Victorian College of the Arts there is a head and shoulders statue of Joan in bronze. She resides on a plinth in the corner and smiles broadly to all who enter. Her expression is keen, interested, encouraging—it's a strong presence. Down the stairs from the Visiting Artist Room one finds the music studios. The medium-sized recital studio is where she used to give her master classes. It lacks the window she always wanted but the beige brick wall now carries her name, a plaque declaring that this is the 'Joan Hammond Room'.

The old recordings, the 78s, the 45s, the LPs, they have re-emerged on shiny CDs—the quality is so refined that train spotters can sometimes detect the rumble of the Underground. Her signature arias appear on 'classic compilations'—box-sets packed with artists of the past and present—which is how a recent CD came to have the name Hammond alongside Barker.

Joan's words of wisdom still float into the consciousness of the singers she taught. Useful, calming or stern reminders will come to them: while waiting in the wings, or opening a new score, or pouring a glass of wine, or running up the scale with 'Noo Nah Noo Nah . . . Her influence will always be with them: in the quality of their work, in the example they set, and in the advice they give to others.

Joan's spirit lives on.

ENCORE:

Peter Coleman-Wright and Cheryl Barker: a 'Noo Nah' duet

PETER: She used to have this scale and I'll never forget it: Noo Nah Noo Nah Noo Nah Noooo. You had to always start with that. If you didn't have a voice that could cope with it, the oooo sound could get a bit problematic . . . She taught us perseverance, diligence, professionalism—

CHERYL: She was very commanding and quite royal in her demeanour, so at first I was a little bit frightened of her . . . I remember knocking on her door and going in to see her and saying 'I'm leaving the college of the arts' and she said 'That's very sad, yes I know.' And then I said 'I'm just wondering whether you'll consider teaching me [privately]' and she said 'Of course I will' . . . She was incredibly generous and wouldn't take any money for the lessons at all . . . And then I went to live in London and I'd ring her from time to time and say, 'I've been offered such and such a role, do you think I should do it?' And she'd say, 'I do' or whatever. I'll never forget just how kind she was and in a way how much faith she had in me.

PETER: By and large for the last twenty years I've never had a teacher. So I would have to say that those three years in that room with Joan gave me the basis of—'me'.

CHERYL: She was more into interpretation in a way—think about the situation, where you are . . . You felt that you were in the hands of a great performer.

PETER: I think she had one of those voices, which I lament now, that was completely personal. It had a real soul. So many voices now are stereotype . . . there was a big period of time when just about every American soprano sounded like the next one because they all had this similar technique. Joan was really individual, like Callas. You'd know immediately it was Joan Hammond. And the voice really, really, really went into your heart. I think as a tone you either loved it or you didn't, and that's what made her a really interesting performer . . . There are still things that I can hear her saying to me in my head. When I was at the Met—and also when I sang the Gunther just recently at Covent Garden—I always say: 'Joan, are you there? This is for you.' Cheryl does as well—

CHERYL: And there's a certain pleasure I took in being able to tell people in the UK that I'd studied with her, you know?—and people would come up to me and say, 'I remember hearing Joan Hammond singing on the end of the pier in Brighton . . . she would come out and she'd be dripping in jewellery and she would have the most beautiful exquisite frocks and just waft past.'

PETER: Talking about her now makes you realise how much you miss her.

CHERYL: Yes . . . She had a light, a glimmer in her eye . . . She'd lift her eyelids and her sparkly blue, keen sharp eyes would be underneath, you know, laughing.

PETER: We always say that we'd love her to suddenly open the door and walk in, don't we.

CHERYL: Yes, yes.

Cheryl Barker and Peter Coleman-Wright
in a scene from *Tosca*

SELECTED RECORDINGS

There are three CDs currently available, all on the Testament label:

Joan Hammond: A Celebration

SBT 1013. Released 1992.
Puccini *Gianni Schicchi*: O my beloved father 1941
Tosca: Love and music 1941
La bohème: Mimì's farewell 1941
Madama Butterfly: One fine day 1941
Manon Lescaut: In quelle trine morbide 1948
Massenet *Thais*: Ah! je suis seul 1951
Offenbach *Les Contes d'Hoffmann*: Elle a fui, la tourterelle 1952
Saint-Saëns *Etienne Marcel*: O beaux rêves évanouis 1955
Cilèa *Adriana Lecouvreur*: Troppò, signori 1949
Giordano *Andrea Chénier*: La mamma morta 1948
Catalani *La Wally*: Ebben? ne andrò lontana 1953
Verdi *Don Carlos*: Tu che le vanità 1952
Aida: Qui Radamès verrà! . . . O patria mia 1956
Tchaikovsky *Eugene Onegin*: Tatiana's Letter Scene 1943
Dvorak *Rusalka*: O silver moon 1952

Dame Joan Hammond By Request

SBT 1160. Released 1998.
Charpentier *Louise*: Act III—Depuis le jour 1942
Massenet *Hérodiade*: Act I—Celui dont la parole . . . Il est doux,
Il est bon 1950
Le Cid: Act III—De cet affreux combat . . . Pleurez! pleurez mes yeux 1951
Korngold *Die tote Stadt*: Act I—Glück, das mir verblieb 1953

Ponchielli *La Gioconda*: Act IV — Suicidio 1949
Verdi *Il trovatore*: Act I — Tacea la notte placida
Act IV — Timor di me? . . . D'amour sull' ali rosee 1955
La forza del destino: Act II — Son giunta! . . . Madre pietosa vergine 1949
Act IV — Pace, pace, mio Dio 1955
Otello: Act IV — Piangea cantando . . . O Salce! Salce! . . . Ave Maria 1952
Cilea *Adriana Lecouvreur*: Act IV — Poveri fiori 1953
Puccini *Manon Lescaut*: Act IV — Sola, perduta, abbandonata 1947
Suor Angelica: Dying thus without a mother's blessing 1955
Turandot: Act II — In questa reggia 1951

Dame Joan Hammond & Charles Craig sing Opera Arias & Duets

Selections from *La Bohème*, *Tosca*, *Madama Butterfly*, *Gianni Schicchi*,
Faust, *Il trovatore* and *Aida*. SBT 1153. Recorded 1956–1961,
CD released 1998.
The Testament web site is at www.testament.co.uk. An internet search will
show further selections, such as:
The Art of Joan Hammond produced by EMI Records Australia which
includes ten popular arias in English plus Panis Angelicus, Ave Maria,
Green hills o' Somerset, By the Waters of Minnetonka, The last rose
of summer, Home sweet home.
EMI 166284 2. Released 1991.

GOLFING HIGHLIGHTS

1929
Junior member of Avondale Golf Club. Winner of the NSW Junior
Championship (aged seventeen).

1930
Winner of the NSW Junior Championship. Winner of the Avondale club
championship. Winner of the best gross score trophy. Qualifies for but is
defeated in the NSW Open Championship—beaten in the second round
by her persistent rival, Odette Lefebvre.

1931
Inaugural winner of the Manly Scratch Cup: Champion of Champions.
Runner-up in the NSW Open Championship. Member of the NSW State
Team (ditto 1933–35).

1932
Joins Royal Sydney Golf Club and wins the club championship;
a regular member in the No.1 grade team she 'generally scored a win'.
Winner of the NSW Open Championship.

1933
Runner-up in the Australian Open Championship. Winner of the
Foursomes Australian Open Championship with Odette Lefebvre.
She won the Yallambie Cup and also won (at various times)
the LGU summer scratch score, notably at Bowral where she
'returned a fine 73'. Member of the Tasman Cup Team representing
Australia against New Zealand.

1934

Runner-up in the *Evening News* Cup—she tied and lost the play-off.
Winner of the Manly Scratch Cup: Champion of Champions.
Winner of the NSW Open Championship. Member of the Tasman Cup
Team representing Australia against New Zealand.

1935

Member of the Australian team versus the visiting British team.
Winner of the NSW Open Championship.

She had considerable success in handicap events during these years
and achieved some record scores. When she withdrew from competition
she held the lowest marker (2) in Australia.

An article in *Golf in Australia* written in 1937 recognised Joan's
substantial influence on the game:

Miss Hammond is one of the most extraordinary, as well as one of the
most outstanding women golfers Australia has produced, certainly the most
electric player seen here . . . it will be many a long day before anyone out here
will see such marvellous golf as she played in the final of the 1934 against
Miss Gowing on Royal Sydney. Her figures in the first nine holes are well
worth recording for all time, and were 2 4 2 4 4 3 5 3 4—31. It is possible
that had this been in an ordinary stroke round she would have gone on to
'break' 70, but as it was, she played a 74 and this was no flash in the pan, for
in the afternoon round she had a 37 on the first nine . . .

[There is] no doubt of the fact that she helped to open up an entirely new
era in golf here, and what is more important, was watched and known to the
younger players in this State, who can set their aim by her attainments . . .
And they can remember that while Miss Hammond had undoubted natural
ability, perseverance, doggedness and intelligence played a great part in her
ultimate success.

ENDNOTES

Key archival sources

National Library of Australia (NLA):

Papers of Dame Joan Hammond

Betty Davison's collection of papers on Joan Hammond

Bertie Lloyd's papers including scrapbooks (4) containing unidentified newspaper cuttings etc.

Pymble Ladies' College archives, Sydney

Performing Arts Collection, Melbourne, Joan Hammond papers

Notes on text

PAGE (v): The opening 'swooning depth' quote is from a review of *Tosca* in Brisbane's *Courier Mail*, 1957.

Chapter 1: Sport and play

PAGE 9: Samuel and Edith Hood are listed in the 1901 UK Census as husband and wife; Samuel described himself as a 'scientific instrument maker' at this time. Samuel's father, Samuel Hood senior, died in 1905, and it appears that Samuel Hood junior adjusted his name fairly soon after. Aurora Hammond says that Samuel and Edith had a son called Julian Hood, but I have not been able to trace his birth. Samuel Hood junior was born on 10 December 1875 and grew up in the Tower Hamlet, Shoreditch area. His mother was Joyce Hood née Calcutt and he had two brothers and three sisters.

PAGE 10: Joan gave an interview in the *New Zealand Listener* in November 1946 saying that Samuel's original intention was to go to Sydney rather than Christchurch; her autobiography, however, says they were bound for New Zealand: *A Voice, A Life*, p. 14.

PAGE 10: Hilda and Samuel were also the godparents.

PAGE 10: Noel and Len/Leonard were aged four and two in 1912.

PAGE 11: The actor Peter Finch attended The Garden School a little later. One of the achievements of the Theosophists was to build the Star Amphitheatre overlooking Balmoral on Sydney's North Shore.

PAGE 12: Samuel was also involved in shipping goods between Sydney and Newcastle; dry ice was invented in 1925. His office was in 350 George Street, an architecturally extravagant building originally owned by the Equitable Life Assurance Society of the US; it even had a ballroom.

PAGE 12: 'Walbrook' was built c. 1918 and still stands at 43 Nelson Road, Lindfield; the pine sapling that Samuel planted in the front garden now towers over the house.

PAGE 12: Palm Beach Golf Club was formed in 1927. The history of the club is recorded in David J. Innes, *The story of golf in New South Wales 1851–1987*, New South Wales Golf Association, 1988, p. 128. Many of Samuel's business friends appear to have been golf enthusiasts.

PAGE 13: When Len Hammond applied for a passport in later life he had to order a copy of his birth certificate. It showed that he'd spent half his life celebrating the wrong birth date. He was actually born on 24 February 1910, not 13 February, as he'd been told. The Hammond boys went to 'Shore'—Sydney Church of England Grammar School, on the North Shore. Interview with Aurora Hammond, Len's daughter, 2 November 2005.

PAGE 13: Bertie Lloyd told me about the Hammonds' reputation for lively argument in our interview of 31 October 2005.

PAGE 16: Hilda bought Joan her first opera scores but it's uncertain when this was.

PAGE 16: Hilda Blandford was born in Cowes in 1887. Her mother, Matilda Blandford née Dennes, had one son and four daughters, all raised on the Isle of Wight, Hampshire; Hilda's brother worked as a labourer in an ironworks in 1901, when aged eighteen; her two elder sisters died from tuberculosis. UK census 1881, 1901 and genealogy searches.

PAGE 17: Joan started PLC Pymble in third term 1926 and was voted Class Captain by first term 1927.

PAGE 19: Mathilde Marchesi famously assisted Nellie Melba in Paris c. 1886 and was instrumental in launching her career. Henri Staëll was 'a pupil of Wieniawski' and gave regular recitals; he was also on the committee that founded the NSW State Conservatorium in 1915. Madame Tasma's claim about her teachers was recorded in PLC 1929 prospectus 'extra subjects', PLC archives.

PAGE 19: Three of Joan's closest friends at PLC were 'Prairie, Lowie and Tommo' aka Heather Field, Sheila Lowe, and Mary Thomas. Some of Joan's friends were 'day-bugs' despite the lower social status.

PAGE 20: Joan understood *Alawa*—the name of her cabin cruiser—to be an Aboriginal word meaning 'I camp here'.

PAGE 20: Joan was elected to membership of Avondale Golf Club on 15 April 1929, David J. Innes, *The story of golf in New South Wales 1851–1987*, p. 146. Female golfers were always 'associate' members; they paid a lower subscription and had fewer rights.

PAGE 22: Palm Beach Golf Club was popular for young golfers during the 1920s and 1930s, champion players included Harry Hattersley and Pat Borthwick. Joan won her first competition there in 1925, aged thirteen. Male golf players tended to strike the ball with far more speed and power than female players.

PAGE 22: Samuel and Hilda visited Japan in 1927 so it's possible they needed a marriage certificate to update their passports. The certificate gave Hilda's 'usual place of residence' as the family home while Samuel gave it as his business address in the city. One of the witnesses to the marriage was H. Wilshire, a founding member of the Pennant Hills Golf Club, the other was J. Brown.

Chapter 2: A powerful drive

PAGE 25: The Palm Beach holiday house, sold c. 1929, became the clubhouse for the Palm Beach Golf Club from 1933 to 1965 when a new clubhouse was built. 'Walbrook' was sold c. 1932.

PAGE 25: 'Renown' still stands at 23 Holbrook Avenue, Kirribilli. The Hammonds' flat was on the fourth floor. It was named after the ship that brought the Duke and Duchess of York (later King George VI and Queen Elizabeth) to Sydney on a royal visit in 1927.

PAGE 26: The orchestra comprised professional musicians and students from the Con and was an early version of what later became the Sydney Symphony Orchestra.

PAGE 27: Odette Lefebvre became a member of Killara Golf Club in June 1929; her coach was Walter Clark. A good tennis player, she won the Alliance Française Championship in 1930. Joan won a squash championship around the same time.

PAGE 28: Bertie Lloyd's scrapbooks contain newspaper clippings featuring Joan's golfing progress, but dates and sources are not identified. Joan's golf club grip was unorthodox because of her damaged arm: both hands went straight down the shaft and the fingers did not intertwine; it was known as the old St Andrews' grip. *The Australian Golf and Tennis Magazine*, June 1933, front cover and p. 201.

PAGE 28: Strict traditional golfing dress codes are discussed in Colin Tatz and Brian Stoddart, *The Royal Sydney Golf Club, the first hundred years*, Allen & Unwin, 1993, p. 12.

PAGE 30: Len Hammond or his parents obtained a copy of his birth certificate from Somerset House in 1926. Like his sister's it gave his surname as 'Hammond' with 'Hood' as a middle name; confusingly, his first name was given as Samuel. Joan never made use of her other middle name: Hilda.

PAGE 30: Joan's singing teacher was Spencer Thomas, an English tenor who returned to England c. 1930.

PAGE 30: Ruth 'Lute' Drummond also coached the tenor, Ken Neate. A friend of Marion Mahony Griffin, she directed performances at the open-air theatre at Castlecrag. In 1936 she produced the first of several opera series for the ABC. Her sister died in 1935.

PAGE 30: Joan's recording of 'Glück, das mir verblieb' from *Die Tote Stadt* is still regarded as one of the best ever made.

PAGE 32: A detailed description of the Williamson Imperial Grand Opera Company season can be found in Alison Gyger, *Opera for the Antipodes: opera in Australia 1881–1939*, Currency Press, 1990.

PAGE 32: The Maestro was Emilio Rossi from La Scala, Milan; one of the assistant conductors was Joseph Post, later conductor for the Elizabethan Theatre Trust Opera Company.

PAGE 33: The price of opera seats had been reduced because of the Depression, and for the first time children were admitted for half price. Tickets sold well for the 1932 season. Twenty shillings equals one pound.

PAGE 34: Two Australian sopranos were given the chance to sing principal roles: the pretty but inexperienced Nora Hill, and the more confident Molly de Gunst who went on to sing in Britain with Sadler's Wells c. 1937. John Brownlee also made some guest appearances in the 1932 season.

PAGE 35: The forceful member of the Ladies' Golf Union was also its President, Miss Una Clift, a terrific woman by all accounts. She wore 'sensible' clothes that had large pockets, and never carried a handbag.

PAGE 35: Joan's best prize-money year for golf came in 1935 when she amassed £25 15s.

PAGE 35: The J. C. Williamson Magazine, Grand Opera Special Supplement for the 1932 Melbourne season included a photo of Joan as one of the Australian Artists (as did the Sydney programme); oddly enough, on the opposite page was an advertisement for the Hecla electric sandwich toaster, suggesting 'a delicious after-theatre supper', price 62s 6d.

PAGE 39: Lindley Evans (1895–1982) had been Melba's accompanist in the 1920s. Evans and Frank Hutchens (1892–1965) were among the first composer-performer teams to be recorded commercially in Australia. See "Hello, Mr Melody Man" Lindley Evans Remembers, Angus & Robertson, 1983, pp. 102–7.

PAGE 40: One of Joan's friends was Jean 'Mickey' McCay, a reporter for the social pages of the Telegraph. She was the daughter of Delamore McCay, Editor in Chief of Sun Newspapers. She later married David McNicholl.

PAGE 40: Joan made her quip about the dangers of taking style too seriously in 'Styles and Swings', an unidentified article in Bertie Lloyd's scrapbook.

PAGE 41: The top players that Joan interviewed were Miss Oliver Kay and Miss Bessie Gaisford. Joan represented her country in the Tasman Cup (played between Australia and New Zealand) in 1933 and 1934, and came up against these two players several times.

PAGE 44: Curt Prerauer was the coach at the Fuller Grand Opera; he went on to pioneer live opera radio broadcasts for the ABC, and was a noted music critic. Molly de Gunst was again recognised as the promising Australian soprano.

PAGE 45: Lady Gowrie (1879–1965) was actively interested in the Girl Guides, Junior Red Cross, Country Women's Association, National Council of Women, Mothers' Union and all organisations for public welfare including religious bodies of all sects from the Salvation Army to the Jewish Women's Guild. Relaxation included golf, tennis and gardening, while in her youth she'd been a skilful horsewoman. She had a distinguished Scottish/Irish ancestry. Her husband, Alexander Hore-Ruthven had a notable military career before becoming Governor of South Australia in 1928, then New South Wales in 1935; the couple had a son, Patrick.

PAGE 47: Miss Leo (Leonora) Wray (1886–1979), won many championships in her youth and middle years, and put much energy into raising the standard of the junior women's game.

PAGE 47: The golf clubs volunteering their services on this night were Elanora, NSW, The Lakes, Manly, Avondale, Pymble, Pennant Hills, Concord, Balgowlah, Roseville, Kogarah, Strathfield, Killara—and Leura had already made a start. Information from Bertie Lloyd's scrapbook.

PAGE 48: The details of Joan's impromptu concert were discussed during my Bertie Lloyd interview, 31 October 2005.

PAGE 49: Joan told Bertie Lloyd that Gladys Moncrieff had said she couldn't sit down all evening because her corset was pulled so tight.

Chapter 3: Innocent abroad

PAGE 52: The Captain of the *Dagfred* was almost certainly Arne Andreassen; the ship and crew went on to experience some very dramatic times during WW2.

PAGE 52: Details about this phase of Joan's life have been drawn from *A Voice, A Life* or Bertie Lloyd's scrapbooks unless otherwise stated.

PAGE 54: Joan wrote letters about the rowdy nights onboard the *Dagfred* to Bertie Lloyd, April–May 1936.

PAGE 56: The last member of the royal family to live at the Schloss Wilhelminenberg was Archduke Leopold I, who died in 1931. The Schloss served as a hospital during WW1 and as a children's home 1927–34. The boys' choir was in residence 1934–38. It is now a hotel.

PAGE 57: The Countess Kinsky (born 1864), stage name Marie Renard, was the daughter of a Graz cabman. Adored by the Viennese, she retired from the stage to marry Count Kinsky in 1900 and remained a prominent, well-loved figure in Viennese society. Popular roles included Carmen, Manon, and Hansel. Mahler's innovations didn't appeal to her—another reason for relatively early retirement.

PAGE 58: Joan recorded the success of her performance at the Schloss in a letter to Bertie Lloyd, 31 May 1936.

PAGE 59: Joan wrote to Bertie Lloyd of her anticipation of the mountain village, 19 June 1936. Joan wrote numerous letters to her mother and other friends during this era but none have come to light.

PAGE 60: Members of the Vienna Boys' Choir had to leave the choir when they reached the age of fifteen but could continue their education at the school till they were eighteen.

PAGE 61: Joan described the Tyrolean festival and the rather demanding mountaineering adventure in a letter to Bertie Lloyd, 6 September 1936.

PAGE 63: The full title of Lady Selby's husband (Sir Walford Selby) was British Envoy Extraordinary and Minister Plenipotentiary in Vienna, it was one of the most important ministerial observation posts in Europe. Selby was a strong supporter of Austrian independence.

PAGE 63: There were four major opera theatres in Vienna. The Staatsoper, established 1869, housed the principal opera company – the Vienna State Opera – where Bruno Walter took over artistic direction in 1936 (Gustav Mahler was there 1897–1907).

PAGE 66: The name of the new singing teacher was probably Dora Keplinger, who was reputed to have taught Lotte Lehmann.

PAGE 68: The tenor was Robert Scott, who had been quite successful in Australia.

PAGE 71: Lilian Baylis (1874–1937) had been manager of the Old Vic from 1898, and reopened Sadler's Wells in 1931 to present opera in English with British singers. She was keen to employ Joan in the foreseeable future, so Joan was especially disappointed when Miss Baylis died a few months later.

PAGE 71: Dino Borgioli married Patricia Mort c. 1935 and they settled in London.

PAGE 72: Sir Thomas Beecham (1879–1961) founded the Beecham Opera Company in 1915 (it became the British National Opera Company after financial problems in 1920). One of Britain's greatest conductors, he was Artistic Director of the Royal Opera House, Covent Garden 1933–39.

PAGE 74: 'I am back in this dismal country . . . The Italian School is the only one.' Letter to Bertie Lloyd, 11 August 1937.

PAGE 75: Joan's two coaches were Alberto Erede (born Genoa 1909) and Erich Leinsdorf (born Vienna 1912); both became highly regarded conductors in Europe and America.

PAGE 75: Joan kept account of her life in a five-year diary from the mid 1930s to mid 1960s; none of them have survived. She switched to one-year diaries in the 1970s.

PAGE 77: The circumstances surrounding Hilda Hammond's overseas trip are unclear. Hilda probably travelled from Australia with Tweet Mcindoe and her mother. Tweet had been a paying guest with the Hammonds in the Kirribilli flat; her parents lived in New Zealand and her father was wealthy. Mr Mcindoe was supportive of Joan and had bought her a dress to perform in for her last Sydney concert. Perhaps he sponsored Hilda's trip in some way. A letter from Joan to Bertie Lloyd indicates that Hilda spent most of her time with Tweet and Mrs Mcindoe in London; letter, 11 February 1938, from Pensione Rigatti, Florence; Bertie Lloyd papers (other pages of letter missing). Hilda was definitely in England between May 1938 and January 1940. Samuel Hammond's finances might have improved by this time, but not by very much.

PAGE 77: Dino Borgioli (1891–1960) was 47 and planning his retirement from opera. Joan suspected (in retrospect) that the Borgiolis hoped to gain some credit from her success, and this did happen to a degree. Pat Borgioli made a point of informing newspapers in Australia that Dino was Joan's teacher, even after Joan had declined to take more lessons. Robert Gard was one of the Australian singers who was coached by Borgioli in later years.

PAGE 78: The Volksoper was built in 1898, originally for drama. Opera began there in 1904, repertoire included operas, operettas and musicals. It was used by the Vienna State Opera for some productions between 1945 and 1955 due to the destruction of the Staatsoper during WW2.

PAGE 79: So many operatic heroines die. Joan's stage falls were done to the right to protect her left arm, and she always covered that arm with some kind of costuming.

PAGE 80: Joan's two test recordings in London were for HMV and (the company that became known as) EMI. The HMV audition was cursory: she sang 'The Green Hills o' Somerset' for Walter Legge, the company's then representative, and didn't feel he gave her a good hearing. The EMI test recording was made at Abbey Road and was more thorough. She sang 'Now in her westering flight', and *'In Quelle trine morbide'* from Puccini's *Manon Lescaut*, both accompanied by Gerald Moore.

PAGE 84: The Howard de Waldens owned Chirk Castle and held a New Year charity concert in aid of the Cottage Hospital. Performers included Keith Falkner and Jan Smeterlin and de Walden family and friends. Joan's memoir says Ivor Newton saved her from spending 'a lonely Christmas'. The McCays had returned to Australia but Hilda Hammond was definitely with her in London at this time; Bertie Lloyd papers.

PAGE 84: My statement about Joan's limited awareness of sexuality is informed by my correspondence with John Crisp, who came to know Joan through his friendship with Ivor Newton. Sexual innocence was the norm for 'nice young girls' like Joan. The 1930s was a world away from the 'sexual revolution' of the 1960s, and the preoccupation with sexuality in later decades.

PAGE 88: Fritz Berens managed to make it to the USA and the watch eventually found its way to him. He became a conductor with the San Francisco Opera and Ballet. Letter to Joan from Berens, October 1987, NLA.

PAGE 89: The Australian mezzosoprano Lorna Sydney was caught unawares at the start of the war in a similar way. The people of Perth raised the money for her to study in Vienna during the late 1930s. She was about to make her debut at the Berlin State Opera when war broke out and she was immediately interned by the Nazis. She made her debut as Carmen at the Vienna State Opera in 1946.

Chapter 4: Blood, sweat and tears — the war years

PAGE 91: The scheme to entertain troops in training centres was not the same as the Entertainments National Service Association (ENSA), which Joan joined later. Florence Austral (born Melbourne, 1894) was a highly successful dramatic soprano during the 1920s and 1930s, but multiple sclerosis restricted her career by the 1940s. She returned to Australia in 1946.

PAGE 93: Joan considered the cost of Dino Borgioli's lessons, as well as his breathing method, to be a problem.

PAGE 93: Joan told Bertie Lloyd that she had urged her mother to go home in a Christmas card, 12 December 1939. Hilda gave a glowing account of her daughter's progress to a journalist in Sydney upon her return. Reportage regarding Hilda's comments were hashed and rehashed by different newspapers, the details inconsistent or inaccurate. One paper said Joan had joined the British Women's Legion, another that she was ill and was going to rest for a while in Italy. Bertie Lloyd papers and scrapbook.

PAGE 93: *La Traviata* translates as *The Fallen Woman*; *La Bohème* as *Bohemian Life*.

PAGE 97: The 'Joan Hammond's soprano has a pure joy of youth . . .' review was retained by Bertie Lloyd in her scrapbook. At Landore, South Wales, Joan sung with David Lloyd and Laurence Holmes.

PAGE 98: 'Joan Hammond was in brilliant form as Pamina . . . She was a distinct success,' Bertie Lloyd scrapbook. *The Magic Flute* was assisted by two other imported artists, Charles Moore, an experienced producer, and Arthur Hammond, conductor. The Dublin Operatic Society was founded in 1928. The chorus was amateur, and performances took place at the Olympia Theatre.

PAGE 98: 'Friendship with Ian . . . happy relationship,' *A Voice, A Life*, p. 107. Ian Blacker, 2nd Battalion, The Tower Hamlets Rifles, died on 22 June 1944 and is buried in the Assisi War Cemetery.

PAGE 99: The name of the friend that assisted Joan in London is unknown but Dowager Viscountess Hambledon had a town house in Eaton Square so the Eaton Mews connection may have emanated from there. Joan referred to it as 'Mews Cottage'; it was a small dwelling added during the Victorian era to accommodate servants working in the main Georgian-built house.

PAGE 100: The Eavestaff Minipiano was made by a British firm and was popular during the 1930s.

PAGE 101: Walter Legge's memo recommending Joan be put under contract, 23 April 1940, EMI Archive; see Tony Locantro's CD cover notes, *Joan Hammond: A Celebration*, Testament, 1992. Walter Legge married the contralto Nancy Evans, and later married the soprano Elisabeth Schwarzkopf c. 1953.

PAGE 106: ENSA was a government-sponsored body responsible for bringing live performances to allied armed forces. The director was Basil Dean (film producer) and Walter Legge was involved in the planning of classical music concerts. Top rank performers were involved in ENSA but the organisation was necessarily spread thin. Some entertainments were substandard, leading to the alternative translation of the acronym 'Every Night Something Awful'. Mary Glasgow headed CEMA initially; the organisation became the British Arts Council after the war. ENSA destinations could be secret—Ivor Newton once found himself on a troop ship bound for the Middle East. The furthest Joan went was Scapa Flow, off the north-east coast of Scotland. She was booked to go to Europe mid-war but became ill following the vaccinations.

PAGE 107: Sir Adrian Boult was conductor of the BBC Symphony Orchestra which was evacuated to Bristol, but then to Bedford after Colston Hall was bombed. Stanford Robinson had studied under Boult at the Royal College of Music.

PAGE 108: Joan pencilled her phrasing alterations in her much-used Ricordi score; signed and with address stamp: c/o Bank of New South Wales, 47 Berkeley Square, London W1. NLA.

PAGE 109: Robertson's review appeared in *The Gramophone*, April 1941, p. 250. *The Gramophone* was also co-edited by Mackenzie, a prolific Scottish author; it incorporated *Vox*, *Radio Critic*, and *Broadcast Review*, and maintained its monthly publication throughout the war, earning a worldwide circulation thereafter.

PAGE 110: Alec Robertson review, *The Gramophone*, June 1941, p. 12.

PAGE 111: Thanks to Tony Locantro for verifying the 'O my beloved father' disagreement between Joan and Legge, email correspondence, 2006.

PAGE 112: Alec Robertson review, *The Gramophone*, December 1941, p. 116.

Page 112: Joan's royalty payment for her recording work was 1½ d per 10-inch and 3d per 12-inch record sold; this amount was fixed so it didn't increase over time.

PAGE 113: Dame Isobel Baillie 1895–1983, Dame Maggie Teyte 1888–1976, Lisa Perli alias concert soprano Dora Labbette 1898–1981.

PAGE 113: Sadler's Wells was kept afloat due also to the help of Tyrone Guthrie; Joan Cross resigned from her administrative position after the war and sang in many of Benjamin Britten's operas.

PAGE 113: Ruth Packer was two years older than Joan. She was married to the lead tenor of the company, Tudor Davies, and had a moderately successful career as a dramatic soprano after the war. Other members of the permanent Carl Rosa company included Helen Ogilvie, Gladys Parr, Hubert Dunkerley and Appleton Moore. Guest artists were generally older than Joan, e.g. Edith Coates born 1908, Gwen Catley born c. 1905.

PAGE 115: Joan's parents gave her an authentic Japanese wig and kimono following an overseas trip during their wealthy phase, possibly the basis for her costume for *Butterfly*.

PAGE 120: 'Joan Hammond' by William Mann, *Opera* magazine, vol. 10, no. 2 February 1959, p. 82.

PAGE 122: Over 100 additional ambulance stations were opened in the Greater London area for use by the auxiliary force, with about 10000 auxiliary personnel; the County of London moved 48 709 war casualties to hospital or First Aid posts during the war.

PAGE 123: Joan's candid discussion about her fear was reported in 'Joan Hammond—Now a singer with a world wide reputation', *Woman's Day with Woman*, 9 September 1953.

PAGE 123: Joan explained how the 'Pippo in a basket' photo came to be taken when she answered a fan's query, but she didn't say which newspaper. Letter to fan, 1988, NLA.

PAGE 126: Alec Robertson review, *The Gramophone*, December 1943, p. 101.

PAGE 127: Alec Robertson review, *The Gramophone*, January 1944, p. 122. The Mozart recordings were made with the Halle Orchestra, at the Belle Vue, Manchester—a venue that had a bad echo—Heward conducting. Claire Dux was born in Poland in 1885, and retired at her peak when she married a wealthy American c. 1923.

PAGE 131: Joan said of her experience performing with Geraldo that he really heeded the dynamics; he was prepared for an *accelerando*, pause or *rallentando*.

PAGE 132: Tony Hammond was awarded the D.F.C. and Bar. He had two daughters by his first marriage, Julie and Jenny.

PAGE 135: Alec Robertson review, *The Gramophone*, January 1945, p. 97. Made with the London Symphony Orchestra, Walter Susskind conducting. The *La Traviata* duets with Dennis Noble were recorded with the Liverpool Philharmonic Orchestra, Cameron conducting.

PAGE 135: Alec Robertson review, *The Gramophone*, March 1945, pp. 119–20. The Liu arias were 'Oh! I entreat thee Fire' and 'Thou who with ice art girdled'.

PAGE 136: There was once a 'difficult' American soprano who received payback from stage management by having her mattress switched to a trampoline when she was playing the part of Tosca—she bounced several times, much to the amusement of the audience. Joan knew of the story and checked her mattress each performance—for safety reasons mainly. Sarah Bernhardt once jumped on to a mattress that wasn't there; the ultimate outcome was a leg amputation.

Chapter 5: Illumination

PAGE 139: John Crisp, friend of Ivor Newton and Joan, told me of Ivor's presumption of a relationship between Joan and Essie in email correspondence, 13 August 2006.

PAGE 140: A sense of Essie's perceived 'oddness' is conveyed through muted comments in correspondence between Joan and friends, NLA.

PAGE 141: An estimated 50000 people died in Belsen concentration camp; Jews the majority, but also homosexuals, the disabled and various political, religious and ethnic groups. Joan undertook a second ENSA tour in Germany early in 1946; newspaper articles, Bertie Lloyd scrapbook.

PAGE 141: There was much power mongering concerning the fate of the London opera companies at this time. Joan Cross was forced out of Sadler's Wells and joined forces with Benjamin Britten; the Royal Opera House was rescued by Lord Keynes, Leslie Boosey, Ralph Hawkes and others who started a campaign which led to the Covent Garden Trust. The 'in favour' soprano was Victoria Sladen, but only briefly.

PAGE 143: Accompanist Jennie Reddin stayed at Eaton Terrace with her daughter immediately after the war when they were homeless. Reddin, rather than Essie, played for Joan during this time but facts and dates are uncertain. Joan gave Jennie Reddin the Minipiano, which was later passed to her daughter.

PAGE 143: One new work Joan incorporated into her preparations for the ABC was *Dies Natalis* (Day of Birth) by Gerald Finzi, 1939; aspiring composers sent their new songs to Joan on a regular basis but very few were included in her repertoire.

PAGE 144: The quoted passages of Britten's *Les Illuminations* are from a translation by George Hall, quoted from CD notes contained in *Britten: Song Cycles, Bostridge, Rattle* EMI Classics 5 58049 2; and see Ian Bostridge's comments on *Les Illuminations*. Britten originally wrote the work for the Swiss soprano Sophie Wyss.

PAGE 145: Footage of Joan's return to Australia appears in Dame Joan Hammond, videoed interview with Robin Hughes, *Australian Biography*, series 1, 1991 VHS/DVD; secondary comment taken from news report. Joan gave her first recital at the Melbourne Town Hall, 9 July; her programme included songs by Fauré, Moret, Cecconi, Pizzetti, H. Wolf, Moussorgsky, Liza Lehmann, Rubbra, Bantock, Armstrong Gibbs, and Bax.

PAGE 146: Raymond Lambert (1908–66) was born in Belgium; he was chief study-teacher of piano at the University Conservatorium in Melbourne from 1932, and official ABC accompanist/associate artist from 1936. His father, Edouard, was concert master of the Melbourne Symphony Orchestra.

PAGE 147: David McNicoll, born c. 1915, a distinguished war correspondent, returned to Australia after the war and started the Town Talk column in the *Daily Telegraph*; became editor-in-chief of Australian Consolidated Press in 1953; long time contributor to the *Bulletin*. Bertie Lloyd interview and scrapbook.

PAGE 148: The concert Neville Cardus reviewed was on 14 August and the first half was broadcast; works included Gluck, Monteverdi, Brahms, Purcell, Rachmaninoff, Rubinstein, Haydn, Scott, Quilter, Parry, and Puccini encores. Neville Cardus (1888–1975) was critic for the *Sydney Morning Herald* and others c. 1940–49; he rejoined the *Manchester Guardian* as its London music critic in 1951. Bertie Lloyd scrapbook.

PAGE 149: Burtta Cheney discussed Lolita's work ethic and abilities in an interview I had with her, 6 October 2005.

PAGE 151: Joan's comments on her repertoire were published in *New Zealand Listener*, 1 November 1946, p. 6.

PAGE 151: Illness disrupted Joan's tour dates: *Les Illuminations* was performed in late November 1946.

PAGE 152: Burtta Cheney discussed Lolita's life-changing decision to go to London in the taped interview, 6 October 2005.

PAGE 153: Len Hammond approached his friend, Bill Northey, to fight the Taxation Department on Joan's behalf. His opening gambit was to ask the judge if he expected Miss Hammond to stay somewhere like the YMCA or the People's Palace. The whole court laughed and he knew he'd win the case. Bill Northey became Joan's friend and accountant in later years.

PAGE 154: Lolita told Peter Burch of her sudden conviction about being destined to support Joan. Interview with Peter Burch, 3 March 2005.

PAGE 157: Joan described Joseph Krips' talent in *A Voice, A Life*, p. 170.

Page 158: Many of Joan's performances during the busy post-war years are recorded in Marcel Prawy, *The Vienna Opera*, Weidenfeld and Nicolson, 1970, pp. 169–70. Schwarzkopf made her debut at Covent Garden in 1947 when she toured there with the Vienna Opera.

PAGE 159: According to Lolita Marriott's publicity blurb—sent to Australia in preparation for the 'thank you' concerts—Joan was the only British guest artist in the Covent Garden 1948–49 season, and the first British guest to sing with the Vienna State Opera for twenty years.

PAGE 159: Joan also sang at PLC Pymble during her Australian tour, fulfilling a promise previously broken, and gave a charity concert for the Red Cross. Four leading golfers, Peter Thompson, Ossie Pickworth, Norman Von Nida and Eric Cremin also assisted Joan's fundraising effort with an exhibition match. Miss Judith Percy served the team well by reaching the semi-finals of the 1950 British Open where she was beaten by the ultimate winner. Leo Wray was the captain-manager of the team. Lindley Evans was Joan's accompanist for Sydney and Bernice Lehmann for Melbourne. Doubtless there were plenty of rehearsals!

PAGE 161: Howard Taubman's review of the Carnegie Hall concert appeared in the *New York Times*, 1 December 1949, a reprint from the late edition of the previous day. Taubman was the paper's music critic for many years.

PAGE 163: Joan's English concert agent was Ibbs and Tillett. The firm focused on the needs of promoters rather than artists and had a virtual monopoly until the early 1950s when the international market changed the scene, bringing big earnings to top artists.

PAGE 164: Kathleen Ferrier's total earnings for her USA tour of March–May 1949 were $17500 (£4375), a sum whittled down to $1500 (£375) after expenses. For comparison, Walter Legge's annual income from EMI was £4000 c. 1953, a sum that Schwarzkopf said was unreasonably low. Ferrier's letter, 15 April 1949, Winifred Ferrier, *The life of Kathleen Ferrier*, Hamish Hamilton, 1955, pp. 114–15.

PAGE 165: Joan discussed finally overcoming vocal insecurity in *A Voice, A Life*, p. 187.

Chapter 6: Love and music

PAGE 171: The McDonnells were a wealthy as well as influential family within the Dublin community, and long-time friends of Joan and Lolita. Interview with Stephen Marriott, 20 October 2005.

PAGE 172: *A Voice, A Life* says Sutherland understudied Joan during the 1959–60 season while Sutherland remembers the date as February 1954—her debut as Aida; the latter seems correct. Letter to author from Dame Joan Sutherland, 4 May 2006.

PAGE 172: Joan continued to be a committed fundraiser for the Freedom From Hunger Campaign launched in 1960 by the United Nations, and sang at various functions to this end.

PAGE 173: Constance Shacklock, the British contralto, was invited to Russia at the same time as Joan; she sang Amneris opposite Joan's Aida.

PAGE 178: The cottage and animals were looked after by dressmakers (twins who went under the name of Gemini), when all three 'girls' were away. Joan and Lolita had their clothes made by Gemini for many years. Joan's clothes, for on and off the stage, were generally designed by Ben Pearson.

PAGE 179: Lolita set up the Nance Marriott Trophies, a pair of silver salvers awarded to the winners of the ALGU Ladies Foursomes Championship of Australia, in honour of her mother.

PAGE 181: Rosemary Wilson (née Wright) reflected on Lolita and her relationship to Joan in phone interviews and correspondence, January 2006. The Wright family lived at 'Coomaroo' on the corner of Albany and Kooyong roads, Toorak.

PAGE 182: Stephen Marriott discussed his impressions of Joan during an interview I taped with him, 20 October 2005.

PAGE 182: Alison Hennegan wrote about Nancy Spain's deliberately codified texts in her introduction to Spain's crime novel *Poison for Teacher*, Virago, 1994. Spain (born 1917) and her partner Joan Werner Laurie ('Jonny') died together in a light plane crash in 1964.

PAGE 186: Spain's interview at the Old Cottage was published in the *Daily Express*, 17 November 1958, p. 8.

PAGE 186: When Joan toured East Africa she said that 'the Mau Mau were still very active . . . I shall never forget seeing some beautifully gowned women in the audience at Nairobi wearing revolvers as casually as a floral decoration.'

PAGE 187: The *Daily Mail's* call for London opera to utilise Joan more appeared in its London edition, 4 October 1958. *Rusalka* premiered in 1959.

PAGE 187: See Alison Gyger, *Australia's Operatic Phoenix*, for the development of ETOC.

PAGE 188: Joan's appraisal of *Salome* originally appeared in *A Voice, A Life*, p. 214.

PAGE 189: Stephen Hall recalled his meeting Joan in Newcastle during phone interviews and email correspondence, April–May 2006. A newspaper referred to Joan and Lolita's vehicle as a 'station wagon'—either way it would have been a top-class car, possibly borrowed from the Marriott 'stable', the caravan probably hired.

PAGE 190: Phone interview with John Rohde, 20 March 2006.

PAGE 192: Taped interview with Greg Dempsey, 10 April 2006. Greg agreed with the 'Art is a jealous mistress' concept; he purposely didn't marry until he was forty. 'You can do the best for yourself as an artist by being on your own, where you don't have "oh we've got to be here, we've got to do that"—you have to just say "no, I'm not doing that".'

PAGE 192: Anecdotes tend to be distorted over time so I was pleased to find that John Bailey's second-hand version of the 'gate-scaling' story was confirmed by Dempsey's first-hand one. John Bailey (ballet dancer and occasional extra with ETOC) also told me that chorus members called Lolita 'Maid Marion'; he can't remember why but it's not a huge leap to couple it with 'Robin Hood'. Joan travelled as 'Miss Hood' a couple of years earlier and when arriving in Australia incognito, she was sprung by journalists at the airport and 'Miss Hood's' photo appeared in the papers—dark glasses and all.

PAGE 195: Joan's impromptu interview has been transcribed from cassette tape copy of outside broadcast radio interview, interviewer unknown, February 1960, NLA. *Salome* was conducted by Karl Rankl, and the Victorian Symphony Orchestra was used throughout the tour; set/costumes Raymond Boyce, Joan's costume Peter Rice (London). The Adelaide and Melbourne seasons alone attracted an audience of 23 000 according to one newspaper. A concert version of *Salome* was performed with Marjorie Lawrence and the Sydney Symphony Orchestra in 1951 but ETOC's was the first full theatrical production. It was sung in English.

PAGE 196: Taped interview with Moffatt Oxenbould, 10 May 2006.

PAGE 197: Joan's call for a national opera company appeared in the *Sunday Mail*, 28 July 1957, p. 25.

PAGE 197: Joan visited Australia at short notice in 1962 when Hilda had an operation and Lolita wanted to attend her father's 80th birthday. Joan's problem with Tony was perhaps to do with his irresponsible behaviour toward his first wife and two daughters.

PAGE 198: Monti Hammond reminisced about boating with Joan during an interview with Christopher Sexton, 25 April 2000. Len Hammond was CEO of Sunbeam.

PAGE 199: Joan had always completely memorised her programme, even though it had been common for concert singers to have their sheet music on stage when Joan started her career. She was distraught at having forgotten her lines.

PAGE 201: Joan and Lolita's press interview on board *Pankina* appeared as an article by Peter O'Loughlin in *Woman's Day*, 12 August 1963 p. 38. The call sign for *Pankina* was MgHv.

PAGE 202: Details of the seaward adventures of Joan, Essie, Lolita, Ivor Newton and John Crisp were shared with me through email correspondence with Commander John Crisp (retired) and Ian Kirk, during 2006.

Chapter 7: 'When I have sung my songs'

PAGE 205: Joan's hole in one at Yarra Yarra was at the 110 yards 4th using a number 8 iron. It helped give her an 81 for the 18 holes—8 over par; her handicap stood at 7.

PAGE 208: The letter to Bertie Lloyd written during Joan's recovery from hospital that appears in the text is extracted from a long letter written 18 January 1965.

PAGE 211: Joan's clarification about the ownership of 'Jumbunna' appeared in the *Australian*, 11 March 1966.

PAGE 211: The result of the 'investigative' journalist's research of 'Jumbunna' was an article entitled 'Joan Hammond goes bush—to the tune of $200 000', *Australasian Post*, 31 March 1966. The photographer was put off by a Keep Out sign and the appearance of a black snake. Joan and Lolita had a bedroom each connected by an en suite.

PAGE 212: Details of Hecla's success and Lolita's finances were given to me by Stephen Marriott. Lolita received £37 000 in 1957 from Marriott shares in Hecla Pty Ltd; she set up trusts through Marriott accountants in order to manage the money effectively, and one such manoeuvre was to assign an indenture sum of £5000 to Joan in 1960.

PAGE 214: Lolita wrote of 'life's cruelties' in a letter to Betty Davison, 11 May 1967. Davison was Joan's adoring fan who worked in a biscuit factory in Sheffield. She'd communicated with and met the trio so often that she, and her female friend 'Rusty', were part of their outer circle of acquaintances.

PAGE 214: Joan wrote of the outcome of her lip surgery in *A Voice, A Life*, p. 236.

PAGE 214: Burtta Cheney told me about the difficulties the 'girls' had in finding suitable domestic staff at 'Jumbunna' during an interview, 6 October 2005.

PAGE 216: One of the anecdotes Joan had previously written detailed her participation in the British Ladies Open Golf Championship of 1948. She had lost to the eventual winner, the then American champion, Louise Suggs. Joan was ahead in the early stages of the game but her story was that the time factor cramped her style—she had to be in Manchester to sing Tosca that afternoon.

PAGE 216: Joan loved poetry; the theme of the opening paragraph of *A Voice, A Life* may have been informed by Rupert Brooke's 1914 poem 'The Great Lover' — '. . . footprints in the dew / And oaks; and brown horse-chestnuts, glossy-new / And new-peeled sticks; and shining pools on grass — / All these have been my loves'.

PAGE 217: Joan expressed her feelings about Australia's loss of conductor Eugene Goosens in *A Voice, A Life*, p. 230–1. In 1956 Sir Eugene Goosens was charged with bringing pornographic material into Australia; he was the victim of a zealous police investigation that had discovered his unconventional (for the times) sexual relationship with Rosaleen Norton, a 'witch' who lived in Kings Cross. The more serious charge of 'scandalous conduct' was never brought, but he was a broken man. *Yerma*, by Denis ApIvor, premiered in November 1961 on the BBC. Joan said the role didn't appeal but accepted because it was a challenge: 'Musically it was the most difficult role I had ever undertaken'.

PAGE 218: Joan wrote of the memorable lack of facilities at Parkhurst Prison in *A Voice, A Life*, p. 227.

PAGE 219: Joan concluded *A Voice, A Life* with a reflective acceptance of her enforced retirement, pp. 234–7.

PAGE 219: Joan spoke later of her concealed despair about being unwell and unable to continue singing in an interview with Robin Hughes, *Australian Biography*, series 1, 1991 VHS/DVD.

PAGE 219: Being awarded the Golden Disc from EMI was a truly exceptional achievement: it was reported at the time that Joan was the only opera and oratorio singer in the world with one to her credit.

PAGE 219: Joan's working title for her autobiography was 'From High Tee to High C'. Gollancz's office was in Henrietta Street, Covent Garden, so there may have been a personal connection. The appendices included a discography and repertoire list; her acknowledgements included a thank you to Lolita and Essie for research assistance and for 'their persistent encouragement'. Essie received four mentions in the book compared to Lolita's fifteen. Her golfing friend, Odette McKay (née Lefebvre), typed the final draft.

PAGE 220: One particular honour Joan received in the period just after her autobiography was published touched her deeply: the prestigious and ancient British order of the Worshipful Company of Musicians gave her the Sir Charles Santley Award, a gift designed for 'retired and active distinguished vocalists'.

PAGE 220: The quoted lines from Verdi's *La Traviata* provide another example of Joan altering the English translation, the Ricordi version has: 'All woe is past, I offer a bright morrow, Yes, in future fortune bright shall smile'.

PAGE 222: Burtta Cheney described being entertained at 'Jumbunna' in an interview, 6 October 2005.

PAGE 223: Stephen Marriott's recollections of the very lively 'Jumbunna' lunches are extracted from a taped interview with him, 20 October 2005.

PAGE 224: Miranda McLeish's anecdotes of the same are extracted from a taped interview with her, 30 September 2005. Interestingly, Miranda's son, Michael McLeish, grew up to be a singer and performer, playing the title role in *Keating!* the popular musical.

PAGE 225: Peter Burch told me about 'lunching' with 'JoLoEss' at Florentino in a taped interview, 3 March 2005.

PAGE 226: Peter Burch discussed his decision to take on the role of joint administrator for the Victorian Opera Company and Ballet Victoria in an interview with Christopher Sexton, 20 May 2000. The Australian Council for the Arts was established in 1968 and headed by Dr H. C. ('Nugget') Coombs and Dr Jean Battersby; its name was changed to the Australia Council in 1973.

PAGE 227: Burch also outlined Joan's role in laying the foundations for a professional opera company in the same interview with Christopher Sexton, 20 May 2000.

PAGE 227: Richard Divall's account of singing Cavaradossi to Joan's Tosca is extracted from Christopher Sexton's taped interview with Divall, c. 2000 (my transcription).

PAGE 228: ETOC singer Neil Warren-Smith commented on Joan's ongoing agitation for the arts, 'If anyone ever earned being Damed for services to music, Joan Hammond did . . . Over a ridiculously long period she proved the points she'd made, and, bit by bit, her advice has been acted on.' See Neil Warren-Smith with Frank Salter, 25 Years of Australian Opera, OUP Melbourne, 1983, pp. 71–5.

PAGE 230: Richard Divall's account of Joan's influence as Artistic Director of the Victorian Opera Company is extracted from his taped interview with Christopher Sexton, c. 2000.

PAGE 232: Peter Burch spoke of his estrangement from Joan in an interview with Christopher Sexton, 20 May 2000.

PAGE 233: Joan's tight financial situation was partly caused by the fact that she was still paying off her UK back-tax in 1974.

PAGE 233: 'Your delightful congratulatory letter . . . how my pals tease me!' Aerogramme from Joan to John Crisp and Ian Kirk in London; this and other material sent to me by John Crisp.

Chapter 8: Master teacher

PAGE 236: John Hopkins (Dean of Music at the Victorian College of the Arts when Joan began teaching there) was born in England in 1927. He was appointed ABC Director of Music in 1963, having conducted major orchestras in Britain and New Zealand.

PAGE 236: The full-time teaching staff listed in the 1978 VCA prospectus for the School of Music was as follows: 'Dean: John Hopkins O.B.E., Principal Lecturer: Keith Field, [Music History and Styles] Pre 1750: John O'Donnell, Post 1950: Dr Richard David Hames, 1750-1950: John Talbot, Piano: Stephen McIntyre, Violin & Viola: Mary Nemet, Voice: Brian Hansford, Master Teacher in Voice: Dame Joan Hammond D.B.E., C.M.G.'; there were also 49 part-time teachers and 3 support staff. The old Police Depot became the Dame Elisabeth Murdoch building.

PAGE 236: Brian Hansford, the other full-time voice teacher at the VCA, won the *Sun* Aria competition in 1956 which enabled him to study with Hans Hotter in Germany; he returned to Australia in 1961 and specialised in German lieder. He taught Cheryl Barker and Peter Coleman-Wright before they transferred to Joan's classes at VCA, and both singers credit him with giving them a strong foundation in breathing technique. Interview with Brian Hansford, baritone and teacher, 13 September 2005.

PAGE 236: Joan was constantly seeking out good teachers for the VCA and after observing soprano Nance Grant in performance, she decided she'd make a good teacher. She invited her on to the staff and it turned out to be a good decision all round.

PAGE 239: Pamela Ruskin's article, based on her interview with Joan, was entitled 'In class with Dame Joan' and appeared, c. 1978, Bertie Lloyd scrapbook.

PAGE 239: Joan was quoted on her belief that artists need genuine competition in 'Dame Joan Hammond' by Pamela Ruskin, printed in *Signature*, the Australian Diners Club Magazine, December 1974.

PAGE 241: Peter Coleman-Wright's anecdotes about his time working as accompanist for Joan are edited extracts from my taped interview with him, 5 September 2006. Peter attended VCA from 1977 to 1979 and was among the first batch of about five vocal students.

PAGE 242: Heather Ross discussed her experience of meeting Joan and being told her voice simply had to be re-trained during phone interviews with me, March 2006.

PAGE 242: Joan's links to the City of Geelong were strong: she served on the committee of the Geelong Performing Arts Centre Trust and assisted with the Geelong Society of Operatic and Dramatic Arts. She also liked to play golf at Barwon Heads.

PAGE 245: 'She taught me *Eugene Onegin* . . . "Joan Hammond taught me that"', Richard Divall interview with Christopher Sexton. Joan resigned from her position as Artistic Director of the VOC in 1976 after a five-year term, she felt she should be accountable for a particularly poor season financially; Alfred Ruskin likewise resigned his chairmanship. It was a symbolic gesture as both remained on the board and Joan continued to give advice. The company re-emerged from the 1976 losses with new personnel and a new name. Richard Divall remained as Music Director, Ken McKenzie-Forbes became General Manager.

PAGE 248: Joan Hammond: *This is Your Life* was produced by Channel 7 (Channel 9 took the programme over at a later date). My thanks to Aurora Hammond for lending me her video copy. Tony Hammond was absent from the line-up; he was a pilot so may have been overseas, though it's also possible he was out of favour with Joan and the rest of the family.

PAGE 250: 'I'd been up in Melbourne . . . "we've got to leave!"', *Australian Biography* filmed interview with Robin Hughes. The local GP was Dr John Eckersley; he was also the doctor to diagnose Joan's diabetes, various top-rank specialists having missed it.

PAGE 254: Peter Burch described the experience of returning to 'Jumbunna' after the fires in the taped interview with me of 3 March 2005. One of Joan's students, Louise O'Loughlin, accompanied Joan and Lolita when they returned to 'Jumbunna' three days later.

PAGE 254: Burtta Cheney discussed the loss of Joan's uniquely valuable library in the taped interview of 6 October 2005.

PAGE 255: James Marriott (Lolita's grandfather) emigrated with his family from Britain at sixteen and continued in the family tradition of wood carving, later turning to the more lucrative art metal trade. His work includes the elegant lamp standards on Princes Bridge and outside Parliament House, Melbourne (1889) and the statue of the Victorian Premier Sir Thomas (Tommy) Bent (1909).

PAGE 255: Documentation detailing the finances of the trio at this time is scant but Lolita's dividend from Hecla, or Hecron Ltd. as it had become, for March 1983 was $14. Joan's income tax bill for 1982 was $2917. *Pankina* had been sold on 1 April 1976; Joan had also sold her eighteenth-century Russian ikon (bought in Moscow) the same year.

PAGE 256: Notes and letters from Lolita's business papers held by Stephen Marriott reveal her determination to quickly, and efficiently, rebuild their lives. For instance, the trio contributed what appear to be unequal amounts for the purchase of the replacement Steinway, a second-hand baby grand — Joan paying most, Essie least; but Lolita asked the retailer to make the receipt in Joan's name only, presumably so it could be claimed as a work expense for tax purposes.

PAGE 257: Lolita's handwritten letter, penned in the aftermath of Ash Wednesday, was provided by John Crisp. The humidity level dropped to 8% on Ash Wednesday; 110° Fahrenheit = 43° Celsius; 75 people lost their lives in total, 47 in Victoria and 28 in South Australia. Joan purchased unit 4.6 at 46 Lansell Rd. Lolita sold her unit (4.3) in 1988, there being no further need for the extra space.

PAGE 257: The trio called the Flinders house 'Farthing Cottage', doubtless because it was relatively small.

Chapter 9: Fate

PAGE 259: Joan sent her letter about the omissions of the ABC's Ash Wednesday report to the *Age*, 19 February 1984. The Salvation Army and the Society of St Vincent de Paul were the two main charities that she wished to thank.

PAGE 261: Joan's paper about the need for a dedicated opera and ballet orchestra in Australia, 'My Utopian Vision', is archived at NLA. The UK government's current lottery system has assisted arts projects immensely.

PAGE 262: A great many of Joan's students continue to sing: the voices she moulded were made to last. Christine Douglas (Musetta) and Cheryl Barker (Mimi) were in Baz Luhrmann's acclaimed production of *La Bohème* in 1993. Steve Davislim went to Joan as a baritone but she said he was destined to be a tenor. She was right, he currently enjoys an international career. Nicole Youl won various international competitions and is one of Australia's favourite sopranos. Apologies for all the names left out.

PAGE 262: Joan had been 'collecting' students' questions for years; the original notes for her proposed book perished in the 1983 fire. The National Library of Australia now holds a later manuscript for 'Question and Answer Singing Book'.

PAGE 264: 1985 had been a tough year for Lolita: her brother, Ron Marriott, died on 12 November 1985, the day after her 70th birthday. Trip Book, NLA.

PAGE 265: 'For me, she was nothing less than the inspiration . . .' speech has been transcribed from a tape recording of the 'Tribute to Dame Joan Hammond', lent to me by Bertie Lloyd. It's well known that Michael Kirby is homosexual; a heterosexual speaker may not have thought to acknowledge a diva's 'secretary and companion of many years'.

PAGE 266: Tributes and awards continued to be many. They included a bronze bust sculpted by Peter Latona (1988), one of a five-portrait series devoted to key artists—e.g. Hiroyuki Iwaki—and Joan was the only female; a Green Room 'Lifetime Achievement Award' (1988); a 'Salute to Dame Joan Hammond Operatic Concert' presented by the VSO with Cheryl Barker, Christopher Bogg, Peter Coleman-Wright, Suzanne Johnston and Stephen McIntyre performing (1992); and a Lifetime Achievement Award for Excellence in Recording from the Australasian Sound Recordings Association (1994). Studios and buildings were also named in her honour; for instance, the VSO named its new rehearsal studio after her in 1992, and there's a Joan Hammond House at PLC Pymble.

PAGE 267: The Granada television series of Joan's Manchester master classes, *A Celebration Masterclass*, was broadcast in 1989. HTV Wales televised Joan's classes with the Welsh College of Music and Drama in 1990.

PAGE 267: Joan once wrote of Essie's 'difficult' behaviour: 'we had tickets booked and cancelled three times and finally she decided not to come. She never HAD to stay back on any occasion. We always had the animals covered, so to speak'. Letter to Nancy McDonald in response to criticisms about Essie's welfare, 2 June 1990, NLA.

PAGE 267: Essie lent Lolita the money to pay for the self-contained unit extension at the Flinders house—another example of the interconnectedness of the three's finances. Stephen Marriott, businessman and accountant, was an executor for all three and assisted with Lolita and Essie's financial matters; he went to great lengths to ensure that Essie's money was repaid when the deceased estates were sorted out.

PAGE 268: Burtta and Alison's letter accusing Lolita of malevolent intent was not sighted by me, but Joan's reply of 21 August 1988 admonished them for their harsh and unfair criticism of Lolita and for calling her 'wicked', NLA.

PAGE 270: 'I must confess to feeling too old to be participating . . . I am sure she will comply with pleasure', Joan's carbon copy of her letter to Peter Burch, 17 May 1990, NLA.

PAGE 271: The gala dinner in Sydney was held on 18 September 1990; the award was a medallion, no cash prize. Leo Schofield was master of ceremonies with Sheila Scotter assisting. Award dinners were held annually until 1998 when the format changed, then funding problems caused the tradition to falter and eventually cease. Winners included Joan Carden, Richard Divall, John Shaw, Donald McDonald, Ken Mackenzie-Forbes, Marilyn Richardson, Kathleen Steele-Scott and Elijah Moshinsky.

PAGE 271: The *Good Weekend* article about the 'Joans'—'Two Dames called Joan'—was written by Valerie Lawson and appeared in the 15 September 1990 issue. Sutherland retired from the stage a couple of weeks later, aged 63.

PAGE 272: Stephen Hall recalled Joan's disclosure about her relationship with Lolita during my phone interview with him, 27 April 2006.

PAGE 274: 'We got there . . . I've never seen anyone so distressed.' Peter Burch interview, 3 March 2005.

PAGE 277: Sir Rupert Hamer's letter was dated 1 July 1993; Joan's reply was 17 August 1993, NLA. See Sheila Scotter's memoir for her view of this exchange, including background problems regarding protocol and the Dame Joan Hammond Award, *Sheila Scotter: snaps, secrets and stories from my life*, Random House, 1998. The VSO merged with the AO in 1996 and became Opera Australia.

PAGE 280: Len Hammond and Peter Burch were 'jointly and severally' Joan's Powers of Attorney, yet the Guardianship Board had the power to overrule their directives.

PAGE 281: The Marriotts were eventually reimbursed for possessions that had been inadvertently sold by Joan's estate, but some family heirlooms, including jewellery, were gone forever. The Steinway, a baby grand, was donated to PLC Pymble and is currently in use.

PAGE 282: 'In my dressing room at ENO . . . we love you very much.' Letter from Cheryl Barker, 19 September 1993.

PAGE 283: The lower part of Joan's right leg was amputated due to gangrene. Monti Hammond interview with Christopher Sexton, 25 April 2000.

PAGE 284: 'JoLo's' shared assumption seems to have been that Joan would die first; Lolita thought she'd be left to organise matters.

Coda: That which remains

PAGE 287: 'Life is all about opposites . . . each of us through our own special talents', Joan as quoted in 'A life of song', *Ita* magazine, August 1992, p. 33.

PAGE 288: Joan's and Cheryl Barker's names appear alongside each other on *The Classic 100 Opera*, ABC Classics, 2006.

Encore: Peter Coleman-Wright and Cheryl Barker: a 'Noo Nah' duet

This chapter is based on edited extracts from a taped interview, 5 September 2006. Cheryl Barker had just begun rehearsals for the title role of Jenufa by Janacek for Opera Australia, Sydney Opera House, September-October 2006. Both singers somehow manage to maintain international careers while bringing up their son Gabriel.

PAGE 290: Peter Coleman-Wright's reference to 'the Met' is of course the Metropolitan Opera, New York; 'Gunther' refers to his role in Wagner's *Götterdämmerung* at the Royal Opera, Covent Garden.

PICTURE CREDITS

All photographs provided by the Performing Arts Collection and the National Library of Australia have been reproduced with the permission of Joan Hammond's estate.

Jacket

FRONT: Joan Hammond as Dido in Purcell's *Dido and Aeneas*, 1950s. Photograph by John Moyes. Courtesy of the Arts Centre, Performing Arts Collection, Melbourne, Joan Hammond Collection.

BACK: Studio portrait of Joan, mid-1940s. Courtesy of the Arts Centre, Performing Arts Collection, Melbourne, Joan Hammond Collection.

Text

PAGE (ii): Studio portrait of Joan by Lotte Meitner-Graf, 1956. Courtesy of the Arts Centre, Performing Arts Collection, Melbourne, Joan Hammond Collection.

PAGE (viii): Studio portrait of Joan in the role of Tosca, 1950s. Courtesy of the Arts Centre, Performing Arts Collection, Melbourne, Joan Hammond Collection.

PAGE 5: Programme for the Fayrfax Recital Club, London's West End, 1962. The club's patrons were Dame Maggie Teyte, Sir John Barbirolli and Alfredo Campoli.

PAGE 6: Joan aged 2½. Courtesy of the Arts Centre, Performing Arts Collection, Melbourne, Joan Hammond Collection.

PAGE 14: Joan before the bike accident. Photograph taken at Glen Carron, The Garden School, c. 1923. MS 8648, file 8/2, courtesy of the National Library of Australia.

PAGE 21: The Hammonds with their motor car in the front drive of 'Walbrook': Joan and Samuel at rear, Len at the wheel, Tony just visible in the back; late 1920s. Acc 97/111, courtesy of the National Library of Australia.

PAGE 23: Joan's 1928 Feldwick prize for singing was an opera score: *Acis and Galatea* by Handel. Courtesy of Pymble Ladies' College archives.

PAGE 24: On the veranda of the Royal Sydney Golf Club after winning the NSW State Junior Championship, 1930. Courtesy of the Arts Centre, Performing Arts Collection, Melbourne, Joan Hammond Collection.

PAGE 29: Joan's golf swing featured on the front cover of *The Australian Golf & Tennis Magazine*, June 1933. Courtesy of the State Library of Victoria.

PAGE 38: Hilda and Joan walking ahead of teenage Tony (his face is just visible) and Samuel; a city street in Sydney c. 1935. Acc 97/111, courtesy of the National Library of Australia.

PAGE 42: The noticeably tall Odette Lefebvre with Joan, Royal Sydney Golf Club, 1930s. Private collection.

PAGE 48: Joan enjoying a bush picnic with friends. Hilda was also in the party on this day, along with Bertie Lloyd's mother and sister. Note the wind-up gramophone at Joan's feet. MS No 8648, File 8/2, courtesy of the National Library of Australia.

PAGE 50: The *Dagfred* leaving Sydney, with family and friends waving goodbye; Joan casting streamers from the deck. MS No 8648, Series 5, Folio 5, Bertie Lloyd scrapbook, courtesy of the National Library of Australia.

PAGE 70: Joan kept this portrait of Lady Gowrie in a leather travel-frame which suggests she carried it with her often. Courtesy of Richard Divall.

PAGE 76: Hilda and Joan with Mrs N. Lloyd (far left, a relative of Bertie's) and Miss Slidwell (far right) at Cowdray Castle, West Sussex, 1938. Photograph by Mrs Eve McCay. Courtesy of Bertie Lloyd.

PAGE 81: This advertisement for a performance of Handel's *Messiah* appeared in the programme for Joan's debut recital at the Aeolian Hall, 1938. Private collection.

PAGE 84: This image shows Joan's transformation; her new 'Snow White' look. This photograph appeared on the poster for the second recital at Aeolian Hall. Joan's inscription is to Bertie Lloyd; 'Terry' was the nickname the Lloyd and McCay families always used. Courtesy of Bertie Lloyd.

PAGE 90: *Daily Telegraph* photograph of Joan at Chelsea Barracks performing for soldiers, September 1939. Courtesy of the Arts Centre, Performing Arts Collection, Melbourne, Joan Hammond Collection.

PAGE 110: Caricature of music critic Alec Robertson by A. P. Lissenden. It was published in *The Gramophone*, December 1953. Courtesy of John O'Brien's archives.

PAGE 118: Joan as Cho-Cho-San—better known as 'Butterfly'—in a wartime production of Puccini's opera. Courtesy of the Arts Centre, Performing Arts Collection, Melbourne, Joan Hammond Collection.

PAGE 124: Joan riding her bike with Pippo in the basket, dressed in her ambulance uniform. Courtesy of the Arts Centre, Performing Arts Collection, Melbourne, Joan Hammond Collection.

PAGE 130: A publicity shot of Joan with an EMI microphone. Courtesy of the Arts Centre, Performing Arts Collection, Melbourne, Joan Hammond Collection.

PAGE 138: Joan's New York agent used this 'soprano with poodle' photograph to promote her post-war USA tour. Acc 97/111, courtesy of the National Library of Australia.

PAGE 150: Studio portrait of Lolita Marriott, 1930s. Courtesy of the Arts Centre, Performing Arts Collection, Melbourne, Joan Hammond Collection.

PAGE 155: Lolita, Joan and Walter Susskind with bouquets after a concert in Sydney, 1953. As this photograph demonstrates, Lolita's attention was often directed towards Joan. Photograph by Norman L. Danvers. Courtesy of the Arts Centre, Performing Arts Collection, Melbourne, Joan Hammond Collection.

PAGE 162: This more sophisticated image of Joan appeared in the late 1940s. A relatively sombre look was fashionable in the post-war era; Kathleen Ferrier had a similar series of 'darker mood' portraits. MS 8646, file 6/1, courtesy of the National Library of Australia.

PAGE 166: Joan in the garden of The Old Cottage, 1950s. Courtesy of Bertie Lloyd.

PAGE 169: An 'at home' publicity photograph of Joan with her pets, 1950s. Photograph by Paul Wilson. Courtesy of the Arts Centre, Performing Arts Collection, Melbourne, Joan Hammond Collection.

PAGE 177: Lolita, Odette Lefebvre, Essie Walker and Joan standing alongside the Rolls-Royce-with-caravan touring combination. Very few photographs of Essie remain and, in those that do, she tends to be obscured or in the background—as in this example. (Odette's married names were McKay and later Inglis). Courtesy of Claude McKay.

PAGE 192: Members of ETOC in Adelaide, 1957. Front row from left to right: Joy Mammen, Eleonora Treiber (choreographer), Joan Hammond, John Young, Max Worthley. Back row: Neil Easton, Jan Ross, Greg Dempsey, Florence Pong, Wilma Whitney, Neil Warren-Smith, John Shaw, Joyce Simmons, Alan Light, Ronald Dowd. Photograph and identification courtesy of Greg Dempsey.

PAGE 198: Samuel and Hilda Hammond with their daughter after a concert in Sydney, 1950s. Hilda genuinely enjoyed Joan's performances but Samuel was less enthusiastic. He once spent a concert counting how many men in the audience were wearing dress suits—he was so impressed by the number that he told his daughter afterwards. Joan wasn't amused. Courtesy of the Arts Centre, Performing Arts Collection, Melbourne, Joan Hammond Collection.

PAGE 203: Advertisement in *Opera*, UK. Vol. 3, No. 12, December 1952. Courtesy of John O'Brien's archives.

PAGE 204: Joan's golf continued to attract attention; this is a publicity shot taken in the late 1950s. Private collection.

PAGE 212: Lolita in the grounds of 'Jumbunna'. Courtesy of Stephen Marriott.

PAGE 220: It was difficult to capture 'Jumbunna' in a single photograph because of its extensive width and unusual shape. Courtesy of Bertie Lloyd.

PAGE 223: This 1970s snap was taken at a Marriott social event. Caught somewhat unawares, Joan's 'stern look' is revealed. Courtesy of Stephen Marriott.

PAGE 225: 'JoLoEss' looking very much at home at 'Jumbunna', 1970s. The frocks are probably one-offs. Joan and Lolita used to buy material when travelling and have clothes specially tailored. Courtesy of Miranda McLeish.

PAGE 234: This photograph appeared in a Sydney newspaper upon Joan's return to Australia from a trip to Britain to promote her autobiography, 1970. Courtesy of the Arts Centre, Performing Arts Collection, Melbourne, Joan Hammond Collection.

PAGE 245: 'JoLo' with their long-time friend Richard Divall (Music Director of the Victorian State Opera). This photograph was taken at the new Flinders house, mid 1980s; the background gives an indication of the remarkable sea view. Courtesy of Richard Divall.

PAGE 248: Group photograph of Joan and some of the guests that appeared on *This is Your Life*. Joan sits with Pauline Grant; behind them, from left to right, are Richard Divall, John Shaw, Ronald Dowd, Donald Smith, Neil Warren-Smith, Stefan Haag and Greg Dempsey. Interestingly, Joan has partially covered the scar on her left arm with the train of her gown, perhaps from force of habit. Courtesy of Greg Dempsey.

PAGE 253: Joan in the ruins of 'Jumbunna' after Ash Wednesday. The fountain stands as a marker of what used to be— before 16 February 1983. The photograph was sent to friends to inform them of the bushfire and to reassure them that 'life goes on'. Newspapers such as the *Age* reported the loss of Joan's home, but as far as is known a photograph wasn't published. Courtesy of Bertie Lloyd.

PAGE 258: Joan, Lolita and their old Labrador on the patio of their new Flinders home, mid 1980s. Courtesy of Richard Divall.

PAGE 276: The handwritten phrases visible on Joan's letter to John Crisp are 'I am devastated' and 'Please do not acknowledge.' There were two forms of this letter, this is the briefer version. Courtesy of John Crisp.

PAGE 278: Joan with her brother Len at the Royal Sydney Golf Club, shortly after Lolita's death. She made a speech in celebration of the Club's centenary. Courtesy of Julie Wyer.

PAGE 286: Joan at the Flinders house. Courtesy of Peter Burch.

PAGE 291: Cheryl Barker as Tosca and Peter Coleman-Wright as Scarpia in a production staged by Opera Australia. Photograph by Branco Gaica. Courtesy of Cheryl Barker and Peter Coleman-Wright.

PAGE 294: Joan playing golf in the late 1980s. Courtesy of Bertie Lloyd.

Illustrated Section

PAGE 1: Joan as Marguerite in Gounod's *Faust*, one of her earliest appearances with Carl Rosa. Acc 97/111, courtesy of the National Library of Australia.

PAGE 2: Joan as Leonora—here disguised as Fidelio—in Beethoven's *Fidelio*. Photograph by Angus McBean. Courtesy of the Arts Centre, Performing Arts Collection, Melbourne, Joan Hammond Collection.

PAGE 3: Joan performing the title role in *Aida*. Courtesy of Stephen Marriott.

PAGES 4 AND 5: This photograph of the *Aida* performance in Moscow appeared in the *Daily Express*, 8 March 1957, when the Suez crisis was in the news. MS No 9832, Press Clippings 1953-64, courtesy of the National Library of Australia.

PAGE 6: Joan performing the title role in *Salome* by Richard Strauss. Photograph by Angus McBean. Courtesy of the Arts Centre, Performing Arts Collection, Melbourne, Joan Hammond Collection.

PAGE 7: Joan as Elizabeth in Verdi's *Don Carlos*. Photograph by Angus McBean. Courtesy of the Arts Centre, Performing Arts Collection, Melbourne, Joan Hammond Collection.

PAGE 8: Joan performing the title role in *Tosca*. Courtesy of the Arts Centre, Performing Arts Collection, Melbourne, Joan Hammond Collection.

ACKNOWLEDGEMENTS

I am particularly grateful to Miss Bertie 'Boo' Lloyd (96 years old at the time of writing) for responding with untiring enthusiasm to my interminable questions, and for allowing me to borrow treasured memorabilia devoted to her friend. Peter Burch has been a wonderful constant in this long process, encouraging me at the start, giving pep talks midway, and cheering me on at the end: thank you Peter! Christopher Sexton conducted some interviews a few years ago with a view to writing a biography but other projects claimed his energies. I'm grateful to Christopher for sharing his interview tapes with me. Many thanks also to members of the Hammond and Marriott families for memorabilia, anecdotes and enthusiasm.

Contributions came from many quarters and in many forms. I am especially grateful to John Bailey, Cheryl Barker, Peter Coleman-Wright, Burtta Cheney, John Crisp, Greg Dempsey, Richard Divall, Aurora Hammond, Stephen Hall, Brian Hansford, Stephen Marriott, Miranda McLeish, Claude McKay, John O'Brien, Moffatt Oxenbould, Heather Ross, John Rohde, Julie Wyer, Rosemary Wilson, Tony Locantro (EMI Classics) and Stewart Brown (Testament). Special thanks also to Alwyn Allford, Jenifer Eddy, John W. Fawcett, Di Gatehouse, Shirley Germain, Gillie Gough, Lord Harewood, Greg Hocking, Suzanne Johnston, Ian Kirk, Doreen L. Metcalf, Lorraine Milne, Roger Neill, Leo McKernan, Beverley Northey, Charles Osborne, Roger Parsons, Joan Pollock, H. Michael Robinson, Alison Searle, Dame Joan Sutherland, Gordon Tuck and Jenny Wareham.

Librarians and archivists in various institutions gave diligent assistance. I'd especially like to thank archivist Anne Cooke for ensuring that my day spent at Pymble Ladies' College, NSW, was such a pleasant as well as productive one. Thanks also to Patricia Convery and staff at the Performing Arts Collection in Melbourne – a particularly valuable resource. I am grateful for the helpful pointers provided by Georgina Binns, College Librarian, and staff at the Lenton Parr Library, Victorian College of the Arts. The general staff and manuscripts librarians at the National Library of Australia did a fine job on all levels (though I hope Manuscripts has a better photocopier by now!). Thanks also to the Open Spaces Department, Burnham Beaches, for confirming the health and location of 'Joan's tree'. Particular thanks to *Opera* magazine (UK) for publishing my letter to the editor concerning my research, and to the people who responded with personal stories and memorabilia.

I am indebted to Julie Wyer and the Royal Sydney Golf Club for generously entertaining me for the day and giving me a crash course—albeit from an armchair perspective—regarding that passion known as golf.

This project may have staggered to a halt without the welcome arrival of a Research and Development Grant from Arts Victoria in 2005. The costs connected with research can be prohibitive so I am especially grateful to Lindis Masterman (Canberra), and Lorna McKenzie and Jenny Lee Heylen (Sydney), for their generosity regarding accommodation; also Michael Pearce for the loan of his car. I'd also like to thank the Australian Centre, School of Historical Studies, University of Melbourne, for the practical support associated with my honorary fellowship (the Baillieu, Music, and Education Resource Centre libraries have been especially useful in this regard). Special thanks—plus cheers—for the support provided by the School of Music, Victorian College of the Arts.

A big thank you to the Allen & Unwin team that brought this book into tangible being. There are many people on that team but I especially want to thank my publisher, Andrea McNamara, whose guidance, care and good humour goes way beyond the call. Special mentions also to Ruth Grüner for another splendid all-round design; and Liza Kennedy—early signs indicate a bright future.

I am grateful to Sylvia Martin for providing feedback on initial chapters; thanks also to my mother, Patricia Hardy, for responding to drafts and offering good counsel.

Resounding thanks to my partner, Lois Ellis, who read every draft of every chapter several times. Her incisive comments and clever suggestions made all the difference to this book.

A tender and loving thank you to friends and family; they know why. I take this opportunity to welcome the arrival of Rosa Emilia Mowszowski, baby sister to Kobi. May the world treat you both kindly.

Finally, I acknowledge the influence of my father, Keith Hardy, and his fine tenor voice: born Somerset 1926, died Wiltshire 1995. It's the music that lives on.

INDEX